DEAD WRONG

Also by Randall Sullivan

The Curse of Oak Island

Untouchable

The Miracle Detective

LAbyrinth

The Price of Experience

DEAD WRONG

The Continuing Story of
City of Lies,
Corruption and Cover-Up
in the Notorious B.I.G.
Murder Investigation

RANDALL SULLIVAN

Atlantic Monthly Press
New York

FIRST EDITION

Published simultaneously in Canada
Printed in Canada

First Grove Atlantic hardcover edition: July 2019

This book was set in 12 pt. Janson by Alpha Design & Composition of Pittsfield, NH

Library of Congress Cataloging-in-Publication data is available for this title.

ISBN 978-0-8021- 2932-1
eISBN 978-0-8021-4700-4

Atlantic Monthly Press
an imprint of Grove Atlantic
154 West 14th Street
New York, NY 10011

Distributed by Publishers Group West

groveatlantic.com

19 20 21 22   10 9 8 7 6 5 4 3 2 1

Dedicated to the memory of
Sergio Robleto and Russell Poole

CONTENTS

PREFACE

I wrote the book *LAbyrinth: A Detective Investigates the Murders of Tupac Shakur and Notorious B.I.G., the Implication of Death Row Records' Suge Knight, and the Origins of the Los Angeles Police Scandal* more than fifteen years ago. At that time, like the investigator who was the book's protagonist, I believed the truth would come out and those murders would be solved long before now.

I was wrong.

Even in 2002, I was incredulous that arrests hadn't been made. I was asking people, "Do you believe that if Frank Sinatra and Dean Martin had been whacked by the Mafia in the 1950s, there's even the slightest chance the killers would have gotten away with it?" In those days, comparing Tupac and Biggie to Sinatra and Martin made sense to only a sliver of the American populace. Today, a far larger segment of our society gets it. But that hasn't made the slightest impact on the investigation of either murder. The only explanations I can conceive of for this are that people don't care enough and that those in positions of power have a vested interest in making sure the facts remain obscured.

In *LAbyrinth*, I followed Detective Russell Poole of the Los Angeles Police Department's elite Robbery-Homicide Division into the maze of lies and corruption that surrounded the Biggie and Tupac killings. As Poole followed the evidence that implicated LAPD officers working for Suge Knight and Death Row Records in the Notorious

B.I.G. slaying, he came up against an institutional stone wall so thick and encompassing that it not only choked off his investigation, but suffocated the man's faith in the organizations and the traditions to which he had dedicated his life. In the Los Angeles of the late twentieth century, the vectors of racial politics and institutional entrenchment had been woven into a thicket so dense that it smothered Poole's probe of the Biggie murder, and of the assassination that he believed was connected to it.

Poole never claimed to be certain beyond all doubt that LAPD officer David Mack had helped arrange the Notorious B.I.G. homicide or that Mack's friend Amir Muhammad had been the shooter. Poole's position was that this theory of the case was the one best supported by the evidence and therefore the one to which he should dedicate his efforts. He was prevented from this at every turn. When Mack was arrested in December 1998 for the robbery of a Bank of America branch near the University of Southern California campus, Poole was denied permission to run forensic tests on Mack's vehicle, to obtain subpoenas for Mack's financial records, or to obtain the ballistic evidence that might have connected Mack to the Biggie murder. He was not even allowed to speak to Amir Muhammad. The best explanation he ever got for that was, "We're not going in that direction."

Gradually, Poole came to believe that Mack's former partner Rafael Perez had been his accomplice in the bank robbery and that Perez might have been part of the Biggie murder conspiracy. Poole became convinced that Mack and Perez were part of a cadre of LAPD officers—"gangsta cops"—who were working for Death Row Records and aiding the record label's CEO, Suge Knight, in commission of crimes that ranged from drug dealing to homicide. Poole was not allowed to investigate the evidence that supported this theory, either. Eventually he found his way to Kendrick Knox, an LAPD officer who *had* investigated the links between the LAPD and Death Row, until his probe was shut down by orders from on high. Like Knox, Poole became convinced that the orders blocking their investigations had come from the very top—from LAPD Chief Bernard Parks.

By then, though, the Biggie investigation had been subsumed by what became known as the Rampart Scandal, in which the central figure was none other than David Mack's friend and former partner Rafael Perez. The Rampart Scandal had been invented by Perez after his arrest on charges that he had been stealing large quantities of cocaine being held as evidence in the LAPD's Property Division and selling it on the street. The Rampart Scandal narrative, largely concocted by Perez—implicating dozens of mostly innocent officers in an epidemic of corruption and brutality—had been swallowed whole by the media in Los Angeles, particularly by the *Los Angeles Times*. In part this was because that narrative was publicly endorsed by the *Times'* main source, Bernard Parks, whose motives were both personal and political. Poole and his investigation were first absorbed and then stifled by the Rampart Scandal.

Because of his insistence on the possible guilt of fellow officers in Biggie Smalls's murder, Poole became a pariah within the LAPD, administratively harassed and personally insulted. Other detectives increasingly avoided any association with him. Nearly broken, he took a leave of absence to consider his options, then returned to the LAPD after being transferred out of the Robbery-Homicide Division. Watching what was happening as Rafael Perez played puppet master to the entire city and the Biggie murder investigation was buried in the process proved to be too much for Poole, however. In 1999, he resigned from the LAPD after nearly nineteen years on the job, walking away not only from the career that had been the core of his identity, but also from the pension he might have attained by remaining with the department for another fourteen months. He filed a lawsuit against the LAPD and Chief Parks that was dismissed on a statute of limitations claim by the City of Los Angeles. At that point, Poole had been marginalized to the point of nonexistence.

There's some irony, I think, in the fact that I found my way to him by a process that was almost a reverse engineering of the one that had at first diverted Poole's investigation of the Biggie murder, then terminated it. In 2000, I was asked by *Rolling Stone* magazine, where

I'd been a contributing editor for many years, to consider writing an article on the Rampart Scandal. I gave a tentative answer of yes, then asked that every article ever published on the scandal be delivered to my hotel room in Los Angeles. I spent several days reading, and what most astonished me was how little *there* was there. Not only was the fabric of the Rampart Scandal shockingly flimsy, but it was obvious that the entire thing rested on the claims of a single individual, Rafael Perez, who was a far-from-credible character.

I made an appointment to meet with Richard Rosenthal, the deputy district attorney who had both prosecuted Perez on the drug theft charges and brokered the deal that resulted in the Rampart Scandal. During our conversation, Rosenthal shared two pieces of information that stunned me. The first was that Rafael Perez had failed not one, not two, not three, not four, but all five of the polygraph examinations to which he had submitted. The second remarkable fact Rosenthal revealed was that what became the Rampart Task Force had originated from the connections that had been made by a former LAPD detective named Russell Poole "between the David Mack bank robbery and the Biggie Smalls murder."

For a *Rolling Stone* reporter that last was, obviously, compelling news. I knew I had to meet this Russell Poole and made arrangements to do so through Poole's attorney, who insisted that we meet at his office in Beverly Hills. I found the lawyer to be unhelpful—his main concern seemed to be maintaining control of both Poole and our conversation. Fortunately, he was called out of the room by his assistant at one point, leaving me alone with Poole. "I need to talk to you without this guy around," I told Poole, and handed him a business card with my cell phone number written on it.

He called me the next day and agreed to meet me for lunch near his home in Orange County. Over sandwiches and beer, Poole told me that he had been the one who arrested Rafael Perez on the original drug charges. He was in a position to make that arrest, Poole said, only because he had been removed from the Biggie case by means that were particularly devious. At first, Poole explained, he was told by his superiors in the LAPD that he was being reassigned from Robbery-Homicide to a special task force that would be dedicated to investigating his theory of the Notorious B.I.G. murder, just as Rosenthal had said. In a matter of days, however, that unit became the "Rampart Task Force," Poole recalled. The Biggie case was unceremoniously abandoned, and "the entire focus of the task force became Perez." That had marked the beginning of his departure from the LAPD.

By the time we had finished lunch, Poole and I were getting on well enough that he told me, "I have something to show you." I followed his pickup truck to a storage facility that was a short distance away. When Poole opened his unit, he gestured toward a wall lined with boxes of documents. That was everything connected to the Notorious B.I.G. and Tupac Shakur murders that he'd been able to copy and carry out of the Robbery-Homicide Division before he was transferred to the task force and taken off the Biggie case, Poole said. I convinced him to let me make my own copies. When I read them, I was astonished and elated. These LAPD files, including the department's main investigative file—its "Murder Book"—of the Biggie case, not only validated what Poole had told me, but, when pieced together, formed a narrative far clearer and more convincing than he'd been capable of describing. They formed the spine of, first, my *Rolling Stone* article "The Murder of Notorious B.I.G." and then my book *LAbyrinth*.

The article and the book each created some sensation. It was the article, though, that convinced Voletta Wallace, Biggie's mom, as well as her attorneys and her representatives, that the estate of Christopher Wallace, a.k.a. Notorious B.I.G., should file a wrongful death lawsuit against the City of Los Angeles. *LAbyrinth* ended there, in early 2002. This new book, its sequel, tells the story of what's happened since. Which is a lot. But not enough. There are people who need to be held to account.

PROLOGUE

In the nineteen years after Russell Poole's 1999 resignation from the Los Angeles Police Department, the nearest approach the investigation of the murder of Christopher Wallace, a.k.a. Notorious B.I.G., would make to justice was during the last week of June and the first week of July in 2005. The events of those fourteen days had unfolded with a suddenness and force that made a major breakthrough feel imminent.

It began on the evening after the third day of testimony in the civil trial that pitted the Wallace Estate against the City of Los Angeles. The trial had lurched forward fitfully after the opening statements on June 21. The combination of a skeptical media and witnesses who were beginning to either duck and cover or simply disappear had compelled the attorneys for the Wallace family, Perry Sanders and Rob Frank, to combat an impression that their case was falling apart almost from the moment the court proceedings began. The jurors should be advised that there would be inconsistencies in the testimony of "reluctant" witnesses who were terrified because those implicated in this case "are incredibly violent people," the attorneys had told the panel in their opening statement. This was driven home when the first important witness for the plaintiffs, Kevin Hackie, took the stand and produced an hour of what the *Los Angeles Times* would describe as "erratic" testimony. The newspaper's coverage of Hackie's appearance in court emphasized the bodyguard's repudiation of his previous sworn testimony that LAPD officer David Mack had worked in a "covert capacity" for Death Row Records. The *Times* made absolutely no mention, though, of how Hackie's testimony began, with the following series of questions and answers:

Q: Do you want to testify in this case?

A: No, sir.

Q: Why not?

A: I'm in fear for my life, sir.

Q: What are you afraid of?

A: Retribution by the Bloods, the Los Angeles Police Department, and associates of Death Row Records.

Things improved from the plaintiffs' point of view on the following day, when retired LAPD detective Fred Miller took the stand and surprised everyone in court, first by praising his former partner Russell Poole's work on the case, then by revealing that, after Poole left the LAPD, he himself had taken the case to the district attorney's office, seeking to have Suge Knight charged with B.I.G.'s murder. Prosecutors had told him that the case was "not quite there," said Miller, who could offer no explanation for the LAPD's subsequent failure to investigate further, replying instead with a blank expression and a shrug of his shoulders. The most startling revelation of the trial's second day, though, came during the testimony of another LAPD detective, Wayne Caffey, who told of having been shown a photograph of a woman posing with David Mack and Mack's former partner Rafael Perez that he understood had been seized from the home of a South-Central L.A. gang member. The woman in the photograph, Caffey said on the stand, was apparently Chief Bernard

Parks's daughter Michelle. "That had the jurors on the edges of their seats," recalled the lead attorney for the Wallace family, Perry Sanders. "They had to wonder what the daughter of the chief of police was doing posing with a couple of gangster cops for a photograph found in a gang member's house."

The atmosphere in court became even more fraught the next day, when a Hollywood screenwriter who had been researching the police scandal for a proposed HBO movie testified under oath that during a private meeting, Detective Caffey had told him that the LAPD was in possession of a secretly recorded videotape. It purportedly showed Mack and Perez present at a meeting in the offices of Death Row Records in which Suge Knight had ordered B.I.G.'s murder.

All that, though, would be utterly eclipsed by what happened that evening.

At dusk on June 23, 2005, Perry Sanders was riding to dinner in an SUV with blacked-out windows, accompanied by two three-hundred-plus-pound bodyguards hired by the Wallace family to protect him during the trial. En route, Sanders took time to listen to his voice mails. One was from the secretary at his office in Louisiana, informing him that three people with tips on the B.I.G. case had phoned that day. Only one caller was anonymous, Sanders remembered, but for some reason it was this person he phoned back first. He almost hung up, Sanders admitted, when the man on the other end of the line began the conversation with the words, "In another life . . ." He had already dealt with too many "'Tupac's been reincarnated' type of callers" in the four years since he had taken this case, Sanders explained, "but then this guy goes on, '. . . I was at a Board of Rights hearing in the basement of L.A. County's Men's Central Jail.'" The LAPD's disciplinary proceedings, Sanders knew, were not ordinarily—not ever, in fact—held in the basement of the jail. Before he said anything further, the man on the other end of the line told the attorney he would require an absolute promise that his identity, should Sanders discover it, be protected. When Sanders agreed to this, the man said he held a position of considerable influence within the LAPD and had a lot to lose, but "felt he just couldn't live with himself if he didn't share what he knew," Sanders remembered. "The guy sounded very credible. He gave me lots of names and dates and other specific details, so I knew that if he was not telling the truth, it would be easy to determine."

After hanging up, Sanders immediately phoned Sergio Robleto, the former LAPD South Bureau Homicide commander who had been hired by the plaintiffs as their lead investigator, and asked him to verify that a proceeding like the one the anonymous caller described had taken place. Robleto phoned back in the middle of the following night to say that he was convinced what Sanders had been told was accurate.

"I showed up for court on Friday morning at seven-thirty," Sanders recalled, "and by noon had a handwritten presentation to make before the judge." District Court judge Florence Cooper, who was presiding over the civil trial, admitted she was flummoxed after reading Sanders's pleading and asked for suggestions about what to do next. Sanders proposed adjourning until Monday morning while both sides investigated what he had been told.

"And by Monday we all knew it was all true."

That weekend, for the first time in memory, the LAPD had locked down an entire division—and not just any division, but the department's most prestigious, Robbery-Homicide—so that U.S. marshals could search it from one end to the other. Sergio Robleto and Sanders's star witness, former LAPD detective Russell Poole, would say later that the lockdown was essentially theatrical, because the Internal Affairs investigators who had secured the scene already knew what was going to be found: more than two hundred pages of documents hidden in two drawers belonging to the LAPD detective who had been heading up the investigation of B.I.G.'s murder since Poole's resignation and Fred Miller's retirement. Most of those pages were related to assorted hearings and investigations that had resulted from the testimony of a prison inmate, named Kenneth Boagni, regarding the confessions of Rafael Perez, the central figure in the Rampart Scandal, to involvement in crimes that included the murder of Notorious B.I.G. "Talk about the shit hitting the fan," Sanders said. "You should have seen the faces of the city's attorneys when we got to court on Monday morning."

The majority of the materials seized from the drawers in the Robbery-Homicide Division would be placed under seal by Judge Cooper, making it impossible to quote from them directly. General descriptions of what Boagni himself had said, though, were offered in other court documents. What these revealed was that in 1999, Boagni had been incarcerated in a special branch of Los Angeles County's jail system, where he was the cellmate and confidant of former detective Perez. During that time, according to Boagni, Perez took pleasure in describing his work for Death Row Records and his participation in various crimes, which included the murder of the rapper he called Biggie Smalls. Perez had detailed his activities and David Mack's, Boagni said, at the Petersen Automotive Museum on March 9, 1997, the night of Biggie's slaying.

What the available record revealed was that an envoy from the LAPD's Officer Representation Section had visited Boagni on a number of occasions at Calipatria State Prison in 2000, and that during their meetings Boagni had described the involvement of Perez and Mack in Biggie's shooting. When a pair of LAPD detectives showed up later at the prison to meet with him, Boagni had testified, he assumed they were the investigators assigned to the Biggie murder. The two detectives, though, were members of the Rampart Task Force, a group committed to validating Perez's claims. He began to suspect a hidden agenda, Boagni would say, because the two detectives seemed determined from the first to trip him up. Eventually, he said, the two did their best to convince him not to testify.

The single most remarkable fact that the judge and the Wallace family's attorneys released to the public was this: Boagni had offered to wear a wire on Perez to see if he could get him to admit he was lying about the accusations he had made against his fellow officers and to implicate himself in the Biggie murder; the LAPD had turned him down. As Sanders and Frank would note in the motion for sanctions they filed with Judge Cooper, "There would appear to be no possible legitimate LAPD motivation for such rejection of help."

The LAPD's attempts to defend itself against these accusations strained credulity to a point where they left the judge shaking her head, first in bafflement and finally in disdain. The Los Angeles city attorney's office attempted to mitigate the damage to its side by arguing that Boagni was an insignificant witness who might easily have been overlooked. The judge would have none of it. The LAPD's claim that the detective in charge of the Biggie murder investigation simply "forgot" about the Boagni materials in his desk drawers was "utterly unbelievable," she ruled: "The detective, acting alone or in concert with others, made a decision to conceal from the plaintiffs in this case information which could have supported their contention that David Mack was responsible for the Wallace murder." The judge listed eighteen of the documents that the LAPD had hidden from the other side in this case, before addressing the city's arguments: "The sheer volume of information attests to the seriousness with which [the police department] treated this informant's statements and belies [the city's] current position that he is just another jailhouse informant seeking favors."

While Judge Cooper was not able to bring herself to award the plaintiffs a default judgment, she felt she had no choice but to declare a mistrial. At the same time, she was awarding the plaintiffs "fees and costs" that would come to more than $1 million as a sanction for the city's misconduct.

Sanders and Frank were at once exultant and overwhelmed. They realized that in the new trial, which they hoped would be scheduled for summer 2006, the City of Los Angeles would be forced to defend itself against a vastly expanded lawsuit before a judge who quite clearly had become convinced their claim possessed merit. "The law of the case is that the LAPD potentially withheld information,"

Frank would explain. "And now there's been a judicial finding of that fact. So we have won the most significant point before we even go to trial. Their lead investigator has been found to be a liar and a cheat."

The addition of Perez as one of the officers implicated in B.I.G.'s murder changed everything, Sanders and Frank knew. After sorting through the Boagni testimony, along with the documents drawn from the sprawling mess that was the Rampart Scandal, the attorneys would realize the lengths to which police and city officials in Los Angeles had gone to protect Perez from those who knew him to be a fabricator. This evidence was now an essential aspect of the Notorious B.I.G. wrongful death lawsuit, Sanders said, and would allow the plaintiffs to demand a vast trove of documents related to Perez's plea deal, his secret testimony, and the investigations that resulted.

Much of the police department's command staff was now likely to face difficult questions. Notations on the Boagni evidence demonstrated that at least nine of the lead detective's superiors, going up to the rank of LAPD assistant chief, were aware of its existence and significance. "He wasn't alone in this," Frank said. Sanders added, "If we catch them withholding other documents, I believe the judge will have to declare a default verdict in our favor."

Such a verdict would be devastating to Los Angeles, as both sides knew. The report submitted to the court by forensic economist Peter Formuzis on B.I.G.'s future earnings potential included a quote from the former president of the company that founded *Vibe* magazine, in which Christopher Wallace was described as "the world's most popular hip-hop artist at the time of his murder." According to his calculations, Formuzis had written to Judge Cooper, Notorious B.I.G. would have been likely to earn at least $362 million during the remainder of his life. The estate's lawyers were prepared not only to claim every penny of that sum, but also to demand punitive damages based on the degree of dishonesty the LAPD had demonstrated in connection with this case. Immediately after the mistrial, Sanders said, he was contacted by a number of "concerned parties"—including political figures in Los Angeles—worried that this lawsuit might bankrupt the city.

Month after month since taking the case, he had absorbed body blows delivered by the city's legal team and the editors and reporters at the *Los Angeles Times*, Sanders said, but now, finally, he could feel the balance tipping in his favor. "We've not only got the case, we've also got the momentum."

CHAPTER ONE

The process by which the Wallace family had chosen the attorney who would represent them in court had as much to do with how the music business operates as with the way the legal profession works. That was probably why Perry Sanders Jr. of Lake Charles, Louisiana, had gotten the job, Sanders perhaps being the one lawyer in America who could truthfully say he had spent many more hours singing into a microphone than he had speaking from a courtroom lectern.

In Sanders's mind, it had all started with Rusty Kershaw. In the mid-1990s, Sanders and Kershaw were two of Louisiana's better-known citizens. A lot of people in the state still thought of Sanders as the musician son of Louisiana's most famous Baptist preacher, Perry Sanders Sr. Years after he earned his law degree at Louisiana State University, the younger Sanders had seemed more committed to his career as a singer-songwriter and music producer than to establishing himself as an attorney. As a college student in the 1970s, he had performed all across the Southern club circuit, and by the time he passed the bar in 1982 was co-owner of the Baton Rouge recording studio Disk Productions, where he and his two partners supported themselves in some style by composing and recording jingles for companies that included Hilton and Honda. Within a few years he had moved on to Nashville, working in entertainment law by day and as a writer and producer at night, and then to Los Angeles, where he was a partner in the studio West Side Sound. By the end of the eighties, though, Sanders had returned to Louisiana, where he set up a law practice in his hometown, Lake Charles, and made a name for himself with a series of civil rights claims that produced local headlines and environmental lawsuits that turned him into a rich man. The police brutality cases he had won in Lake Charles and New Orleans were especially closely watched in those cities' black communities, which had a lot to do with how Sanders had been drawn back into entertainment law. The case in which he represented the New Orleans–based rappers Beats by the Pound and won back an assortment of copyrights from Master P's No Limit Records was especially well known in Louisiana, and only in part for the unlikely success Sanders had achieved. In that case, as in others, the attorney had driven a hard bargain with not only his opponents but also his clients. He took all his cases on contingency and generally paid the costs out of his own pocket. He got paid only if he won, Sanders would point out, but if he won he got paid big. In the lawsuit against No Limit, Sanders had taken half of the copyrights he'd won back.

Rusty Kershaw was an even more favorite son in Lake Charles. The guitarist and his fiddler brother Doug had become regulars on the *Louisiana Hayride* show during the mid-1950s. By 1957, Rusty & Doug had joined the Grand Ole Opry and were recording a series of songs that made the country charts, including their top ten hit "Louisiana Man." Outside the South, Kershaw was known for his work on Neil Young's album *On the Beach*, in particular for his playing on what a lot of aficionados considered Young's greatest song, "Ambulance Blues." In 1992, Young had returned the favor by playing with Kershaw on Rusty's solo album *Now and Then*. Though widely loved among other musicians, *Now and Then* was not a commercial success, and Kershaw's discouragement had turned into bitterness about what he saw as a failure of support from the Domino Records label. By the time he got Sanders on the phone, Kershaw was complaining that "the producer had taken not only most of the money, but also most of the credit" for the album, as the attorney recalled it.

That producer was one of the best known and most respected in the music business, Rob Fraboni, celebrated for his work with Bob Dylan, the Band, Eric Clapton, and the Rolling Stones, among others. Fraboni actually owned Domino Records, Sanders discovered, a label he had created to record some of his favorite Louisiana artists, Kershaw among them.

Moved by Kershaw's story and aware that the target of the musician's ire was a man with deep pockets, Sanders was preparing to file a lawsuit against Fraboni when he made a phone call to his client Charles Vessels, a legendary record promoter who now ran an artist management company out of Beaumont, Texas, just an hour down the interstate from Lake Charles. The two of them agreed that *Now and Then* was a great record that for some reason had underperformed in the marketplace, Sanders recalled, but as soon as he mentioned that he had accepted Rusty Kershaw as a client and was about to sue the owner of Domino Records, who had also produced the album, Vessels became upset. "He told me, 'Don't do that. Rob Fraboni is a friend of mine. He's also a great guy who would never cheat a musician,'" recalled Sanders. "Charles says, 'Let me make a call.'" Only about an hour later, Vessels phoned back to say Fraboni would be flying to Lake Charles the next day and wanted to meet for lunch.

Fraboni, it turned out, was every bit as cool a fellow as Charles Vessels had claimed he was. "He says, 'Look, I want Rusty to get what he needs. This was just a misunderstanding,'" Sanders recalled. "Within minutes we had an agreement—probably the easiest settlement of a case I've ever had. I was headed up to New York on some other business, and Rob and I agreed I'd bring all the paperwork and we'd get it signed then."

While he was in New York, Fraboni asked Sanders if he liked Les Paul. Who doesn't like Les Paul? asked Sanders, for whom the "father of the electric guitar" was a personal hero. His good friend, the musician and electrical-systems whiz Gregory Ercolino, was close to Les, Fraboni said, and could get Sanders a table on the floor of the tiny Iridium Club in the basement of the Empire Hotel, where Paul was performing. By the time Sanders left New York, he not only owned three Gibson guitars signed by Paul ("To Perry, Keep on Rockin'"), but had formed a lasting friendship with Ercolino, who would soon marry one of the other people Sanders had met that night at the Iridium. This was the eminent music attorney Terri Baker, whose long list of famous clients included Notorious B.I.G. Soon both Baker and Ercolino would become significant people in Sanders's life. It was Baker who introduced Sanders to Dan Pritzker, the owner of the legendary Vee-Jay Records label, whose catalogs included the music of Jimmy Reed, John Lee Hooker, and Little Richard. Vee-Jay had a copyright case that needed to be filed in New Orleans and wanted a Louisiana attorney to handle it, explained Pritzker, who became a big Sanders fan after the attorney won back all the copyrights, trademarks, and master recordings that were in dispute.

In the months after the Vee-Jay case was settled, Sanders and Ercolino traded visits, with the attorney recording his album *After Mother* at Ercolino's old farmhouse in upstate New York, "with two open mics and him playing pots and pans and me on Neil Diamond's old guitar," Sanders recalled. Ercolino came to Louisiana to stay for two weeks with Sanders in Lake Charles at his converted barn on English Bayou. The two of them spent a lot of those days racing Sanders's speedboat to the Gulf of Mexico, but their vacation was interrupted by a deposition the attorney had to take in a civil rights case he was prosecuting. Just for a kick, he brought Ercolino along as his "legal assistant," Sanders recalled, and "Greg thought it was just about the most exciting and interesting thing he'd ever been part of."

All those pieces were in place in June 2001, when *Rolling Stone* magazine published my article "The Murder of Notorious B.I.G." Recalled Sanders: "I get a call from Terri Baker, who asks me, 'Perry, have you heard that cops might have been involved in the murder of Notorious B.I.G.?' She said she and Greg were just sitting there flabbergasted. She said, 'I want you to read this and tell me what you think.' So she faxed the article to me. I read it and thought, 'Whoaaa.'"

He advised Baker that "it would be a tough case to make, because you would have to get the city of Los Angeles on the hook," Sanders recalled, but also told her that if even half of what had appeared in the *Rolling Stone* piece was true, there was plenty to work with and a huge upside if they won in court. She would need the family's approval, Baker said, but she thought he might be the perfect attorney to represent the slain rapper's estate, given his unusual background, which included handling both civil rights and copyright cases, along with his experience in the music business.

Sanders and his sometime associate, Colorado attorney Robert Frank, were at that moment embroiled in a massive environmental lawsuit against the Schlage Lock Company, however, and neither lawyer was sure he could afford the money or the time the B.I.G. lawsuit would demand. Baker pressed Sanders to meet with Biggie's mother, Voletta Wallace. Sanders asked Frank, who was in Boston at the time, to drop down to New York and introduce the two of them to Mrs. Wallace.

That would be no easy task, considering the extreme contrast the pair of attorneys presented. The ebullient Sanders was a singular character in just about every regard, including his appearance. Nearing fifty, he was still athletically built, with a shaved head and hardly any eyebrows. His chiseled features lent him the aspect of an actor who'd been hired to play Lex Luthor as a protagonist. "Perry isn't just larger than life. He also thinks big picture better than any lawyer I've ever met," Frank said. "It endlessly amazes me how often he makes a brilliant decision without needing to think about it very long, usually based more on intuition than analysis."

Sanders, though, knew better than anyone how much he depended on Frank to bring his often scattered attention into focus. Frank, then in his late thirties, disguised his considerable killer instinct with a blond beard, slumped shoulders, and a relentlessly self-deprecating attitude. He publicly played the part of a skilled legal technician who handled most of the briefs and motions, generally but not always deferring to Sanders in matters of strategy and presentation. It was the younger attorney alone, though, who made the decision that instead of taking the short hop to New York, he would first fly to Los Angeles for a meeting with Russell Poole, the former LAPD detective who had been featured in the *Rolling Stone* article. "I felt the first thing to do was to look at his evidence and see if there really is a case," Frank explained.

Frank booked a hotel in Long Beach, about halfway between LAX and Poole's home in Orange County, and was waiting there the next day when the ex-detective showed up with what he called "my files." "I thought he'd come in with a two-inch stack of papers," Frank recalled, "but Russ comes in with boxes. We needed a cart to carry it to my room." He and Poole spent nearly seven hours going through the documents in the boxes, Frank remembered. "When we were done, I called Perry and said, 'I don't know for sure, but this Russell Poole guy sure seems credible to me, and what he's put together looks like a real case,'" Frank recalled.

"Rob always understates," Sanders would say later. "If he says something looks like a case, you can be pretty sure it is." At his partner's urging, Frank flew back across the country the next day to meet with Voletta Wallace at Terri Baker's office in Manhattan. The mother of Notorious B.I.G., Frank discovered, was a tall, slender woman of proud carriage who looked him straight in the eye and seemed never to blink, let alone glance away. "Voletta was as impressive as anyone I've ever met," Frank recalled. "She had a grace to her, and a power to her. And her ability to articulate what her son meant to her and so many other people, what had been lost when he died, was remarkable. After the meeting, I reported back to Perry that I still wasn't sure we had a winning case, but we certainly had a winning client."

Before Biggie's murder, Voletta Wallace said, "I trusted everyone. I trusted the Los Angeles Police Department. I had to believe they wanted to find out who the murderer of my son was." Almost immediately after reading about former LAPD officer David Mack's alleged involvement in her son's death, though, Wallace said, she decided to pursue a civil action. "I wasn't thinking about the world I was taking on, only that something was not right and I have to make it right. If I have to sue them for that, I was gonna do it."

By early 2002, Sanders had weighed what he and Frank had learned from Russell Poole and Voletta Wallace and had arrived at the decision to file a civil rights claim in the federal district court of central California. "We wrote twenty-seven or twenty-eight drafts before we got the one we submitted," Frank recalled. Said Sanders, "Rob and I both knew it was a long shot, but it was a long shot worth takin'." The two lawyers were up against a statute of limitations deadline, and in the end had go with the best version they could deliver on time, a lawsuit accusing the LAPD of "policies and practices" that had permitted officers to obtain employment with Death Row Records and enabled at least one of them, former LAPD officer David Mack, to conspire with his friend Amir Muhammad to murder Notorious B.I.G. "Even then we didn't appreciate the magnitude of what we were getting ourselves into," admitted Frank.

They got a quick lesson when the City of Los Angeles answered their suit first with an attempt to "force us out on statute of limitations," Sanders recalled, then followed with a voluminous filing for summary judgment, the main grounds being that it could not be proved that David Mack—even if he was involved in the murder of Christopher Wallace—had acted under "color of law." Judge Florence Cooper made a tentative ruling in favor of the city, but she scheduled a hearing to allow the plaintiffs to persuade her to change her mind.

"I went to Perry and asked, 'Is this even worth going out to argue?'" Frank remembered. "Perry said, 'Hell yes, it is.'"

What followed was a long and contentious disagreement over how their reply to the city's motion should be couched. Sanders wanted to contend that if Mack had employed "cop tools and cop knowledge" as an accomplice in the Biggie murder, this satisfied the federal statute's color of law requirement. Frank did not think that would work. "We sat in a room going back and forth about it for thirteen solid hours," Frank recalled. Said Sanders, "By the time we finished, my butt was as sore as a butt could be. I didn't want to sit down for the entire next week."

"Long story short, Perry won the argument, and he was right," Frank said.

For the next several days, Frank said, he "prepared like crazy," then flew out to L.A. for the hearing before Judge Cooper. "I went to the courtroom very early to observe the judge, to see how she handles her business," Frank remembered. He had been sitting for some time before the city's lead attorney, Paul Paquette, showed up in the courtroom. "He didn't know who I was, and he was talking to some other attorneys about how this was a bullshit case and the judge was going to dismiss it for sure," Frank recalled. "He said she should have already. That got to me. If I wasn't charged up enough already, I was after that."

When Frank was given the opportunity to speak, he did, for nearly an hour. "I took the court through a survey of how color of law worked, then argued that as long as the murder was accompanied by some use of authority or knowledge granted by the state—'cop tools and cop knowledge'—it would satisfy the color of law requirement. And that argument changed her mind. She allowed the case to continue. It was one of those big victories that help you keep going when other things aren't working out so well."

Immediately after that ruling, Sanders hired a tech to set up the website BiggieHotline.com, where individuals could post tips about the murder, anonymously if they chose. "We got a lot of publicity after we filed and after the judge said the case could go forward, so clues started coming in like crazy," Sanders recalled. What most amazed and frustrated the attorney was the number of people who called or wrote to say they had seen Tupac Shakur alive and well in a Florida parking lot or a Maryland crab market or some other place in just about every state of the union. "A lot of the callers were spooky, strange, and totally useless to us," Sanders remembered. "We weren't prosecuting a lawsuit about Tupac's death. Almost nobody who came in on the hotline said they'd seen Biggie. I guess he was a little more difficult to mistake for somebody else."

Right around the time the hotline was put up, Sanders began to hear warnings from Voletta Wallace and Biggie's widow, Faith Evans, along with their New York attorneys and investigators, that his life was in danger. He tried to shrug it off with the same response he used during the Beats by the Pound lawsuit, Sanders recalled: "They'd ask me, 'Aren't you afraid?' Of all the gangbangers who surrounded Master P, they meant. I'd say, 'Are you afraid?' They'd say no, and I'd say, 'Then I'm not afraid. Because if they kill me, you'll just hire another lawyer, and they know that. But if they kill you, the case goes away.'"

He was shaken, Sanders admitted, after he was contacted on the hotline by a California prison inmate who said he'd been the cellmate of David Mack's former LAPD partner Rafael Perez and had a good deal of information about Perez's involvement with the Notorious B.I.G. murder. "I was interested, of course," Sanders recalled. "But there was something about a girlfriend or wife in Lake Charles who was gonna come and see me, and that scared us off. There are Bloods everywhere, and we thought it was a setup. I was really afraid I was gonna get killed if we agreed to that meeting. So, we didn't."

That would prove to be a problematic decision, though how significant the problem was Sanders wouldn't know until three years later.

Heartened by Judge Cooper's first major ruling, Sanders and Frank were even more encouraged when they learned that the Federal Bureau of Investigation was looking into B.I.G.'s murder. Shortly after the publication of the *Rolling Stone* article, a young agent in the FBI's Los Angeles office, Phil Carson, received permission to launch an investigation of the murder under federal civil rights laws. Sanders's anticipation was blunted, though, when Carson phoned to request a meeting in Louisiana, adding that he would be accompanied by two detectives from the LAPD's Internal Affairs (IA) Division. "You had to figure the LAPD guys were coming to run us off the case," the attorney explained. "And that if Phil Carson was bringing them along, he probably was going to tell us to go away, too."

He was flabbergasted, Sanders admitted, when Carson began the meeting in Lake Charles by saying, "We think you've sued the right people for this murder." To which one of the IA detectives quickly added, "And we believe there are others involved."

CHAPTER TWO

P hil Carson had not even been an FBI agent when Notorious B.I.G. was shot to death outside the Petersen Automotive
Museum. Carson, a compact man with sandy hair, elfin features, bright blue eyes, and a buff physique, was at that time working
in Orange County as a bond trader for Titan Value Equities. He
hadn't entered the FBI Academy until June 1997—three months
after the Biggie murder—at the age of thirty-three, yet still had
managed to finish first in his class in physical training and defensive
tactics. His assignment to the bureau's Los Angeles office, though,
had plunged the probationary agent into the maelstrom of police
corruption cases swirling through Southern California. Carson had
worked on several such investigations, most notably one centered
on Ruben Palomares, an LAPD officer suspected of organizing more
than forty home invasion robberies perpetrated by his gang of fellow
cops. The investigation conducted by Carson and partners from the
LAPD's Internal Affairs Division had compelled a guilty plea by
Palomares that resulted in a thirteen-year prison sentence for him on
the condition he testify in court against his associates. On the basis of
what Palomares told the judge and jury, one of his associates would
be sentenced to nearly ninety years in prison.

Carson would eventually receive the U.S. Department of Justice's
annual Exceptional Service award (presented to him by Attorney
General Eric Holder) for his work on the Palomares case, but he

was still a young agent in the early stage of his career in June 2001, when "The Murder of Notorious B.I.G." was published in *Rolling Stone*. Carson, admittedly "not much of a reader," had not learned of the Biggie case until a couple of months later when the VH1 network aired a documentary that drew heavily on the magazine article. He was "pulled in" by the implication of David Mack in Detective Russell Poole's investigation of the Biggie murder, Carson said, because of all the connections he saw to the LAPD corruption cases he had investigated during the previous three years. "It was the number of similarities," Carson explained. "The tactics, the players, and, especially, the criminal culture that had been cultivated inside the LAPD, in particular among cops working with celebrities." He wrote a long outline of how the earlier cases he had worked seemed to be intertwined with the Biggie murder, Carson recalled, "then went in to my bosses and said, 'You guys gotta look at this. I know there's something here.'"

His FBI supervisors agreed. Carson asked that two LAPD investigators he had worked with on the Palomares case, Roger Mora and Steve Sambar, be assigned to the investigation with him. The police department granted the request. Carson was further encouraged when the LAPD's number two man, Deputy Chief Jim McDonnell, helped him, Mora, and Sambar set up a ruse that permitted them to examine the department's investigative file—its "Murder Book"—on the Biggie case. "William Bratton, who had just been appointed chief, said, 'Hey, I'm new here. I want to see all the unsolved high-profile cases, one being the Biggie Smalls murder,'" Carson recalled. "'Give me that entire case so I can peruse it.' Then what McDonnell did was have it brought over, surreptitiously, to the FBI office. Mora and Sambar and I were sent into a conference room to look through it. McDonnell told us, 'You can't make any copies, you can just look.'"

Among the details that jumped out at him, Carson recalled, was the report by Russell Poole in which he described how a large cache of GECO ammunition—the unusual brand of bullets that had been fired in the Notorious B.I.G. slaying—had been recovered from the garage of David Mack after he was arrested for the November 6, 1997, armed robbery of more than $722,000 from the Bank of America branch just north of the USC campus. It was the FBI that had first actually identified the GECO ammunition when the bureau's agents searched Mack's home after LAPD officers arrested him. The LAPD, as Poole noted, had simply left the ammunition sitting in the garage without even noting its brand.

GECO, Carson knew, was German-manufactured ammunition intended mainly for the 9-mm Luger, though it would work in nearly any 9-mm automatic pistol. Seven GECO shell casings had been collected from the scene of the Notorious B.I.G. shooting. GECO bullets, Carson learned from FBI reports, were "extremely rare" in the United States—so rare that there was not a single mention of their use in a crime in the entire FBI database, with the exception of the Christopher Wallace murder. Only two stores in the Unites States sold GECO bullets, Carson discovered: one in New Jersey and the other in Corona, California, the city where Death Row Records director of security Reggie Wright Jr. lived, and where Amir Muhammad had conducted a good deal of his mortgage brokerage business.

By the time he had finished paging through the Biggie Murder Book, Carson recalled, he was certain of three things: "The first was that one person could not possibly have pulled off this murder by himself, even if he was a police officer. The logistics were just too complicated. You had to know how to move and manipulate law enforcement to be able to do it and get away. There was just no way it could have been done otherwise. The second was that the LAPD had done absolutely nothing on this case for the past two years, since it was assigned to Steve Katz as the lead investigator. The Murder Book was literally collecting dust. The third thing I realized was that Russ Poole had done a lot of great work, work that was right on, and they had shut him down before he could finish his job."

Within days, Carson had arranged for Poole's designation as what the FBI called a "137 source," essentially making him a confidential witness brought in to aid the investigation. "I got enough money from my bosses to copy Russ's entire case file," Carson remembered, "and after I looked through that I was really impressed. I made it clear to my bosses that David Mack and Amir Muhammad were going to be targets of my investigation, along with other police officers, and my bosses signed off on it."

He found Poole to be a tremendous asset, Carson said, but also a tremendous pain in the ass. "Russ was a good guy, but he could just *not* let go," Carson explained. "And I couldn't blame the guy, because he had sacrificed so much to try to make this case. But he was always calling me, and saying, 'Did you think of this? Did you talk to him? Have you considered this? Have you looked at that?' And sometimes he would get upset with me because I couldn't tell him things. It was an ongoing investigation, and I'm bound by the FBI's confidentiality rules. But Russ had a hard time accepting that, and he started to get frustrated with me. And I started to get tired of him."

Not long after setting up the Murder Book ruse, Jim McDonnell had been replaced as Carson's main point of contact with the LAPD command staff by Michael Berkow, recently appointed by William Bratton as his new deputy chief. Bratton had hired Berkow away from his position as chief of police for the city of Irvine, in Orange County, making him "the first outside sworn deputy chief in the history of the Los Angeles Police Department," as the LAPD website described it. What that press release hadn't mentioned was that Bratton had placed Berkow in charge of the department's most sensitive division, Internal Affairs, giving his man control of all claims of LAPD misconduct or corruption.

Berkow and Bratton agreed to let the Internal Affairs Division investigators, Mora and Sambar, accompany Carson to Louisiana to meet with Perry Sanders. "Roger and Steve were great detectives and really good guys, both totally straight," Carson said. "So I figured the LAPD had to be pretty committed to this investigation if they would give me a couple of guys like this to work with. Roger and Steve were just as enthusiastic about talking to Perry Sanders as I was. Just like me, they wanted to see what leads Perry was following or not following, but mainly what we wanted was an avenue to people who wouldn't talk to law enforcement." Carson and the IA investigators were particularly interested in gaining access to two key witnesses to the Notorious B.I.G. slaying: Eugene Deal, who had been working as the bodyguard for Sean "Puffy" Combs on the night of the murder; and rapper James "Lil' Cease" Lloyd, who was riding in the same vehicle with Biggie when the shooting happened.

"And Perry was great about that," Carson said. " Once he trusted us, he basically gave us everything he had and all the help we asked for."

Carson and the two LAPD detectives also traveled to Colorado Springs, to meet Rob Frank and go through the documents he had obtained in discovery. When they returned to Los Angeles, however, Carson learned that Deputy Chief Berkow had pulled Mora and Sambar off the case. "I was stunned," Carson recalled. "All I knew was that Roger and Steve had shown Berkow everything we'd gotten in Louisiana and Colorado, and he'd immediately told them they were no longer part of the Biggie murder investigation." Mora and Sambar were not available even to consult on the investigation, although one of them did confide, Carson said, that, "'if this case gets made, the effects could be catastrophic for the LAPD.' And now Berkow, and presumably Bratton, knew we *were* making the case."

He still could not at that point process the LAPD's position, Carson admitted. "I had had almost entirely good experiences working with LAPD. As I said, Roger and Steve were top-notch guys. So I wanted to work with LAPD on the Biggie case." Then Berkow paid a visit to Carson at the FBI office. "He said, 'Look, I'd like to give you Mora and Sambar back, but we're short of bodies,'" Carson recalled. "'So, what I want you to do is put together a PowerPoint presentation and show me what you've done and what you plan on doing, then I'll see what I can do.'"

Carson went to his FBI supervisors with Berkow's request and was relieved when his bosses told him that there was no way they were giving the LAPD the blueprint of their investigation. Carson still hoped to get Mora and Sambar back on the case, so he suggested offering the LAPD brass an olive branch. "Through Perry Sanders, I had access to witnesses who wouldn't talk to the LAPD, because they thought LAPD was involved in Biggie's murder. I said we should help the LAPD find out what these people knew." His boss, Steve Gomez, agreed. Carson placed a call to Katz, the Robbery-Homicide Division detective who had supposedly been in charge of the Biggie investigation for the past two years, and asked if they could look at the Murder Book together. Katz agreed.

"So I go over to LAPD to sit down with Katz and go through the Murder Book," Carson recalled. "And very quickly I'm in shock." Numerous photographs that were part of the book when he had examined it at the FBI office were now gone, Carson realized. "These were photos of police officers who were inside the Petersen Museum on the night of the Biggie murder," Carson recalled, "plus a photo of Big Gene Deal standing with the person he identified as Amir Muhammad outside the museum by Puffy Combs's vehicle. All of those photos had been removed."

He couldn't tell Katz that he knew the photos were missing, Carson explained, because he was not supposed to have seen the Murder Book previously. Only when he found a report in the Murder Book in which Katz had made reference to the missing photographs did Carson ask the detective where those pictures were now. "Katz told me he had no idea what I was talking about," the FBI agent recalled.

For a few moments, Carson sat stunned, trying to gather his thoughts. "And then I actually tried to convince Katz he should work with me. I tell him, 'Hey, this is where I am, this is what I've got. If you guys want to reengage your Murder Book and work with me on this case, I'm open to it.'"

As a result, Carson was invited to what he understood would be a meeting with Katz and Robbery-Homicide's commanding officer, Captain Al Michelena. His main purpose in going, Carson said, was his hope that he could persuade the LAPD to run a ballistics test on the GECO shell casings recovered from the scene of the Biggie murder and still in the police department's possession.

"I brought Steve Gomez with me, and when we get to Robbery-Homicide we're shown into this room where ten or twelve of these old-school, crusty, keep-everything-close-to-the-vest kind of RHD [Robbery-Homicide Division] guys are sitting around the table," Carson recalled. "And they're looking at me like I'm the plague. I look at my boss like, 'I didn't expect this,' and he looks back at me like, 'I didn't, either.' The tension was insane. I mean, these guys, if eyes could kill, I'd have been a dead man."

He quickly realized that the men in the room understood that the FBI believed Russell Poole's theory of the Biggie case was supported by enough evidence to warrant opening a federal investigation, and that this made him their enemy, Carson recalled: "They get that we don't investigate homicides unless there's a federal nexus, and the involvement of police officers is one of the things that creates that federal nexus. So they know we must have some real evidence of police involvement in the Biggie murder. They realize that the FBI has decided to pick this case up where Russell Poole left off, and they're both terrified by and furious about that. And they let us know that they have absolutely no intention of helping us in any way, shape, or form."

He and Gomez were each in a daze after they walked out of that conference room, Carson said. "But Steve told me, and I agreed, that we should try to maintain an amicable relationship with the LAPD, if that was possible."

Shortly after that meeting, Carson was approached by the most decorated television reporter in Los Angeles, Chris Blatchford, with a request that he appear in a special that Blatchford was putting together on the Biggie murder for KTTV, the local Fox network affiliate. "My bosses and I agreed I should do it, because, the thinking was, this is local and it could generate some leads. We didn't know how many, but at least dozens, we figured. Maybe hundreds." As part of his ongoing effort to show the police that he wanted to work with them, not against them, Carson approached the LAPD to suggest they set up a joint hotline that would be publicized on the KTTV special.

"So we come to an agreement that I thought even at the time was crazy," Carson recalled. "I would do the interview, but LAPD would handle the hotline." A few days after the special aired, Steve Katz informed Carson of the results. "Guess how many leads the LAPD said they got from that special? Zero!" Carson recalled. "Guess how many phone calls the LAPD said they got? Zero. They didn't even try to pretend. They could have said, 'Oh we got fifteen calls and twelve were crazies and the other three wouldn't give their names,' and we wouldn't have known for sure they were lying. But they didn't care."

Carson would not truly begin to realize what he was up against, though, until he tried to interview Reggie Blaylock, the Inglewood police officer who had been working as part of the Puffy Combs–Notorious B.I.G. security detail on the night of Biggie's murder. Blaylock, who was at the wheel of the black SUV that was serving as the "trail car" in the Bad Boy Records entourage as it left the Petersen Museum that night, had disappeared from the scene by the time LAPD investigators arrived. Weeks would pass before the LAPD could compel Blaylock to provide a statement. His description of the events surrounding Biggie's murder ran to six pages but offered almost nothing useful to the investigation. He claimed never to have seen the shooter's face and could only describe his complexion as "lighter than mine."

Just as Russell Poole had been, Carson was most troubled by Blaylock's failure to give chase after the shooting. "You're a sworn law enforcement officer carrying a gun sitting at the wheel of a vehicle that is right behind a vehicle in which the passenger is shot to death and you don't go after the shooter?" Carson wondered. "No way does that make sense unless there's something else going on. So of course I want to ask Blaylock about it. But the LAPD kept him so wrapped up that I could not get to the guy. They literally shielded him from me. That was when I first began to understand that the LAPD was not simply refusing to assist me in my investigation, but was actually doing what they could to obstruct me."

Perry Sanders and Rob Frank received a bracing lesson in where *they* stood in the eyes of the Los Angeles Police Department when Judge Cooper granted their first major discovery motion and ordered the LAPD's Robbery-Homicide Division to share its entire case file on the Notorious B.I.G. murder investigation.

"We arrive at Robbery-Homicide and there's file cabinets lined up that are filled floor to ceiling," Sanders recalled. "They put us off in an interrogation room in the corner, and all the cops are outside sneerin' at us."

"They were trying to intimidate us for sure," said Frank. "It was a completely hostile atmosphere. I was waiting for them to lock the door on us."

In Sanders's recollection, "It was plenty tense and a total blast. I mean, there we are in the bowels of RHD, in the belly of the beast, and they have to deal with us. I love that stuff."

The fun ended when the files began to arrive in the interrogation room, one after another, "like on some crazy conveyer belt," Sanders recalled. "It's comin' at us so fast we have to make quick decisions on what to have copied. We're both speed-readin' through this stuff that is ninety-nine percent baloney."

"There were so many horses all we could do was look for zebras," Frank remembered. "Anything out of the ordinary we grabbed. We could only hope we were guessing right."

The day was a template for how the City of Los Angeles would answer the Notorious B.I.G. lawsuit, satisfying the letter of the law with as little actual cooperation as possible. Perhaps because he sensed it would be this way throughout, Sanders had earlier decided that a court reporter should be present at the Rule 26 conference. These conferences are face-to-face meetings between the attorneys for the plaintiffs and the defendants in federal cases, held immediately before the discovery process begins. "Under the rules, the city had an obligation to disclose any relevant evidence," Frank explained. "I went through it painstakingly, asking every conceivable question." The transcript of the Rule 26 conference eventually came to be among the most significant pieces of evidence placed before the court.

"But we had absolutely no clue it would be that way at the time," Frank said. "Bringing the court reporter in was an absolutely brilliant decision by Perry."

"Just a wild-assed hunch," Sanders said. "I figured I was probably wastin' money, but somethin' told me to do it."

Once they had the Robbery-Homicide files in hand and began to bring in more discovery, much of it based on the list of documents cited in the back of my 2002 book *LAbyrinth*, Sanders and Frank realized that the next big step was to hire the right private investigator. Everybody he knew in L.A. said that was Anthony Pellicano, Sanders remembered. When he spoke to Pellicano in early 2002, though, the investigator's aggressive grasping made him uneasy, the attorney said. "Pellicano wanted a twenty-five-thousand-dollar retainer right now," Sanders recalled. "I mean, he wanted it *right* now." Something about how intensely Pellicano demanded the money gave him pause, said Sanders, who by the time he flew back to Colorado Springs a few days later had decided to tell Frank they should go in another direction. Instinctive or reasoned, the decision would prove a wise one. Within the year, Pellicano would be arrested for illegally possessing grenades and plastic explosives, and the subsequent federal investigation would spiral into wiretapping and racketeering charges that added another fifteen years to the P.I.'s prison sentence. More than a dozen of Hollywood's best-known power players—Michael Ovitz, Brad Grey, and Ron Meyer, among them—would be drawn into the biggest scandal the entertainment industry had seen since the arrest of Hollywood madam Heidi Fleiss. One of those put through the wringer was Bert Fields, considered by many the most powerful attorney in show business, who had used Pellicano as his investigator for years. "I can't remember how many times Rob thanked me for not getting us into that mess," Sanders said.

Sanders, in the midst of relocating to Colorado from Louisiana, was house hunting in the Colorado Springs area when Russell Poole phoned to say that he was visiting a relative in Denver and offered to drive down for a meeting. "I had the same reaction that Rob did," Sanders recalled. "There was a plain decency to Russ that made me feel real good about how he'd come across as a witness in court." It was Poole who suggested that Sanders and Frank consider hiring Sergio Robleto as a consultant and an expert witness. His former supervising lieutenant in LAPD's South Bureau Homicide was one of the sharpest and most dedicated cops he'd ever worked with, Poole told the attorneys, and absolutely the best he'd ever worked under.

Seventeen hundred unsolved murders were on the books when Robleto arrived at South Bureau, a number he publicly declared to be "completely unacceptable." That apparently hundreds of killers were escaping justice in South-Central L.A. created an impression that the LAPD didn't care about the mostly young black men who were their victims, Robleto said, or the law-abiding people who had to live in fear of gang members with guns. He immediately established an unsolved murder unit, one that he closely supervised, often working right alongside his investigators. Within a matter of months the number of murder arrests in South Bureau skyrocketed, as did the number of unsolved cases that were closed.

This success had made Robleto a hot commodity in the department, where many believed he was destined for an eventual appointment as the LAPD's first Hispanic chief. Sergio had surprised and disappointed a good many people, Poole told Frank and Sanders, when he resigned in 1995 to take a position at Kroll Associates, the New York–based "risk consulting" firm that had become popularly known in the media as the "corporate CIA." The attorneys, though, were delighted to learn that Robleto had spent four years (1998–2002) heading up Kroll's Los Angeles office before leaving to establish his own private investigation agency. Kroll's fingerprints were all over the LAPD, Sanders and Frank knew. Not only had the company won the contract to monitor the department's compliance with the consent decree imposed on it by the U.S. Department of Justice in the aftermath of the Rampart Scandal (placing the LAPD under the supervision of a federal monitor), but the man chosen to succeed Bernard Parks as LAPD chief in 2002 was Kroll executive William Bratton, who had formerly served as police commissioner in both Boston and New York. Among many other things, Robleto might help them understand the politics of the LAPD, Sanders and Frank agreed. And if he was as good an investigator as Russ Poole said he was, it seemed there could be no better choice.

The attorneys became somewhat skeptical, though, when Robleto showed up in Colorado Springs to examine the investigative files they'd received in discovery. "I'd talked to Sergio on the phone, laid out our case," Frank remembered. "He said he'd come out and see me. I assumed he was going to set up a meeting, but he's at my office at nine the next morning. I shake hands with this short and slightly chubby Guatemalan guy, smiling and jovial, and suddenly I'm not sure about him. I thought maybe he wasn't serious enough. But he asked to have all the Murder Book files moved to the conference room so he could spread them out and study them, and I figured, why not? Four hours later he comes in to see me and starts asking a series of questions that I hadn't even thought of and couldn't answer. And he did it with a precision and clarity that absolutely astonished me."

That twinkle in Robleto's eye, Frank and Sanders quickly learned, masked an ability to combine focus and ferocity that they had encountered in few other people. "On top of that, I came to know Sergio as one of the best human beings I've ever met," Frank said. "People think I hate cops, because I've sued a lot of them, but I don't. And I always put Russ Poole and Sergio Robleto at the very top of the list of cops I've met."

Robleto had first become familiar with the Notorious B.I.G. murder investigation and the politics surrounding it back in 2000.

That was when Poole had contacted him to ask for support. "Russ said there was an article coming out in the *L.A. Weekly* about how the LAPD had ostracized him and refused to let him fully investigate the murder," Robleto recalled. "He knew that making sure every major crime gets fully investigated is something near and dear to my heart. I preached tenacity, as Russ was well aware. Russ was in full battle mode at the time, and he was a pretty intense fellow anyway. He asked me to talk to the reporter writing the article and 'tell him what you know about me.' So I did. I told the reporter that Russ was one of the finest investigators I had in South Bureau, that there was none better. He was absolutely tenacious, absolutely honest, absolutely committed. I didn't fully understand what was going on with Russ at the time, though, so I wasn't willing to talk about Chief Parks, which may have disappointed Russ a little."

When he arrived in Colorado Springs, there were fifty-four volumes of the Biggie Smalls Murder Book, Robleto remembered, the most he'd ever seen connected to a single case: enough four-inch blue binders to fill a pair of file cabinets. It took him two solid weeks to read through those and the forty-four boxes of other materials from the LAPD stacked in a conference room. By the time he was done, Robleto was prepared to tell Frank and Sanders that this was by far the most politicized and compromised murder investigation he'd ever seen.

"The most glaring thing, the most shocking, was the number of percipient witnesses who were never interviewed and the number of major clues that were never followed up," Robleto recalled. "People who had been at the scene at the time of the murder were never interviewed because they were never called back, and then the LAPD lost track of them. That, to me, was unbelievable."

He recalled another case in South Bureau where there had been a hundred witnesses to a murder, Robleto said. His detectives had interviewed fifty of those before saying they found the killer, Robleto remembered. "I interviewed the rest and found he wasn't the guy. That's why you talk to everybody. That's also why in this case I found myself asking, 'How it is it possible that they didn't even bother to call up witnesses who said they knew who committed the crime?' That's absolutely deficient. Reckless, almost.

"Leads that name a suspect we call 'category one' leads," Robleto explained. "Seeing how many of those the LAPD investigation just let slide gave a lot of credence in my mind to what Russ was saying about not being allowed to go and follow leads, because of the politics."

In his entire career, he had never seen a case where the LAPD had "chosen to obfuscate or block a murder investigation," Robleto said. "To me, that was something to be proud of. But I couldn't see any other reason why the department had walled off this investigation, telling a detective, basically, 'Don't go there.'"

What excited Frank was Robleto's determination that the Notorious B.I.G. assassination was the furthest thing from a gangbanger murder; it had been too well planned and well executed to have been the work of anyone but professionals. "The level of foreknowledge and sophistication in the Christopher Wallace murder was the most significant thing to me," Frank explained. "Sergio was able to show that whoever committed this murder knew things about Christopher Wallace's security and whereabouts. That was just amazing. The precision of the killing and the escape afterward suggested this was a far, far cry from some thug murder. It also suggested access to communications equipment and police frequencies. In order to pull up alongside Christopher Wallace's vehicle when he did, number one, the driver had to have known when the Wallace vehicle was leaving the Petersen Museum. And the spot where the shooting took place had to have been staged, with the communications and the escape route all laid out in advance. There were police everywhere, on the corners and in the parking lots, and more police coming in response to shots fired. And yet no police came across the killer's car, even made eye contact with it. The killer or killers knew where the police were. That was significant for a lot of reasons, but especially the whole color of law claim we were making. Some aspects of this murder required someone to use authority or pretense of their authority, and it would also have required police communication equipment or its equivalent. There had to be somebody who was either a cop or was helped by cops. This was all part of what we were going to need Sergio to testify about."

Said Robleto, "The description of the original response in the documents I'd seen was confusing. There were fifteen hundred people packed into a room and sixty police officers on the scene. With that many policemen, how the hell did somebody not notice something was coming down?"

A gunshot fired on Orange Grove Avenue just minutes before the murder was a partial explanation, Robleto said. Russell Poole apparently had been the only LAPD investigator who believed that the Orange Grove shot was not an unrelated event but rather a deliberately staged distraction. Robleto found himself agreeing with his former detective. Other investigators had accepted the explanation of the young man who claimed he had fired the shot after his gun had fallen out of his Ford Explorer's map pocket to the pavement and he had discharged a round into the air to make sure his weapon was still working. To Robleto, though, this sounded like "a perfect way to stage such a distraction and get away with it."

What Robleto found most difficult to fathom was that the Robbery-Homicide Division hadn't taken the case right from the start. He'd learned from the LAPD reports he'd read in Colorado that the RHD captain and one of his lieutenants "were there that first night." But, recalled Robleto, who had worked in Robbery-Homicide in 1983–84, "they were gone by the next morning and didn't come back to the case until an entire month had passed. In thirty years I had never seen that: a murder case involving a major celebrity that wasn't taken over by Robbery-Homicide right out of the gate."

And in this case the major celebrity was the victim, which made it even harder to fathom. "There was no other possible explanation other than that this was a political decision," Robleto said. "Clearly this case was beyond the resources of Wilshire Division." He could see that plainly in the LAPD's own documents, Robleto said. "You had people removing evidence and handing it over to the police later, which basically makes it useless. There were witnesses who had given a description of the shooter, but no one seemed to follow up on it. I mean, the killer had been identified as either belonging to or wanting to appear to belong to a certain group, the Nation of Islam, but no effort was made to follow up on that until Russ Poole came on the case a month later. They wasted time chasing a theory that the Crips had done it when everything pointed away from that. They had a helluva lot of good clues in Wilshire, but they weren't able to do much with them, in part because they were overwhelmed. Then when Russ came in, he was being set up to fail almost right from the first."

CHAPTER THREE

What had become clear to Sanders and Frank in the first round of discovery and witness depositions was that the Los Angeles Police Department had no real interest in solving the murder of Christopher Wallace. Nothing made this more evident to the attorneys than their questioning of the detective who had been in charge of the case since 1999, Steve Katz. Sanders and Frank were startled by Katz's admission that he'd made three trips to Houston in connection with a pair of "primary suspects" named Richard Daniels and Tony Draper, who had been seen driving a Bentley Coupe near the Petersen Automotive Museum on the night of the shooting. What made this so astonishing was that neither Daniels nor Draper had been implicated in the crime by even the tiniest shred of evidence. In dozens of documents, including search warrants, the LAPD had identified the vehicle driven by the killer that night as a black Impala. Katz couldn't offer an even remotely persuasive reason why the investigation should focus on Draper and Daniels. "All we could think of was that it made Katz look like he was keeping busy, and it gave him and his partner a series of paid vacations in Texas," Frank said.

Phil Carson put it this way: "My interest had forced the LAPD to start pretending they were investigating the case. They had to do something, even if it was nothing."

Robleto was even more perplexed than the attorneys by the LAPD's focus on the two Houston men and their Bentley. "I really tried to understand and be open," Robleto said. "I still wanted to believe in the police department I'd given most of my career to. But there was absolutely no evidence that pointed to the two Houston guys. And the difference between a Bentley and an Impala SS is huge. Nobody's going to mistake one for the other." He was disgusted, Robleto said, when he saw reports on how LAPD investigators had reconstructed the shooting scene in an alley to try to figure out whether the trajectory of the bullets that killed Biggie matched up with the window height of the Bentley better than the Impala's. "If you look at the street where the murder occurred, you see that the pavement drops toward the curb, where it's about a foot lower than in the center of the road," Robleto said. "The vehicle Christopher Wallace was sitting in was on the high part of the road, and the shooter's car was by the curb on the lower part of the pavement. Yet they did the reconstruction on perfectly level ground. Their approach was at best flawed and at worst stupid. It was a complete waste of time and money, but when you looked through the records of their so-called investigation, it looked like that was exactly what they wanted to do, waste time and money."

Katz and the LAPD certainly weren't investing any resources in the theory of the Biggie Smalls murder that Russell Poole had put forth in his original investigation of the crime. For nearly everyone who had followed the case, Eugene Deal's identification of Amir Muhammad as the "Muslim-looking guy" whom the massive bodyguard had encountered outside the Petersen Museum just before the shooting had been a bombshell. But neither Katz nor anyone else from the LAPD had ever contacted Nick Broomfield, the documentary film director who had shown Deal the photo lineup from which he'd identified Muhammad. According to Katz, Deal "didn't give a real hundred percent identification, but he said he felt that it was him." In fact, Deal was definite: "That's the guy," he'd told Broomfield. "That's the guy who came up to me." When Broomfield asked if that was "definitely him," Deal nodded vigorously. "Yep," he said.

When Katz finally did interview Deal, he left the big man embittered and skittish. After they spoke, Deal said, Katz called Deal's superiors at the New York State Parole Department to report him for working as a bodyguard to Notorious B.I.G. That wasn't true, said Deal—he was Puffy Combs's bodyguard on the night of the shooting—but Katz's claim had been enough to embroil Deal in a protracted dispute with his employer, which accused him of working too many hours outside his regular job.

To Sanders, the strangest part of the Katz depositions had been his explanation for why he had never questioned Amir Muhammad. Katz explained that since the FBI was focused on the "Mack-Muhammad theory" of the case, the LAPD had made a decision to let it handle that part of the investigation.

"Oh, I see, they *let* us handle it," Phil Carson would say when Sanders told him what Katz had said. "What about the two years Katz had the case before there even *was* an FBI investigation?" Wasn't it true, Frank asked during one Katz deposition, that Phil Carson had sent him a note suggesting that Suge Knight's attorney David Kenner may have made mortgage payments for David Mack or Amir Muhammad? It was, Katz acknowledged, but the LAPD never looked into that claim.

The LAPD was in possession of documents in which Amir Muhammad had identified his work address as 1297 Steiner Drive in Chula Vista, wasn't that correct? Frank asked. Had the LAPD determined whether that was correct? No, it hadn't, Katz answered, "because that is inclusive of some of the things that the FBI is doing." Had the LAPD made any attempt at all to contact Amir Muhammad subsequent to August 15, 2003? Frank asked. It had not, Katz answered, because the FBI was "working that angle of the investigation." And besides, the detective added, he didn't consider Amir Muhammad to be the "primary suspect" in the murder of Christopher Wallace.

But Richard Daniels and Tony Draper *were* primary suspects, Frank observed. Katz's only reply was a slight smirk.

A moment later the detective said he had recently planned to interview Amir Muhammad, only to be asked by the new commander of the Robbery-Homicide Division, Captain Michelena, to "hold off" for sixty days to let the FBI complete its investigation. But he still planned to interview Muhammad at some point in the future, Katz said. "Does that mean a month, two months, six months?" Frank asked. "I couldn't tell you," answered Katz, who then mentioned that he had been considering placing a wiretap on Muhammad.

Why would you do that? Frank asked. Because Muhammad was still a suspect in the murder, answered Katz, contradicting what he had said just moments earlier.

Frank and Sanders would depose Katz at length three times prior to trial, and yet in all those hours there was only a single revelation that either attorney found remarkable. At one point, Katz for some reason mentioned that a hidden microphone had been placed in Suge Knight's cell while he was being held in the L.A. County Jail. Why had that been done? Frank asked. It was because the LAPD had obtained "information that indicated that he may have been involved in the murder, but not enough to sufficiently arrest him," Katz answered.

Suge Knight was far more isolated and vulnerable than he had been during the years Russell Poole was investigating him as the man behind the murder of Notorious B.I.G. A good deal of Suge's new circumstances had to do with the attrition of his thugs. Aaron Palmer, better known as "Heron," had been the first to fall, shot dead at the wheel of a Toyota 4Runner stopped for a red light at a Compton intersection at dusk on June 1, 1997, less than three months after the Notorious B.I.G. murder. Heron was heading home from a Death Row party when two men jumped out of a blue van and emptied their semiautomatic pistols into him. He was thirty years old.

The next to go down was William "Chin" Walker, who, just after midnight on April 4, 2000, was sitting next to fellow Blood Wardell "Poochie" Fouse in a white Chevrolet van parked on a dead-end street in Compton, when two men ran up on both sides of the vehicle and emptied their pistols though the windows. Walker, in the driver's seat, had bled out by the time he made it to the hospital. He was thirty-seven. Though gravely wounded, Fouse survived. Three weeks later, Vence "V" Buchanan had been found facedown in a Compton graveyard. Word on the streets was that Buchanan, although a Blood himself, was allied with a renegade group of Death Row bodyguards and drug dealers from the Fruit Town Piru Bloods set that had turned against Suge and the Mob Pirus. V, it was said, had helped arrange the shooting that left Chin Walker dead and Poochie Fouse in a wheel-chair for three months.

According to eyewitnesses, men wearing police uniforms had grabbed Buchanan off the street at the intersection of Central and 135th avenues, cuffed his hands behind his back, and forced him into the back of a dark-colored Cadillac. By the time his body was found in the cemetery, V had been tortured, mutilated, and finally executed with a bullet to the back of his head. Alton "Buntry" McDonald, Suge's number one thug, and his partner David "Brim" Dudley reportedly had made a videotape of Buchanan's torture and execution that they were playing for audiences of fellow Mob Pirus.

Brim escaped the vengeance of the Fruit Town Pirus for nearly another year before he was shot dead on March 25, 2001, outside Buntry's house. Just over a year after that, on April 3, 2002, Buntry was filling the tank of his black GMC Denali at the big Shell station at the corner of Rosecrans and Atlantic avenues when two men walked up with pistols and shot him four times in the chest before fleeing in a pickup truck, leaving the hulking gangster dead at thirty-seven.

Henry "Hen Dog" Smith became Suge's new top thug, but occu-pied that position for only six months. On the afternoon of October 16, 2002, Hen Dog was wearing a Death Row medallion around his neck and sitting at the wheel of a burgundy Jeep parked next to a fried-chicken stand in South-Central L.A. while his girlfriend used a nearby pay phone. The girlfriend's infant son was lying on the backseat when a young man stepped up next to the Jeep, leaned in through an open window, fired six shots, then fled on a bicycle. Thirty-three-year-old Hen Dog was dead on the spot.

By the summer of 2003, Poochie Fouse had largely recovered from the wounds he'd suffered in the 2000 shooting that claimed Chin Walker's life. Early on the evening of July 24, he was riding a motorcycle on Central Avenue when a car sped up from behind him and the young man in the passenger seat began firing. Poochie, now forty-three, was hit ten times in the back and died in a puddle of blood on the pavement.

Even those of Suge's thugs who survived were unavailable to him because of their prison sentences. Travon "Tray" Lane and Roger "Neckbone" Williams, each of whom had participated in the stomping of Southside Crip Orlando Anderson* on the night of the Tupac Shakur murder, were behind bars after armed assault and weapons convictions.

Knight himself had spent nearly all of the past six years behind bars. He'd done five of those years as part of his sentence for assaulting producers George and Lynwood Stanley at Solar Records in Hollywood. During that period, Suge was held in jails and prisons all over the state. His longest residence was at Mule Creek State Prison in Ione, a small town in central California that in earlier incarnations was known as Bed Bug, Freeze Out, and Hardscrabble. In May 2001 Knight landed at the federal prison in Sheridan, Oregon, to be processed back into society.

Upon his release in August of that year, Suge did his best to project an air of confidence about the revival of his renamed record company, Tha Row. "Welcome Home Suge," read the billboard above

---

* Anderson, shot to death himself in 1998, has been and continues to be the primary suspect as triggerman in the Shakur murder.

Tha Row's Wilshire Boulevard offices on the day of Knight's return to Los Angeles. "Better days is coming," Knight told the *Los Angeles Times.* "It's like we're getting ready for the Super Bowl. Preparing for the game. We're going to win the big one. Going to sign some new young producers to come up with some tough new stuff." The reality, though, was that with Tupac Shakur dead, and Snoop Dogg and Doctor Dre moved on to other companies, Tha Row had become a second-tier rap label where the nearest thing to a star was the modestly talented Kurupt.

Within fourteen months of Suge's release from prison, Buntry and Hen Dog had been shot dead by the Fruit Town Pirus, and Knight himself was a hunted man. In November 2002, fifteen months after his release, Suge was caught up in the net cast by the Los Angeles County Sheriff's Department in the Eric "Scar" Daniel murder case. Daniel, one of the Fruit Town Pirus believed to have pulled the trigger on Buntry, had been shot dead on June 7. The Sheriff's Department issued arrest warrants in connection with the killing for eight men, all Mob Piru Bloods and Suge Knight associates. One of them was Knight's bodyguard Kordell Depree Knox, who had been fired from his job as a Los Angeles County sheriff's deputy only a couple of weeks earlier. In the course of searching Tha Row's offices and the nine-thousand-square-foot home in Malibu where Knight was currently living, sheriff's investigators put together a case that Suge had violated the terms of his parole by associating with convicted felons and known gang members. He was arrested on December 2, 2002, and locked up in Los Angeles County Jail, where he would be spending Christmas.

Suge had seemed to sense immediately that the Sheriff's Department was overreaching. His arrest was a desperate effort to salvage the bungled investigation of the Scar Daniel murder, Suge told the *Los Angeles Times* in an interview the day after Christmas. When he last met with his parole officer, Suge said, a gang investigator had showed up to threaten him with a long jail sentence if he didn't tell what he knew about the killings of Scar, Buntry, Hen Dog, and V Buchanan, among others: "I told him, 'You better handcuff me right now. Because I don't know a thing about it.'" The Sheriff's Department admitted that Knight was not a suspect in any of the murders. The case it had made against Suge was based entirely on photographs seized from the Malibu house and Tha Row office that showed Knight posing with various Bloods, all of them making what were described as "gang signs." The pictures were from a rehearsal for his rapper Crooked I, Suge said. The cops were so clueless that "they think anything with fingers in the air is a gang sign," he explained. If "I have to stop dealing with people from the hood, I might as well shut down my business," Knight added. "I can't turn my back on the people I came up with. Rap comes from the same place that I did—the ghetto."

Suge sounded more plaintive than defiant when he told the *Los Angeles Times*, "I ain't no gangster. I'm too damn old. I'm a grown man trying to run a business."

What Suge didn't say was how immensely galling it had to have been that, while he was struggling to sustain a floundering rap label on the West Coast, his hated East Coast rival Puffy Combs was sitting on top of an ever-expanding entertainment empire. Bad Boy Records continued to put out one hit record after another, many of them featuring the owner himself, who these days was calling himself P. Diddy, soon to be simply Diddy. Combs's Sean John clothing line was being distributed by high-end department stores, while he himself appeared in advertisements for the company in magazines like *Vogue* and *Vanity Fair*. The Sean John line's 2001 runway show was the first to be televised nationally, and in 2002 the *New York Times* had a front-page story on Combs and his company. For several years in succession, Sean John had received a Designer of the Year nomination from the Council of Fashion Designers of America. And now Puffy was talking about adding a line of fragrances. He was no longer dating Jennifer Lopez but was partying regularly in the Hamptons and on the Upper East Side. They were even putting the homely little motherfucker in movies, Suge marveled.

The worst thing, though, was that while Knight remained a favorite target of law enforcement in Los Angeles, Combs seemed to be getting a pass from the cops in New York. Puffy was dealing with at least one lingering headache, however, and that was his connection to the last remaining effort to bring the killers of Notorious B.I.G. to justice. Perry Sanders was determined to depose Combs in preparation for the civil trial in Los Angeles, and Combs seemed just as determined to avoid it. "What happened the night of the murder was the main thing," Sanders said. "But I also wanted to talk to Puffy about him tellin' other people who were there, 'If you're a witness, you're fired.'" (When he was interviewed by the LAPD in New York, Gregory Young, who had been sitting right next to Biggie when he was shot, stated, "Puffy has told us that if our names even appear on a witness list, we're out of a job.")

Sanders tried at first to set up the deposition through Biggie's former manager Wayne Barrow, who was also close to Combs, but Puffy continued to bob and weave behind his phalanx of lawyers. "So I sent him a letter sayin', 'You either voluntarily show up for the deposition or I'm gonna sue you,'" Sanders recalled. "Somebody who knew him called me after he got the letter and said you could hear him screamin' all over New York. This person said, 'He is so pissed off he doesn't know what to do.'"

Combs would finally agree to sit down with Sanders on June 10, 2004, in his attorney's offices at 99 Park Avenue in Manhattan. "With almost no advance notice, we had to fly straight out to New York," Sanders said. Still, the deposition almost didn't happen. "All these LAPD officers showed up," Frank recalled, "and Puffy refused to do the depo with cops in the room." Two of the LAPD officers were detectives assigned to the department's Risk Management Section, which was coordinating with the city attorney's office in opposition to the *Estate of Christopher G. L. Wallace v. City of Los Angeles* lawsuit. The third was Detective Steve Katz. Combs and his attorney were not happy about having Katz in the room. Only when the three detectives agreed to wait outside could the deposition proceed.

During the next couple of hours, Combs proved to be unfailingly polite and consistently unhelpful. He added "sir" each time he answered one of Sanders's questions, until the attorney told him it was unnecessary. But it took seventy pages of transcript just to get Puffy to identify the people who were with him in L.A. at the time of Biggie's murder and to acknowledge their relationships to him and to his company. Even then he was vague and uncertain, adding "to the best of my recollection" to nearly every answer he gave. When Sanders asked if he remembered Biggie being booed at the Soul Train Awards ceremony on the night of the murder, something that thousands had witnessed live and millions had seen on television, Combs answered, "No." He also denied the confrontation with Nation of Islam members that had taken place as he and his entourage were leaving the Shrine Auditorium that night, an incident already testified to by other witnesses. He maybe had seen Mustapha Farrakhan sometime that weekend, Puffy said, but couldn't remember exactly when. What Combs seemed to most want to make clear, though, was that he was in no way responsible for Biggie's security: "I wasn't involved in his whereabouts. He was on my label. I wasn't his parent or anything like that."

He had heard "rumors" about an East Coast–West Coast, Bad Boy–Death Row feud, Puffy allowed, but never experienced it personally. "Hype" was how he described the feud, adding, "I didn't play any role in the hype." He also had no knowledge of Biggie or Suge Knight or Tupac Shakur playing any role in the hype, Puffy managed to say with a straight face, the same one he wore when he told Sanders, "To be honest, I don't really know who killed Biggie, to be perfectly honest."

As Frank would observe, "Generally when a person says 'to be honest' twice in the same sentence, they're lying. But it was obvious pretty quick that we weren't going to get anything of value out of Sean Combs, so Perry just turned him over to [Los Angeles assistant city attorney] Paul Paquette."

Paquette got even less cooperation than Sanders had from Combs, who said he couldn't even remember how many vehicles had been in his entourage the night of Biggie's murder or what kind they were. "All Puffy wanted was to make sure he didn't get called as a witness at trial," Sanders said. "And by the time we finished that deposition, everybody in the room knew he probably wouldn't be."

Combs seemed to warm up when the deposition was over. "I sat around with him after and we talked a little," Sanders recalled. As it happened, Puffy was in the best shape of his life at that moment, training to run in the New York City Marathon five months later. "So he was eatin' real healthy and whatnot," Sanders remembered. "That day he was eatin' some soup. And he had an extra container of tomato soup. So he looked at me, then passed the soup over to me, and said, 'Here. Don't say I never did anything for you.'"

Sanders's biggest remaining concern about Sean Combs was that Puffy might have bullied Eugene Deal into silence. The big man suddenly seemed determined to disappear from public view. Efforts to arrange an interview and on-camera deposition had been fruitless. Deal was gruffly defiant on the phone and clearly felt that cooperating with the authorities had cost him far more than doing the right thing was worth. Combs, for whom Deal had worked on and off as a bodyguard nearly as long as he had been a parole officer, had fired him for talking to the cops and to Nick Broomfield. On top of this, the rumors that had been spread about him being some sort of police snitch made his life more difficult and more dangerous. "People that I meet on the street, who was fans of Biggie and Tupac, they look—they look at me in a derogatory manner," Deal would explain. "I've come out and found my car, you know, on flats, windows busted."

It was only through the intervention of Voletta Wallace that Rob Frank had been able to arrange a face-to-face meeting with Deal in a suite at the New York Hilton. Things began to move in a potentially disastrous direction, though, the moment Sanders showed up to join them. Stepping through the hotel room's door, Sanders took a look at the size 16 EEE basketball shoes Deal was wearing and immediately informed the big man, "I can whup your ass in one-on-one."

"What the fuck did that cracker just say to me?" Deal asked Frank. Deal, who stood six feet seven inches tall and weighed over three hundred pounds, had attended the University of Tennessee at Chattanooga on a basketball scholarship. Even in his forties, he continued to be one of the most feared playground players in New York City.

"I said I can whup your ass in one-on-one," Sanders told him.

"You crazy motherfucker," Deal replied, but now he was smiling.

The contest between Sanders and Deal would take place at Basketball City at the Chelsea Piers in New York. Deal won six out of eight games and broke Sanders's nose, but loved the way the smaller man battled him. "You showed me somethin'," Deal conceded.

Deal's deposition took place on Valentine's Day 2005. To the immense relief of Sanders and Frank, Deal not only repeated his story about encountering Amir Muhammad outside the Petersen Museum on the night of Biggie's murder, but also gave the most detailed sworn account yet of what had taken place. Right at the start, Deal debunked the recurring claim that Puffy and Bad Boy had hired Crips to provide security in Los Angeles. Never happened, Deal said. Puffy used only off-duty or retired law enforcement officers.

Deal said he had first come out to Cali in February 1997 to provide security during the shooting of Biggie's "Hypnotize" video. There'd been some gang members hanging around, some Crips, some Bloods, but no problems. He returned to New York after the video wrapped, but then got a call from Bad Boy's head of security, Paul Offord, asking him to come back to L.A. and stay until Puffy and Big were ready to leave. So Deal took some vacation time and flew west again.

He still recalled the night of the Soul Train Awards after-party at the Petersen Museum vividly, Deal said. He'd been concerned from the moment Puffy said they'd be attending the party. Part of that was the size of their entourage. With the addition of "some guys from Philly" who'd worked their way into the group, "it was like twenty-three of us that went to that party," Deal said, which made it difficult to keep track of everybody. Rob Frank steered Deal to the events that took place after the Bad Boy group quit the party and stepped outside the museum. He had made sure the drivers parked right in front of the doors, Deal said. Why? Frank asked. "Because I had a bad feeling about that night," Deal answered. "I had a feeling that somebody from Bad Boy or one of us had to die because that was our last night in the city. I had got a couple of phone calls from friends and other people that somebody was sending somebody out there to get us." It made him "extra cautious," Deal said. "I was on point the whole time."

His concerns only increased when he saw the "Nation of Islam–looking guy" who was trying to check them out, Deal said. "While the cars was loaded up and Big and them was waiting to get in the cars . . . I took a walk out the parking garage," Deal recalled. "I made a right, looked up and down the street. And this guy in blue and white was walking by hisself . . . and he came into the garage. And then Paul said, 'Yo, did you see the guy in blue and white?' I said, 'Yeah, I got my eye on him.'" He recalled a light-skinned black man "dressed like he was from the Nation of Islam" who had strong cheekbones and a square face, and was "serious-looking," Deal said.

He stayed outside on the sidewalk until all the others were loaded into the cars, Deal said, and that was when he saw the Muslim-looking guy coming "close to Mr. Combs's vehicle . . . And he looked me in my eye," Deal remembered. "I looked him in his eye. He didn't say anything to me. And I showed him my weapon. He looked at me again and turned around and walked down the street the other way where he came from," in the direction of Fairfax Boulevard.

When Deal got in the lead SUV, sitting directly behind Puffy, he told Kenny Story, who was driving, "Yo, Kenny, don't stop at this light. Keep going. Run the next three lights." Story was running the first of those lights, at the intersection of Fairfax and Wilshire, when he and the others in the vehicle noticed that Biggie's car wasn't fol-lowing, Deal remembered. He looked back and saw that Biggie's SUV was stopped along the curb on Fairfax, where three young women stood. "Next thing I know I hear Tone [Anthony Jacobs] say, 'Yo, somebody pulling a gun on Big and them. Yo, he pointing a gun at Big and them.'" Story braked to a stop, Deal recalled, and then "next thing you know, I heard something go *bap-bap-bap-bap-bap-bap*. Then I'm trying to open the door, and Kenny just stepped on the gas. Me and Tone were screaming at him. Puff ducked down. Me and Tone were screaming, 'Yo, what you doing, man? They shooting at Big and them. And he said, 'We don't know who they're shooting at.' We said, 'Man, they're shooting at Big. Turn this car around.'"

Story did as told, Deal said. "And as he's turning around, we see the [shooter's] car going around the corner." Tone said it was an Impala, Deal remembered. "We stop right in front of Big and them's car, right. Big's car look like an airplane now: everybody doors is open except Big's . . . We get to the car, see Big right there. Big's in the car laid back."

He and Jacobs jumped back into their vehicle with Tone driving now and chased the Impala, Deal recalled: "Tone seen where the car went, turned, you know. So we followed him. We see the car just flyin' and we goin' after the car." But their rented SUV had a governor that prevented the vehicle from accelerating to a speed above ninety miles per hour, Deal explained, "and it's like every time the truck would get up to a hundred, it would go back down to ninety. So now I say, 'You know, Tone, we ain't going to catch him, man.' You know, the guy was out of there. So we went back."

When they returned to the corner of Wilshire and Fairfax, they saw Puffy and all the others still standing outside the SUV where Biggie lay, eyes wide open, in the passenger seat. "Everybody was askin', 'Big, you all right? You all right, Big? You all right?' I don't see no blood, I don't see nothin'." (An autopsy report stated that Biggie had so much body fat the blood couldn't seep through to the surface of his skin.) An ambulance had been called, but Story jumped into the driver's seat of the SUV and told his wounded friend, "Big, I'm going to get you to the hospital," Deal said. Then Biggie spoke his last words, "Just do it." Puff sat next to Biggie all the way to the hospital, Deal remembered, telling him, "Big, keep your eyes open. Keep your eyes open." But by the time they made it to the hospital's emergency entrance, Biggie's eyes were closed. They never opened again.

He knew the man he'd encountered outside the museum as they were preparing to leave had been the killer, Deal said, as soon as he and Lil' Cease had a chance to speak. "Lil' Cease had said a guy from the Nation of Islam shot Big. And I said, 'The guy with the blue suit, blue bow tie, and the white shirt with the white handkerchief? With the peanut head?'" Lil' Cease asked how he knew that, Deal recalled, "and I said, 'He's the one walked up to Puff's car.'" After he showed the Muslim his gun, Deal told the others, the guy had walked away toward "exactly where the shooting was, that same direction."

Deal told Sanders and Frank that he had given the LAPD statements on three separate occasions and was convinced the L.A. cops were more interested in discrediting him than in listening to what he said. The first time the LAPD officers showed him the composite drawing they'd made of the suspect, Deal said that he "told them that [it] was not a clear identity of the guy, that they had his bone structure in his face wrong, that he was a lot slimmer and stronger in the face, not fat in the face."

He'd never seen a photograph of Amir Muhammad, Deal said, until Nick Broomfield showed one to him as part of a six-pack photo-lineup card. Broomfield had waited until the cameras were rolling to let him see the lineup card, said Deal, who immediately recognized Amir Muhammad as the "Nation of Islam–looking guy" he had seen the night of the murder. The LAPD came to New York to interview him shortly after Broomfield's film was released, recalled Deal, who demanded to know why the police had never showed him a photograph of Amir Muhammad. The last time Steve Katz interviewed him, the detective had told Deal that "they might need [him] to come out to do a lineup or just to come out to L.A. and do a lineup on this individual." Deal said, "But I've never heard from the police after that day."

CHAPTER FOUR

The ways in which Gene Deal had been punished for standing up and speaking out infuriated them, Sanders and Frank would say. Nothing the forces of the other side did, though, would enrage the two lawyers like the coordinated effort to discredit and discourage another of their key witnesses, Mike Robinson.

It would not have been inaccurate to say that the Wallace family's case against the City of Los Angeles had begun with Robinson. In spring 1997, the man known to many as "Psycho Mike" was working as one of the most successful police informants in Southern California. Certainly no other informant was more beloved by his handlers. There were two of these: a Los Angeles County sheriff's deputy named Richard Valdemar and a special agent from the FBI's L.A. office named Tim Flaherty.

Valdemar was Mike's main point of contact with law enforcement. They had met in the early 1990s. Robinson had been brought to Los Angeles from a state prison up north because it was believed he could help solve one of the most vexing murder cases in the city's history. This was the 1985 slaying of Sheriff's Sergeant George Arthur, who had been assigned to the Men's Central Jail at the time. At just around 10 p.m. on the night of June 1, Arthur was killed during the drive home after finishing his shift at the jail. An assailant hidden in the back of Arthur's van had attacked him while he was negotiating an on-ramp to the 10 freeway. Witnesses said the van began to careen wildly before colliding at full speed with a center divider. They had seen a second man, bleeding from a head wound, climb out of the wreckage of Arthur's vehicle and escape. But the witnesses were unable to offer any better description, because it was dark and they were driving past at high speed. Medical examiners first believed Arthur had died from injuries suffered in the crash, until an autopsy revealed that a gunshot had killed him. Evidence of a violent struggle was recovered from the van, along with blood and other "biological evidence" that did not match Sergeant Arthur's. Still, somehow, the murder would go unsolved for almost fifteen years.

It was a case that Valdemar took personally, because Arthur was his former partner and a close friend. Arthur had gotten involved in a shootout with members of the Black Guerrilla Family gang and survived, but two of the men shooting at him hadn't. "George was convinced that the gang had put out a contract on him," Valdemar recalled. "He told me, 'If anything happens to me, you know who to look at. It'll be them.'"

Mike Robinson, Valdemar had been told, was a former BGF member who had undergone some sort of religious transformation in prison and started warning law enforcement when he believed police officers were being targeted by the gang. Psycho Mike's story was considerably more complicated than that, as Valdemar would learn. Mike had grown up in Compton as one of eight children, all of them criminals. He started stealing bicycles at "five or six," Mike said, and at age eight went into the first of several California Youth Authority (CYA) institutions where he would do time. He became a professional auto thief by the time he was twelve and joined the Compton Crips in his teens. Not long after his twentieth birthday, he was convicted of murder. That crime, like everything else about Mike Robinson, contained elements that created a measure of sympathy for the perpetrator. He had been driving a stolen van on a street parallel to Artesia Boulevard when he was flagged down by two of his "aunties," Mike would explain. They were the ones who told him his twin brother had just been shot to death on the next block by a gang member named Lorenzo. Less than a minute later, Mike had killed Lorenzo with a hail of bullets that left the woman he was with paralyzed. Robinson would spend seventeen and a half years in state prison for that crime.

Mike had endured an upbringing that included horrific abuse by his father. Unable to obtain the slightest traction in school, he was still totally illiterate, in part because of his dyslexia. Yet there was a certain savant quality to him that had been evident even when he was a young boy. While in CYA, he had been featured on the 1980s television show *That's Incredible* because of his uncanny ability to completely disassemble a Porsche in less than five minutes. "Mike knew every tool and every part," Valdemar said. "He was far from stupid."

He was definitely dangerous, however. While in prison, Mike had satisfied the "blood in" requirement for admission into the BGF by stabbing another inmate fourteen times, then stoically accepting the twenty-eight-month stretch in solitary confinement that was added to his sentence. After he got out of solitary, though, Robinson was a changed man, according to prison authorities. Valdemar attributed this to a prison doctor who had come up with a cocktail of drugs that cured Mike's chemical imbalance. Mike himself said it was divine intervention. When an interrogator suggested that he had made "a decision to leave [his] life of crime behind," Mike quickly corrected him: "I didn't make a decision. God made the decision for me."

However Mike had become who he was, Valdemar was impressed from the first by the man's encyclopedic knowledge of the California prison system's gangs. It turned out that in the George Arthur murder, though, no gang members had been involved. Fourteen years after the crime, DNA evidence would reveal that Arthur had been killed by a fellow deputy, Ted Kirby, in what was apparently a dispute over a woman. Kirby shot himself in the head before he could be arrested. Valdemar's relationship with Mike Robinson, though, was already so strong that the deputy made a pledge to be at the prison gates when Psycho Mike completed his sentence, and to give him a ride home. Valdemar not only kept that promise, but also became

Robinson's personal advocate after the former inmate was settled in Long Beach. Because Mike could not read or write, he needed help filling out the forms to qualify for disability insurance and Section 8 housing. More importantly, he needed someone who would make sure he got the medications that kept him sane. Valdemar and FBI agent Flaherty assisted with that and also helped Mike obtain the truck that was the foundation of his business, Half Head Towing. In addition, the sheriff's deputy and the FBI agent put Mike to work as a paid informant, initially for the federal task force that was trying to penetrate the Mexican Mafia. "Mike was just one of many informants we had," Valdemar said, "but he was one of the most reliable, right from the first, even though people often didn't believe he could get what he got."

Mike discovered that his reputation as a violent crazy man was the best protection he could have on the street. He had been diagnosed in prison as a paranoid schizophrenic and encouraged people to call him Psycho. Mike also made sure everyone knew he'd done prison time on a murder conviction. Yet a large part of what made him such a good snitch was that, for Mike, it had become a religious mission; getting as many bad guys off the streets as he possibly could was his way of trying to get right with the Lord, he explained. One way Mike proved his dedication, Valdemar said, was by refusing to touch alcohol or drugs, for fear that they would upset the chemical balance he had achieved through medication.

By his own count, Mike would help put "dozens upon dozens" of criminals behind bars. That number included two federal agents and a sheriff's deputy who had been criminally charged and convicted in corruption cases where Robinson was the main prosecution witness. "He was that good," said Valdemar, who would observe that Mike seemed to possess a sixth sense about people with bad intentions. A case that stuck in his mind, Mike's handler said, was one involving a "white motorcycle gang guy who was building bombs to target a rival gang." When Valdemar's colleagues questioned Mike's claims, he took them to the room he had just rented, from which he was able to look directly into the lab where the motorcycle gang member was assembling the explosive devices. "Nobody believed Mike could testify in court, with all his problems," Valdemar remembered. "Well, he went and testified in that case and he was better than most policemen. He was exceptional." Mike had proved this to a wide swath of Southern California law enforcement by the time of his enlistment in the task force that was attempting to put together a racketeering case against the murderous Bloods set who called themselves the Bounty Hunters. Most of the forty-seven arrests in that case had been made on the basis of evidence produced by Mike Robinson. His four days on the witness stand would result in twelve convictions; all of the others he was prepared to testify against had pleaded guilty. By the late nineties, the L.A. County Sheriff's Department, the LAPD, the FBI, and the DEA, along with assorted task forces and anti-terrorist groups, had all used him as what they called "a reliable informant."

Mike had first become involved in the Biggie Smalls murder investigation within days of the killing, when he told Valdemar he knew who had committed the crime: a professional hit man from the Nation of Islam named Amir. "I typed up a report and sent it to Robbery-Homicide Division at LAPD," Valdemar recalled. By July 10, 1998, when the LAPD sent a detective to interview Robinson, Mike was locked up at the Wayside Honor Ranch, serving time for a parole violation. (The one crime Mike hadn't sworn off was trafficking in stolen automobiles.)

Valdemar rode out to Wayside with Ted Ball, the RHD detective who was to interview Robinson, but Ball asked him to leave the room after being introduced to Mike, the sheriff's investigator recalled. Because of that, Valdemar couldn't be absolutely certain that Mike had not, as Ball wrote in his report, said the Biggie Smalls killer was someone named "Amir or Ashmir" whose real name might be Abraham. Mike would later state under oath that the only name he had given Ball was Amir.

Valdemar believed his informant. "For two reasons," he explained. "One, the only name he had given me was Amir, and Amir was the only name in the report I sent to LAPD. Also, the report [Ball] wrote blatantly misrepresented what *I* had told him. When I read the report, I was stunned. I thought he had deliberately changed what I said, but I had no idea why. So I was pretty well inclined to believe it when Mike told me that what he had said was not accurately reported, either."

It would be almost a year after he got out of Wayside before Mike Robinson encountered Amir Muhammad face-to-face. The "confrontation," as Mike called it, had taken place during a party at the home of a Death Row Records employee named Rick James. This James was an individual he knew better as "a crook" who sold PCP on the side, Mike said, out of a place on Peck Street in Compton that he'd turned into a sort of party house. He had heard that Amir Muhammad would be at the party that night, Mike recalled. Even though they'd never met, he and Muhammad had heard of each other, Mike said. One of his younger brothers had been a contract killer before being slain himself, Mike explained; prior to his death, this brother told Mike that Amir Muhammad was an assassin for hire also. Muhammad may have been a stranger to him, but "he wasn't a stranger to my brother," Mike said. "Two killers was in the same group. He knew who I was."

It was "a big stripper party" at Rick James's house that night, Mike recalled, noisy and crowded. He spotted Amir Muhammad standing near the pool table, approached him, and asked him straight out if he'd been the one who killed Biggie Smalls. According to Mike, the first thing Muhammad said was, "Yes, I did it." Then he smiled and said, "No, I didn't." Muhammad was speaking in "a killer's whisper," Mike would remember, that dropped even lower when he leaned in and spoke directly into Robinson's ear: "He said if my brother was alive, I'd be dead. I would not be talking about it."

Another three years passed before the FBI approached Mike Robinson to ask him what he knew about the Biggie murder. By then, he was certain that Amir Muhammad had been the shooter, Mike recalled, and told that to Tim Flaherty. Soon afterward, his FBI handler brought another agent to his house at the corner of Rosecrans and Madris, Mike said, right across from the Norwalk Auto Auction complex. This new agent was Phil Carson.

"Tim Flannery was a friend of mine," Carson recalled, "and he told me Psycho Mike was money, the best informant he or anyone else in the L.A. office had ever worked with. Tim and Richard Valdemar gave me a list of all the cases this guy had done, and it was amazing. They one hundred percent believed him when Mike said the killer was Amir Muhammad, and after I talked to Mike so did I." After Flaherty told Carson that "Mike had taken a liking to me," the agent remembered, he and Valdemar persuaded the informant to join the Biggie murder investigation.

In March 2004, Carson acquired an address in the San Diego County city of Chula Vista, where Amir Muhammad was currently living. Still being encouraged by his FBI bosses to work with the LAPD, Carson placed a phone call to Steve Katz and told him, "I've found Amir Muhammad, and I have a source that's willing to wear a wire and go talk to him." Katz scoffed. "He tells me, 'You didn't find Amir Muhammad,'" Carson recalled, "and I said, 'Yes, I did.' Katz goes off to consult with Michelena and Berkow, then they all three come back and tell me, 'We don't think Amir Muhammad was involved in this murder and we want nothing to do with this.'"

He was perfectly happy with that answer, Carson said: "I'm fine with this being an FBI operation. The LAPD wants to leave it to us, good." The day before he and Flaherty were to drive down to Chula Vista with Mike, however, "the LAPD calls and says, 'We want to be part of your source going down there,' Carson remembered. "And I say, 'The problem is the source won't do it if LAPD is part of it. So I can't include you guys.' They get all pissed off and I say, 'Talk to my bosses.' And the bosses tell them, 'Look, Phil offered you guys to be part of it, and you said no. So you're not going to be part of it.'"

To appease the LAPD, Carson agreed to provide the department with a transmitter that would permit its officers to listen in on any conversations Psycho Mike was able to have with Amir Muhammad. "Only the transmitters we had back then didn't work so well," Carson recalled, "so when I told the LAPD where to be, I knew it was too far away for them to pick up what was being said. But now they did know that Amir Muhammad was in Chula Vista, just not the exact address."

That first visit was fruitless, though. Muhammad was not at home when Mike knocked at his front door, and a woman answered. After a cordial exchange, Mike left a note with his name and phone number.

Carson, Flaherty, and Psycho Mike made a second trip to Chula Vista a couple of days later. "And this time Amir Muhammad does answer the door," Carson recalled. "He and Mike had a conversation that never got near the subject of Biggie. Mike keeps it friendly, but Tim and I, listening in, are now certain that these two guys really do know each other, that there's a relationship between them. They talked about meeting at Rick James's house, and some of the other people who were there, about women they both knew, stuff like that. Everything Muhammad said coincided exactly with what Mike had told us. Then after a few minutes Muhammad cuts the conversation short. It's obvious that by then he's wondering what's going on, why Psycho Mike is in Chula Vista."

When Carson returned to Los Angeles, his FBI bosses told him he would have to brief LAPD deputy chief Berkow. "This turns into a big meeting at the FBI, in the office of our ASAC [assistant special agent in charge) Lou Caprino," Carson said. "Berkow came with Roger Mora and Steve Sambar, and some female lieutenant. I had our FBI legal team, our press information team, my bosses, and my bosses' bosses with me. We started out talking about the case in general and how I had kept trying to reach out to LAPD to be part of this operation. Berkow snapped. He said, 'That's a lie, Carson. I'm tired of this shit. You've never reached out to us. You wouldn't let us be part of this operation. We wanted to be part of it, and you wouldn't let us."

To Carson's immense relief, Roger Mora spoke up: "Phil's right, chief. He did reach out to LAPD and we told him we didn't want to be part of it." Sambar nodded in agreement. "I was so grateful to those two guys," Carson said. "It took balls to speak out like that to a deputy chief."

Berkow, though, responded by storming out of Caprino's office. Carson turned to his supervisor, Mary Jo Marino, and said, "I gotta go out there and talk to this guy." When Marino nodded, Carson followed Berkow out into hallway. "I said, 'Chief, I've been one hundred percent transparent and always up front with you.' Berkow won't even answer. He just looks at me like I'm shit he scraped off his shoe. Then one of my bosses came out after us to say the meeting was over."

The meeting may have ended, but Berkow's fury was far from exhausted, and that fury extended through most of the Los Angeles Police Department.

"What people have to keep in mind," Carson said, "is this: If LAPD is involved in the Biggie murder, and the Biggie murder is solved, LAPD is done. They're over with. Financially, they cannot survive. They'll be taken over by the Sheriff's Department or the federal government, and there will be no more LAPD. For them, this was a battle to survive, not a murder investigation. They don't want to make the case, because they can't make the case. That's what happened with Russ Poole. They saw that 'This guy is going down the right track and he's not gonna stop.' So, they had to stop him. And now they had to stop me."

A few days later, Carson and Flaherty sent Mike Robinson south again at the wheel of a rented Mercedes sedan, wearing a wire. They had tried to arrange some sort of "chance meeting," Carson recalled, where Mike might run into Muhammad at a mall or gym or movie theater. Muhammad, though, didn't keep a regular schedule, and the cost of maintaining surveillance on him was already way over what the FBI had budgeted for the operation. "So we made sure Muhammad was home and sent Mike to his front door a third time," Carson recalled. On this occasion, Muhammad refused to respond. "Mike calls us and says, 'He ain't answerin' the door.' And I say, 'We know he's there. You keep pounding on that door.' Because I know we won't get a fourth shot at him."

Finally, the same woman who had answered the door the first time opened it again. Mike saw Muhammad inside, his back reflected in a mirror behind the wall he was using to conceal himself. When Mike shouted at him to come to the door and talk, though, Muhammad replied by calling the Chula Vista Police Department.

"Mike did great when the cops showed up," Carson recalled. "He told him he was with the FBI, that there were agents down the street, and that they have to play along. He really did an excellent job of communicating all this to the cops without alerting Muhammad, and got them to act like it was a normal call. When they came back out to the street I met them, told them what was going on, and told them to just go about business as usual."

After taking an incident report from Muhammad, the Chula Vista police left. Mike went back to the front door and began knocking again. The door remained shut.

"So finally we give up and start driving back to L.A.," Carson recalled. "We haven't gone far when Mike gets a call from the Chula Vista Police Department. The guy on the other end says, 'Hey, this is Amir. Don't do anything crazy. I'll call you back in a couple of hours.'" The caller didn't sound like Amir, though, Mike told Carson. "And it wasn't," the agent said. "Somebody else had made that call, somebody I'm pretty sure was working for the LAPD."

Muhammad *was* at the Chula Vista Police Department by then, though. Carson learned this just a few minutes later, when he took a call from a detective who said, "Something fishy's going on here. This guy Amir Muhammad came down here and filed a report claiming Mike Robinson was harassing or threatening him, and gave us

Robinson's name and number, plus the license plate on the Mercedes he said Robinson was driving."

Carson explained what was going on, "and the detective agreed to cover for us. He got off the phone with me and told Muhammad that the title on the Mercedes Mike was driving had been transferred and belonged to somebody else. And Muhammad tells the detective, 'You're fucking lying. Because I called LAPD and gave them the plate and they gave me the name.'

"I hear this, and I think, 'Muhammad just fucked himself.' And he fucked the LAPD, too."

The detective who related all this to Carson finished by saying that he had done as the agent requested and said, "Your name's Amir Muhammad. Did you used to go by Harry Billups?" According to the detective, the reaction this produced was astonishing. "He tells me that Muhammad's demeanor changed one hundred percent in an instant," Carson recalled. "That it was like he became a different person. That he went stone cold and said he didn't want to talk anymore and he wanted out of there. I could hear in the detective's voice how amazed he was by it."

During the rest of the drive back to Los Angeles, Carson became certain he knew what had happened. "I was convinced that Berkow had put surveillance on us the second time we went down to Chula Vista, and that was how the LAPD found Muhammad. I was also sure that after that second trip, somebody from LAPD, at Berkow's instruction, had alerted Muhammad to what we were up to with Psycho Mike and had told him not to answer the door if Mike knocked again. I'm no conspiracy theorist. It was just that I had been briefing Berkow on our every move, because my bosses had instructed me to. He was the only one besides me and Tim Flaherty who knew what we were doing. Our own bosses didn't know."

Any doubts that remained in Carson's mind when it came to Berkow vanished several days later, on March 20, 2004, when the *Los Angeles Times* published an article under the headline "FBI Probes Rap Star's '97 Killing." The thrust of the story was that the feds were "pursuing a six-year-old theory" that former LAPD officer David Mack and his friend Amir Muhammad had killed Notorious B.I.G. at the bidding of Suge Knight. None of the facts that implicated Mack and Muhammad in the assassination were mentioned in the article. Muhammad and Knight, though, were given ample space to deny their involvement in the slaying. The section of the article that created consternation, however, was the part that described how the FBI had "wired an informant in an attempt to elicit incriminating statements from" Muhammad at his home near San Diego.

"Even if Mike's name was never mentioned, Muhammad knew he was the informant," Valdemar said. "And as soon as Muhammad knew, so did a whole bunch of other very dangerous people." Mike never really worked as an informant after that day, Valdemar recalled. "You have to understand, Mike never truly trusted cops. His experience in Compton was with people like Reggie Wright, dirty cops who will do anything for money. After that article, he decided all cops were pretty much the same."

He would remember that Saturday morning "until the day I die," Carson said. "I'm getting ready to go to the gym and I get a call from Perry Sanders and he's livid with me. I think Perry's a great guy and we had gotten along fine up to that point, but he's furious at me now. He tells me about the article and I have him read it to me."

The section of the article that most astonished and enraged him, Carson recalled, was a quote from Deputy Chief Berkow, who had told the *Times* that the informant sent to Amir Muhammad's home had been part of "a joint FBI-LAPD investigation" and that the LAPD was "cooperating with the feds 100%."

"That was just a damn lie," Carson said. "I told Perry, 'There is no way in hell the LAPD was involved. The only person who would know what we were doing, and who must have been the *Times*' source, is the same person directly quoted in the article, Berkow, because I briefed him on it."

Mike Robinson was even more furious at Carson than Sanders was. He first heard about the *Times* article, Mike said, when a deputy from the Sheriff's Special Intelligence Task Force "came and got me early in the morning and told me that I had a contract out for my life." Since then, "I don't know where to go," Mike said. "I'm running from my life. I feel like I have to carry a gun. I don't trust LAPD. I don't trust the newspaper."

He had immediately blamed the FBI agent who had sent him to Amir Muhammad's home in Chula Vista, Mike said: "I confronted Phil Carson, and I wanted to jump on him."

When Mike accused him of having "penned me out," Carson swore it wasn't him. "I told him, 'Mike, why would I ever give up an FBI informant?' Tim and I got him calmed down, but he was worried about his life. And rightfully so."

Carson was so indignant that he did something extraordinary by FBI standards: he provided Sanders and Frank with a declaration in which he publicly accused the LAPD of having outed Mike Robinson as an informant in order to damage the Mack-Muhammad theory of the Biggie murder. "The declaration was actually written by the FBI, which provided it first to the city attorney's office, which then passed it on to Perry Sanders," Carson recalled.

The *Times* article had contained "information and procedures" that were "singular in nature," Carson's declaration read, "known only to me and one person I informed at the Los Angeles Police Department. To the best of my knowledge, no other person, including my peers and supervisors at the FBI, possessed this information."

Much as Sanders and Frank appreciated what Carson had done, the attorneys were frustrated by the FBI's refusal to name Berkow as the "one person" at the LAPD to whom Carson had described the San Diego operation. Still, "Phil Carson's declaration was great to have," Sanders said. "It would show the jury how far the LAPD was willing to go and how complicit the *L.A. Times* was in what had happened to Mike Robinson."

For Sanders, his adversarial relationship with the largest newspaper in California had become the defining struggle of the entire lawsuit. "It's been so far beyond anything I've ever seen or imagined," he said. "We knew this was going to be difficult. We knew going up against the second-biggest city in the country in court was going to be an uphill struggle. But it's been made ten times harder by the *L.A. Times* doing everything it possibly could to undermine our case. And that includes giving free rein to the most corrupt journalist I've ever met to work hand in glove with the LAPD to accomplish that."

CHAPTER FIVE

Chuck Philips had entered the Notorious B.I.G. story on May 3, 2000, when an article with his byline was printed on an inside page of the *Los Angeles Times* under the headline "Man No Longer Under Scrutiny in Rapper's Death." The story appeared almost five months after the *Times* had run its one and only story on Russell Poole's working theory of the Biggie case. Though Poole was "in shock" at how that earlier article had distorted what he'd told the *Times* reporters—"They made it sound like the case was about to break wide open, instead of describing how the investigation had been thwarted"—the appearance of the story at least made public the idea that police officers working for Death Row Records might have been involved in the murder of Notorious B.I.G. Philips's article, though, appeared to at once discredit Poole's theory and depict Muhammad as the innocent victim of an overzealous police investigation. This was not entirely welcome among the newspaper's staff: Chuck Philips's editor from the *Times* Business section and editors from the Metro section had contested the content of Philips's article to the point of a screaming match in the middle of the newsroom.

The article quoted the current lead investigator on the case, Detective Dave Martin, as saying, "We are not pursuing [the Mack-Muhammad theory] and have not been for more than a year." Muhammad was quoted as saying, "I'm not a murderer, I'm a mortgage broker," and described his visit to Mack at the Montebello City Jail as nothing more than an expression of concern after his former college roommate was arrested on bank robbery charges. Philips either hadn't asked or wasn't interested in printing the answers to the two most pertinent questions his article raised. The first was *why* the LAPD wasn't "pursuing" Poole's theory. No explanation whatsoever had been offered by Martin. The second, and equally obvious, question was why, if Muhammad's visit to Mack in jail was an innocent contact between two old friends, the man had used a false address, a false Social Security number, and an out-of-service phone number to arrange it.

In 2005, while researching what became the *Rolling Stone* article "The Unsolved Murder of Notorious B.I.G.," I asked Philips why he hadn't reported this information. The *Times* reporter at first said he hadn't been aware of it. When I pointed out that it had been included in the newspaper's earlier article on the Poole theory, Philips said he was concerned that Muhammad might have ended the interview if he was asked questions that challenged him on those points. What most baffled me—and Russell Poole as well—was that Philips's article had led the rest of the Los Angeles media to publicly dismiss the Mack-Muhammad theory of the Biggie murder. "It was like the cover-up had been covered up, this time by the media," Poole said.

Philips's next article on the Notorious B.I.G. murder was a two-part series appearing in September 2002 on the *Times'* front page under the headline "Who Killed Tupac Shakur?" The gist was that the rapper had been murdered by Crips, who had been offered $1 million to do it—by Biggie. On the night of Tupac's slaying, Philips reported, a Crips "emissary" had visited B.I.G. in the penthouse suite at the MGM Grand Hotel in Las Vegas, where the rapper promised the money on the condition that Tupac was killed with Biggie's gun—then placed a loaded .40-caliber Glock on the table.

No one was identified in the article as the source of the claim about the alleged meeting at the MGM Grand. Nearly three years later, when I interviewed them for *Rolling Stone*, Philips and his editor Marc Duvoisin would say that their sources were two Crips whom Philips had met at a park in Compton; neither journalist would reveal the gang members' names. I asked if Philips or anyone else at the *Times* had attempted to obtain some independent verification of Biggie's presence in Las Vegas on the date of the alleged penthouse meeting and was stunned when Duvoisin said no, no one had.

"You don't think that if a flamboyant rapper who weighed almost four hundred pounds and traveled with an entourage had been staying at the MGM Grand that weekend, people would have noticed and remembered?" I asked. Duvoisin's reply left me flabbergasted: the question of whether Biggie was in Las Vegas that night "wasn't an issue until our article was published," he said. It took me a moment to gather myself before I said, "That's right, Marc. Your article *made* it an issue. And before you made it an issue, by reporting that on a certain date Biggie met with the Crips in Las Vegas and offered them a million dollars to kill Tupac, don't you think you should have made some effort to establish that Biggie was actually *in* Las Vegas at that time?"

Within a few days of the publication of the Biggie-killed-Tupac articles, at least some of Duvoisin's colleagues at the *Times* were asking that same question. Immediately after Philips's articles appeared in print, Voletta Wallace was contacted by several of her dead son's friends, who said they had watched the Tyson-Seldon fight with Biggie at his home in New Jersey, roughly an hour before the *Times* said he was in Las Vegas offering the Crips $1 million to kill Tupac. By the next afternoon, the estate of Notorious B.I.G. had produced invoices showing that on the weekend when Biggie was supposed to have been at the MGM Grand in Las Vegas, he was in fact working on a recording for Puffy Combs in New York's Daddy's House studio. Biggie's family was even able to provide MTV with a digital tape of the song "Nasty Girl" that the rapper had recorded during that session.

Five days after the *Los Angeles Times* published the claim that Biggie had paid Crips to kill Tupac, the newspaper ran a story reporting that the Christopher Wallace Estate had offered evidence that Biggie was in a New York recording studio when Philips had claimed he was in a Las Vegas hotel. Sanders called it "a non-retraction retraction" and complained it had been buried on the lower half of an inside page, while the Biggie-killed-Tupac articles had run on the *Times'* front page.

Voletta Wallace certainly was not mollified. "It was so ridiculous," she told me. "My son is Notorious B.I.G. If my son is gonna go to Las Vegas, don't tell me nobody didn't see him."

Sanders and Frank were even more astonished by Philips's article "FBI Probes Rap Star's '97 Murder" exposing Mike Robinson's attempt to gather evidence against Muhammad Amir. The warning that the article's publication had put Robinson's life in danger was swiftly proved accurate by "two or three good attempts on his life," Valdemar said. One involved a drive-by shooting in which Mike and a group of friends and relatives standing on a corner in the Nickerson Gardens housing project were sprayed by an AK-47 on full automatic. Mike was not hit, but one of his granddaughters was. Two cousins caught bullets also, one in the abdomen, the other in a leg. "Another of Mike's cousins got his teeth knocked out," Valdemar recalled.

Part of what put Mike at such risk was that "he didn't like hiding," Valdemar said. "He'd rather meet you face-to-face. But he was also worried about his family. Mike may not have been much of a father, but he was as devoted a grandfather as he could be. He insisted on taking his grandkids to school. Every time he did that, he risked his life." And now Mike knew he was risking the lives of his grandchildren as well.

"Chuck Philips was saying that his article had nothing to do with whatever happened to Psycho Mike, but the guy is full of shit," Phil Carson said. "And one hundred percent it was Berkow who gave Philips the Mike stuff for that article. They were both guilty. And in a way so was I. I gave the LAPD the benefit of the doubt, and I paid for it. But Mike *really* paid for it."

It was mainly to protect his family, "but also himself," Valdemar said, that Mike began insisting that he would not testify in court if the Wallace family's lawsuit went to trial. "Everyone knew we were going to have to put Mike on the stand," Sergio Robleto recalled, "but nobody wanted to tell him."

Valdemar retired from the Sheriff's Department in 2004 and shortly afterward was hired by Robleto as one of his operatives. Among his duties was to serve as a liaison between the Wallace Estate and Mike Robinson. It was Valdemar who drove Mike to the deposition scheduled for February 3, 2005. "Mike was mad because he didn't want to go and do the thing," Valdemar remembered. "In the car he started screaming, having a meltdown. We were parked at a mall next to the freeway where I'd picked him up. He shouted in my face, 'Testifying is gonna get me killed or my family killed. You told me I didn't have to testify. Now you're making me testify.' At one point he threatened to kill me if I didn't let him out of the car." Valdemar had brought along a blue ballistic vest that he wanted Mike to wear and it was "a struggle" to get the informant to put it on, he recalled, though Mike finally did.

Robleto had arranged for the deposition to be held in a suite at the Crowne Plaza in the city of Commerce, a compact community in southeast Los Angeles County that was just north of the blue-collar suburbs Downey and Bellflower. The hotel was part of a complex that included one of Perry Sanders's favorite places on the planet, the Commerce Casino, where he liked to play high-stakes poker while receiving backrubs from the masseuses who worked for the casino. "Perry was always going off to get a 'poker massage,'" Frank recalled.

"But Perry didn't know where the Robinson deposition was going to be," Robleto said. "None of the lawyers did. We were that concerned about security. We just arranged to pick them all up and drive them to the hotel."

"All we knew about Mike Robinson was that he was at some double-secret location," Rob Frank recalled. "I realized how seriously Sergio and his people took the threat to Mike when they picked us up in three separate SUVs that went in three different directions."

Robleto had stationed fifteen armed personnel at various spots in the hotel ahead of Robinson's arrival. "We knew the other side knew what an important witness Mike was going to be," he explained. "There were a whole lot of people who wanted him dead."

Through Valdemar, Robleto had gotten to know Robinson, and a certain affection had developed between the two men. "On my side for sure," Robleto said. "There was just something about the guy. I liked his attitude, I guess. I'm all about facts and not real big on speculation. And Mike was like that, too, in his own way. He wasn't just honest—he wanted to be a hundred percent right."

The main precaution Sanders had taken was to arrange for the deposition to be videotaped. He didn't bother to say what everyone knew: if Mike were killed, that videotape would be the only way to offer his testimony in court.

The direct examination portion of the deposition went fairly quickly. Mike described hearing from multiple "sources" that the killer of Biggie Smalls was Amir Muhammad, and that Suge Knight had paid for the hit; then he described how he passed that information on to Richard Valdemar and Tim Flaherty. He recounted his two face-to-face encounters with Muhammad and what he had told first the Sheriff's Department and then the FBI about them.

When it was his turn to ask questions, Assistant City Attorney Don Vincent repeatedly pushed at places where he thought the witness might slip or trip, but Psycho Mike held steady. The only name of the killer he had heard on the street was Amir's, Mike said, and that was the only name he'd given to the LAPD detective who'd interviewed him at Wayside. Detective Ball "wrote what he wanted to write" in his report, Mike said.

Who had told him the killer was Amir? Vincent wanted to know. "Different people," Mike answered, some from the Southside Crips and also guys from a smaller set called Power Rule. He'd heard it from Bloods as well, Mike added.

"These were people that were in jail with you?" Vincent asked.

"No, sir," Mike answered. "These are people on the streets."

When Vincent asked if he had told the FBI "who you think did" the murder of Notorious B.I.G., Mike answered tersely, "I don't think anything. I know who did it. Amir did it." Vincent got under Mike's skin, though, when he asked about the trip to see Amir Muhammad at his home in San Diego County and why it had been unsuccessful. Mike answered with an accusing look, then said he guessed "somebody told him I was coming."

Sanders sat as expressionless as he could, trying not to let Vincent see how pleased he was with the way Mike was handling his interrogation. "Ten minutes into that depo, I knew this guy was going to be an absolutely great witness for us in court," Sanders said. "He came across as someone who was just going to tell it like it was, and to hell with you if you didn't like it."

Mike even managed to throw a few things at Vincent for which the city's attorney was clearly unprepared. At one point he spoke about security firms that "hire crooked police officers." When asked if he knew of "any LAPD officers that were involved in this crooked activity," Mike replied, "Mack one." David Mack was "in the same circle" with the Reggie Wrights, Sr. and Jr., Mike added. What circle is that? Vincent wanted to know. "Crooked," Mike replied. "They take money, they take dope, they do all kinds of things. They kill people for a living." Police in Los Angeles County had been hearing for years that the Wrights lived as well as they did by stealing from drug dealers and selling their stuff on the street. That Reggie Wright Sr. continued to serve as a sheriff's deputy was for many Crips and Bloods evidence of how corrupt the cops were.

When the subject of Rick James's party house was brought up, Mike mentioned that he'd seen David Mack there once with Amir Muhammad. He'd seen Suge Knight there also.

"So if you went up to Suge Knight and said, 'Hi, Suge,' he'd say 'Hi, Mike,' right?" Vincent asked.

"Yeah," Mike answered, then added, "I don't know about now because of what you people done to me. He probably would kill me now."

Mike showed tremulous emotion only when he was asked why he was helping the FBI and the Wallace family's attorneys. "I might as well finish it because I'm already exposed," Mike replied. "I'm done. So I might as well, you know, do the right thing. Maybe somebody might have some kind of peace or justice in their lives by me doing the right thing."

Vincent goaded Mike with questions about the risks he was taking by talking about the Biggie murder. The stress and anger in Mike's voice became increasingly audible. Finally, he asked for a break.

Sergio Robleto took him into the hotel suite's bedroom, where Mike sat on one corner of the mattress and "began to weep and weep and weep," Robleto remembered. "I tried to calm him down, reassure him that we were going to do everything we could to protect him. But he sobbed for half an hour."

Then suddenly Mike "jumped up, ran out of the room and down the stairs," Robleto remembered. "I figured he needed air. I told my guys to stay loose, don't try to stop him. The freeway was right across the street, and Mike runs down the embankment right onto the freeway. He ran right into the oncoming traffic. At that point we ran onto the freeway chasing him, but he just kept running. He ran on the shoulder for a couple of miles. Then he got off the freeway and ran for another mile. He finally slowed down and we caught up. He was sobbing again and shouting, 'They're gonna kill me! They're after me!' The only one who could talk to him was Richard Valdemar. Richard calmed him down to the point where he was listening again. That took a couple of hours. Then Richard took him home, because no one else was supposed to know where he was staying."

It was the last time Robleto ever saw Mike Robinson.

Chuck Philips, though, wasn't done with Mike. On June 3, 2005, just as the case of *Wallace v. City of Los Angeles* was approaching trial, the *Los Angeles Times* ran an article by Philips under the headline "Informant in Rap Star's Slaying Admits Hearsay."

The essence of the story was the headline: the secret informant who told the police that Biggie's killer was a Nation of Islam member named Amir—"or Ashmir," as Ted Ball's report had it—had acknowledged in a sworn deposition that his information wasn't first-hand. What made the article fundamentally deceptive was Philips's description of how Mike had "admitted" under cross-examination that he was only repeating what others had told him. But Mike had made that clear from the very beginning. "It was exactly what he told me and exactly what I told the LAPD," said Valdemar, "that Mike had heard it was Amir Muhammad from people on the street. But the *Times* article made it sound like he had tried to hide that."

Philips detailed some of Mike's background—how he had gone to prison for murder, and earned his membership in the Black Guerrilla Family by stabbing a man fourteen times, and had been diagnosed as a schizophrenic. The reporter, though, left out any mention of how successful Mike Robinson had been as a police informant and a witness in court, the long list of criminals and corrupt law enforcement officers he'd put behind bars, and Mike's consistency when he was questioned by the attorneys attempting to discredit him.

What most infuriated Sanders was that every bit of Philips's information had been drawn from Mike's deposition, a deposition that Judge Cooper had ordered sealed and to which no one had access other than the attorneys on both sides of the lawsuit and their clients. Sanders and Frank had no doubt that someone on the other side had given Philips a copy of Mike Robinson's "confidential" deposition. "This is how outrageous it's become," Sanders said at the time. "They release a sealed transcript immediately before the case it involves is scheduled to go to trial, knowing that the *L.A. Times* will use that transcript to distort the facts and make our case look ridiculous in the eyes of the public."

Sergio Robleto was even more outspoken. The release of the sealed transcript was "tantamount to jury tampering," he said. Robleto was not given to extravagant statements, but "this case has really gotten to me," he explained. "I've learned things I really wish I didn't know."

No one was more devastated by the article than Valdemar. He was stunned, the former deputy said, that Philips had used his informant's street name, Psycho Mike. "Before that, Mike at least had some deniability," Valdemar said. "It was basically his word against the word of Amir Muhammad that he was a government informant. There were a lot of people who didn't believe it. But once it was in print that the informant was known as Psycho Mike, he was a dead man if he showed up on the streets."

For Sanders and Frank, the main consequence of the "Informant . . . Admits Hearsay" article was that Mike Robinson disappeared immediately from the place where he was hiding out. Even Valdemar couldn't find him. It meant that Sanders and Frank would be unable to call him as a witness, and would have no choice but to offer only his deposition into evidence—if the judge allowed it. "That article was the single worst thing that happened to our case," Sanders said.

Months later, Mike Robinson contacted Valdemar. He was tired of running, Mike said. Did they have any safe place for him? Valdemar found him a house in California City, a town of about thirteen thousand on the desolate eastern edge of the Antelope Valley, closer to Death Valley than to Compton. "A place the term 'middle of nowhere' was made for," Valdemar said. Mike never got comfortable there, though. "He was constantly looking over his shoulder, always on the lookout for the people who would be coming after him," Valdemar said. "The stress ate him up."

Mike lived for only about another year before dying of a heart attack on December 5, 2006. He was forty-nine.

Valdemar and Tim Flaherty attended Mike's funeral, the only white faces in a surprisingly large crowd. "What I will always remember is Mike's grandkids sobbing and hugging the casket," Valdemar said.

Valdemar vented his rage and grief in an article for *Police* magazine in which he wrote, "Chuck Philips did all he could to twist the witness statements, expose the sources and protect his pals at Death Row. His *Los Angeles Times* editors failed to see that obviously his view was biased . . . As a result of the *Times* articles and Chuck Philips, Mike Robinson was attacked physically on more than one occasion. He was shot at, cut in the face and head with a razor, and his front teeth were knocked out. The assailants even mentioned the *Times* article during one attack . . . It is my belief that Michael Robinson died as a result of the stress and anxiety caused by his exposure and identification in Chuck Philips's hit piece."

CHAPTER SIX

S pecial agent Phil Carson's life and career both began to blow up on the day the attorneys for the plaintiffs' side in *Wallace v. Los Angeles* listed him as a witness. According to Carson and two other agents in the FBI's Los Angeles office, Berkow had twice asked the head of the criminal division at that office, Lou Caprino, to shut down Carson's investigation of the Biggie murder. Caprino refused both times. When Carson's name appeared on the witness list, the city attorney's office got involved. An assistant city attorney named Louis Li arranged a meeting with Carson and his bosses at the FBI office. "Li told us, point-blank, 'We cannot let Agent Carson testify, because if he does, we stand a better than fifty percent chance of losing upwards of six hundred million dollars in this lawsuit,'" remembered Carson, whose recollection was confirmed by another FBI agent at the meeting. "'It would ruin the LAPD, and the relationship between the LAPD and the federal government, including the FBI.'"

When Carson's FBI bosses equivocated, a larger meeting was organized, one attended by not only the highest-ranking FBI officials in L.A. but also the senior command staff of the LAPD and the attorneys defending the city in the *Wallace v. Los Angeles* lawsuit. The LAPD representatives and city attorneys spoke at length about the relationship between the police department and the FBI, the various federal programs and task forces the two agencies were involved with

together, and the enormous amount of money that had been committed to these projects, remembered Carson and a second special agent
who was present. The FBI and the LAPD were "interdependent," one
of those on the city's side of the table argued, and it would be insane
to jeopardize all that "just to solve the murder of a four-hundred-
pound black crack dealer turned rapper."

"Those were the exact words used," Carson recalled. A second
FBI agent who was at the meeting confirmed this.

Carson's bosses acceded to the city's demand: he would not be a
witness in the *Wallace v. Los Angeles* civil trial, the agent was informed.
Officially, it was Caprino who had made that decision, but Carson
believed "it went higher up than Lou, to people back in D.C."

By then, Carson's greatest concerns were not about what the
LAPD and the city attorney's office were doing to his case, but about
the threats against his career being made by Chuck Philips. Carson
recalled, "Philips started phoning me constantly and asking me questions about the case that I couldn't answer. When I explained that to
him, he started calling Cathy Viray, who was the head of the press
information unit at our FBI office, and telling her, 'I'm going to ruin
Carson.'" Viray, who confirmed Philips's threats, and Steve Kramer,
who was then the assistant chief counsel at the FBI's L.A. headquarters, both explained to Philips that Carson couldn't say more than
he already had said.

Philips, though, continued to threaten that he would destroy
Phil Carson's career if he didn't get answers, remembered Viray.

Finally—"and this was absolutely unprecedented," Carson
said—Caprino arranged for a conference call during which every
one of the supervisors at the FBI office, along with its legal and press
teams, would answer what questions they could for Philips.

The agents who participated in that conference call were filled
with dismay and fury when, just days later, an article by Philips ran
on the front page of the *Los Angeles Times* Metro section. "FBI Ends
Probe into Killing of Rap Star," read the headline. In the article,
Philips revealed that the FBI had shut down its investigation of the

Christopher Wallace homicide, the first time this news had been made public.

The FBI had decided to drop the probe, Philips wrote, "after learning that Agent Philip J. Carson had discussions with lawyers for Wallace's mother, Voletta Wallace, and had been subpoenaed to testify in her wrongful-death lawsuit against the city." FBI officials had already informed Sanders and Frank that Carson would not be permitted to testify in open court. According to Philips, Carson's bosses had also instructed him to have no further contact with the Wallace family's attorneys.

Those lawyers, Sanders and Frank, were enraged by the article. "We had heard, and had to assume, that enormous pressure was being brought to bear on the FBI for something like this to happen," Sanders said. "Phil Carson called me at one point and said, 'This is political at the highest levels you can imagine.' He said he still believed we were right about who was responsible for Biggie's murder, but was being hassled in a major way by people who wanted him to stop going in that direction."

For the record, the head of the FBI in Los Angeles, Richard T. Garcia, stated that the results of Special Agent Carson's eighteen-month-long investigation had been submitted to the U.S. attorney's office, which "determined that the evidence was insufficient for [criminal] prosecution."

That much was true: Carson *had* submitted the results of his investigation to the U.S. attorney's office. By then, he knew the case was being followed at the highest levels of the bureau, Carson said. That had become obvious when the name of FBI director Robert Mueller began to appear in the email chain of memos concerning the Christopher Wallace murder investigation. "The politics of the case had become mind-boggling," said Carson, who was "stunned" when the U.S. attorney's office answered his submission of the case with a letter stating it saw insufficient evidence to prosecute.

"I knew I had the case," Carson explained. "We definitely had enough to prosecute." The standard procedure—universally observed—was that when the U.S. attorney's office turned down an FBI case, it provided a "letter of declination" laying out the reasons for the decision. In this instance, however, the assistant U.S. attorney who had been assigned to the case, David Vaughn, a former Los Angeles County assistant district attorney, refused to provide such a letter.

"I had a meeting with the assistant director and all my bosses to go over the investigation page by page," recalled Carson, whose recollection was confirmed by another agent in attendance. "After the assistant director heard and read the evidence, he looked at me and said, 'Why isn't this case being indicted?' I said, 'Good question. Go ask the U.S. attorney's office. They won't explain why.' He said, 'Well, don't you have a letter of declination?' I say they won't give me one, and he looks me in the eye for a long time, then says, 'You get that letter of declination.' Because at this point he's not going to let this come back on the FBI. There is obviously a case here that should have resulted in an indictment, and if there isn't one the U.S. attorney has to take responsibility for it."

He asked—and eventually implored—Vaughn multiple times to provide the letter of declination, Carson recalled, and was refused on each occasion. "That just doesn't happen," Carson said. "I talked to my fellow agents and to my bosses, and they all said they'd never seen a decision not to prosecute an FBI case where the U.S. attorney's office had refused to provide a letter of declination. It was unique to this situation."*

After the March 11, 2005, publication of Philips's article "FBI Ends Probe," Carson had been at least slightly consoled by the anger that spread through the FBI's Los Angeles office. In particular, his

---

* In May 2018, I asked Vaughn, now a defense attorney in Los Angeles, to explain why he had refused to provide the letter of declination. In what sounded like a panicked voice he insisted that he did not know what I was talking about, then said he couldn't discuss it over the telephone, asked me to send my questions in an email, and hung up. I immediately sent an email to Vaughn at his law firm, laying out the claims made by Carson and other current and former FBI agents and asking him to reply. He never did.

Los Angeles colleagues were offended by Philips's suggestion that Carson had behaved improperly and had based his investigation on information provided by Sanders and Frank. The section of the article that the FBI agents believed most unfair to Carson, though, was a lengthy paragraph in which, according to Philips, David Mack called Carson "the most inept or laziest agent I had ever met." Carson, Mack claimed, had offered to seek a reduction of his fourteen-year sentence on the Bank of America robbery conviction if he cooperated with the FBI's investigation of the Wallace murder.

"Not one word of that is true," said Carson, who noted that Philips's article failed to mention that there was another FBI agent, from the local office in Alabama, with him during every second he spent with Mack at the Talladega Federal Correctional Institution, where Mack was currently incarcerated. Carson's bosses at the FBI's Los Angeles office vehemently disputed that Carson had ever offered Mack anything at all.

He had approached Mack with extreme caution, Carson said. He'd heard early on from Perry Sanders that people the attorney had spoken with seemed to be far more afraid of Mack than they were of Suge Knight. He was especially impressed by two inmates who said they preferred to accept twenty-year prison sentences rather than make a deal to testify against Mack, Sanders said: "They told me, 'Twenty years is a long time, but dead is forever.'" What he'd heard from Sanders had been repeated again and again as he'd moved forward with the Biggie investigation, Carson said. "People I wanted to talk to about Mack told me flatly, 'No, I say one word about David Mack and I am a dead man.'" Rafael Perez's ex-partner Nino Durden had told him simply, "You don't fuck with Mack," Carson recalled.

When they arrived at the Talladega prison to interview Mack in person, Carson recalled, "the other agent and I had to walk across this huge grass field where there were three little cells on the other side. Mack was in one of them." He remembered Mack's long braids and "sadistic smile," Carson said. "When I looked into Mack's eyes, I have never been more sure in my life that I was looking at a cold-blooded killer than I was in that moment." Mack, "a charming guy and a totally frightening one," had of course given him nothing, Carson recalled.

Immediately after interviewing Mack, Carson had taken a call from Paul Paquette: "He tells me he just got a call from David Mack and Mack wants to take a polygraph, but he doesn't want LAPD to be part of it. And he'll only do it if these four other people are polygraphed also." His bosses told him to advise Paquette they weren't interested at this time and would let him know if they were. Unknown to Carson at the time, Paquette had made up the whole "Mack wants a polygraph" story. That would come out eventually, and Paquette would be removed from the case. In the meantime, though, the threat Chuck Philips posed was at the forefront of his thoughts, Carson said.

In his March 11 article, Philips reported that there had been a meeting in September 2004 in which FBI officials questioned Carson's "conduct of the investigation" and expressed their concern "that Carson might have been influenced by the Wallace lawyers and that his contacts with them could embarrass the bureau."

When I interviewed him for *Rolling Stone*, Caprino, who had been Philips's main source for the "FBI Ends Probe" article, told me his statements had been "grossly distorted and misquoted" by the reporter. "That article really pissed off a lot of people, including me," said Sergio Robleto, who had met Agent Carson for the first time at Rob Frank's law office in Colorado Springs, where they were reviewing the discovery materials from the LAPD at the same conference table. "Phil Carson was an absolutely stellar FBI agent, above reproach, incorruptible."

Cathy Viray sent a lengthy letter on FBI stationary to the *Los Angeles Times* demanding assorted corrections and clarifications. After a series of "delays and excuses," Viray told me, the newspaper informed the FBI that it was refusing to publish the letter. "I don't know of another instance where the *Times* has refused to publish a letter sent on behalf of the federal government," she said. "It really makes you wonder what they're afraid of."

As a result of the article, the FBI's Los Angeles office—"on my orders," Caprino said—informed Philips it would have no further contact with him. In Carson's view, at that point "Philips says basically, 'Screw it. Now I'm really gonna go after this guy.' He was calling Cathy Viray again and again and telling her how he was going to ruin my career." Viray confirmed this.

Carson appealed to the L.A. office's assistant director, Rich Garcia, who made another unprecedented decision: he sent the office's assistant chief counsel, Steve Kramer, along with Viray, to meet with Philips. The rendezvous took place in a corner booth of a downtown bar at just past eleven on a weeknight. "Cathy told me they began by telling Philips, 'Look, Carson is not a bad dude. We don't want you to ruin his career,'" recalled Carson, whose recollection was confirmed by Viray. "'We'll try to answer any questions [about the Biggie murder investigation] that we can, but you gotta understand there are limits to what we can tell you.'"

Viray called him just before midnight, Carson remembered, and said, "'We just got done meeting with Chuck Philips.' How did it go?" Carson asked. "And Cathy tells me, 'You're done. He's going to ruin you.'"

He decided on the spot that he had to meet with Philips himself, Carson recalled. "I told Cathy, 'You need to talk to the assistant director and get his okay for that, because nobody else is going to save my career. I have to do it."

Garcia gave his permission for Carson to meet with Philips. It was after midnight by then. He phoned Philips, but the call went straight to voice mail. "I left a message that 'I know about the meeting with Steve [Kramer] and Cathy, and I understand you're going to write an article that's going to ruin me. And I'd appreciate it if we could at least sit down and you could actually see me and put a face with my name and understand what you're doing to a real person.'"

Philips phoned back fifteen minutes later, said he had just gotten out of the shower, and added, "Boy, that's a phone call I didn't expect to get." He and Carson agreed they would meet early the next morning at a coffee shop near the Los Angeles Times Building. Carson picked Viray up the next morning at around five o'clock and the two were at the coffee shop before six. "When we sit down," Carson recalled, "Philips immediately starts asking questions about the Biggie case that he knows I can't answer. And I tell him that he knows I can't share details of an ongoing investigation, and he's trying to make my refusal to say things that could get me fired into a reason to ruin me."

Ten minutes into the conversation, Carson got a call from the woman who had been the face of the FBI in Los Angeles for years, public affairs specialist Laura Eimiller. "Laura asks, 'What are you doing?'" Carson remembered. "I tell her I'm in a meeting and she asks, 'Who's with you?' I tell her Cathy, and she asks, 'Are you guys meeting with Chuck Philips?' I say, 'Yeah,' and Laura tells me, 'Well, Mike Berkow just called the assistant director and chewed him a new asshole. He's pissed off you guys are meeting with Philips. I hand the phone to Cathy and I watch her face change. She starts bawling and telling Chuck Philips, 'You motherfucker! You're going to get me fired, you piece of shit!' She's losing it. I take the phone and Laura tells me, 'You guys need to get out of there right now.' When she hung up, I told Philips, 'You called Berkow, didn't you? And you told him about this meeting.'"

Philips had to have made that call sometime between one and six in the morning, Carson thought, which said something about the relationship he had with Berkow.

He and Viray got up from the table and left the coffee shop. "I'm literally carrying Cathy down the sidewalk toward our car, and Chuck is chasing after me, saying, 'Phil, Phil, look, I can explain. Just listen to me. I got something I need to show you, and it's up in my office.' I tell him to just get away from me and I keep dragging Cathy away, because she's turning around to go off on him. And Philips is telling me, 'Just look at what I have to show you. It will explain everything.' But I won't stop. Then he says, 'Someday I will tell you about how I found out about your operation in San Diego, about Psycho Mike.' That was the moment when I knew for certain that Berkow had told him."*

By the time he got back to the FBI office, his "pager was blowing up," Carson recalled. "Chuck Philips is doing anything he can to get hold of me. The guy won't quit, and finally that night I answer his call and say, 'What the hell do you want?' He says, 'You need to meet with me and see the stuff in my office I want to show you.' I'm thinking, 'Okay, the case is closed, I can't get a letter of declination, you and Berkow are trying to ruin my career; it's almost like I have nothing left to lose."

So he agreed to meet with Philips again early the next morning on the sidewalk outside the Times Building. Philips showed up and the two rode the elevator up to the newspaper's nearly vacant editorial department. Philips had brought him there not to "see" anything, Carson discovered, but rather to hear. What he wanted the FBI agent to listen to was a series of recorded phone conversations between the reporter and LAPD deputy chief Mike Berkow.

"Berkow is telling him things like, 'We have to make sure Phil Carson is totally noncredible. If he ever testifies, the LAPD will be destroyed. We have to wreck this case,'" Carson remembered. "I mean, these two guys were conspiring not just against me, but against the entire Wallace side of the case, against the murder investigation itself. To Berkow, I was just collateral damage. Ruining my life meant absolutely nothing to him. In one conversation I hear Berkow talking about Mike Robinson, and what he told Philips to shut down the third meeting with Amir Muhammad in Chula Vista, and by that point I was so pissed off that I could barely contain myself. He also tried to show me some photos, but by then I wanted out of there so badly I didn't look at them. I just walked out, shaking with rage."

---

* Michael Berkow's defense against the accusations made against him by Carson and others is considered in detail in Appendix A.

During the next two weeks, Philips called him repeatedly, dozens of times, said Carson, who refused to take the reporter's calls. Finally, though, realizing the mistake he had made in not looking at the photos, Carson called Philips back from the U.S. attorney's offices and said he'd like to see them. The reporter showed up minutes later with an envelope full of photographs. "They were the same ones that I had seen the first time I looked at the Biggie Murder Book," Carson said. "They were from the Petersen, on the night of the party. Philips pointed out various people in cheaper suits that he said were police officers. Then he showed me a picture of Amir Muhammad. I felt literally sick, and I wanted Philips away from me, so I walked away. I should have taken the photos, but I didn't."

He realized in a flash what Philips was doing, Carson explained: "He wanted me to be his new inside source, and he was willing to sell out Berkow to land me. The whole thing just made me sick and disgusted, and I knew I was done with it all. I never spoke to either Philips or Berkow again after that day."

A short time later the FBI agent requested and received a transfer to Orange County. "L.A. was poisoned for me," he explained. "I didn't believe anybody in the whole damned city."

By June 2005, the run-up to the impending trial in *Wallace v. Los Angeles* had become increasingly frantic and frustrating for the plaintiffs' side. "It was hard to find people and it was hard to find information," Rob Frank said. The City of Los Angeles and the LAPD were throwing up every roadblock they could find. What made getting to the people the attorneys needed most wearisome, though, was the cloud of fear that surrounded the case.

One witness Sanders and Frank were certain they wanted to put on the stand was Kendrick Knox, the now retired LAPD senior lead officer who had conducted an investigation of Death Row Records in 1996. Knox's investigation had established beyond doubt that it was widely known among the police department's highest-ranking officials, well before the murder of Notorious B.I.G., that a significant number of LAPD officers were working for Death Row Records, in spite of an official policy that forbade it, and that the police department had deliberately turned a blind eye.

What had begun for Knox as a "civil abatement" case involving conflicts between condo dwellers and gangbangers in the vicinity of Death Row's Encino, California, recording studios had morphed into an investigation into the murders of Tupac Shakur and Notorious B.I.G. When the LAPD command staff learned of this, Deputy Chief David Gascon had distributed an intradepartmental memorandum stating that only a single LAPD officer had ever worked for Death Row Records. Knox knew that this was not true, and knew also that Gascon's boss and longtime ally, LAPD chief Bernard Parks, knew it was not true. Shortly afterward, Knox had been ordered not to discuss his Death Row Records investigation with anyone inside or outside the police department without official authorization. Knox also had been ordered to turn over all the files in his possession that related to Death Row Records. "They closed the lid on him" as Russell Poole put it, leaving Knox so "disturbed and frustrated" that he had given Poole both the notes that had survived his investigation and Kevin Lewis, the informant working for Death Row who had provided him with accounts of what was happening inside the record company. Most of Knox's work, though, had disappeared when the hard drive on his work computer was wiped clean while he was on sick leave, Knox had told Poole.

This last event had left Knox deeply shaken. The officer became increasingly concerned that information about him and his investigation was being leaked to Suge Knight by other members of the police department. "Knox had become convinced that his life and his wife's life were endangered," Sergio Robleto explained.

In the weeks before the lawsuit's trial date, Robleto and his operatives devoted many hours to surveillance of Knox's home, but saw no sign of the man. "We heard he had gone to Mexico to avoid our subpoena," Robleto recalled, "but we wondered how he knew exactly when he needed to be gone in order to do that."

Sanders and Frank would say publicly that they had no doubt that someone on the other side of the case had alerted Knox that he was about to be subpoenaed and encouraged him to abscond. "However it happened, his disappearance has hurt our case and helped theirs," Frank said.

CHAPTER SEVEN

For Perry Sanders, preparation for the Notorious B.I.G. wrongful death lawsuit was turning into the most surreal experience of a life that had long been lived large. It was quite a bit of fun at the beginning. He and Frank were staying in a spectacular ocean-view condominium in Santa Monica that had been formerly owned by the NFL great Anthony Muñoz and, as Sanders put it, "havin' a ball." Sanders was spending at least a couple of nights a week playing poker at the Commerce Casino. Traveling to and from court, he was watched over by the hulking bodyguards the Wallace Estate had hired to keep him safe. That the bodyguards were Bloods gang members confused him at first, Sanders recalled, but he knew Voletta Wallace and Biggie's widow, Faith Evans, were determined to see him protected, "so I trusted they were the right guys."

Sanders himself began to take the danger, and the commitment of his bodyguards to protect him from it, more seriously one afternoon while dining at Enterprise Seafood in the Abbot Kinney section of Venice. He was meeting with Lil' Cease over the meal to talk about the rapper's trial testimony. "I'm pourin' champagne for Lil' Cease when one of my bodyguards sees somebody come in he thinks might be a threat. I got a bottle of champagne in my hand when the bodyguard grabs me by the back of the jacket and literally carries me out to the car, with the bottle still in my hand."

Lil' Cease's manager Wayne Barrow had invited Sanders to the Hollywood Boulevard Club where the rapper's new album was being previewed. "So I show up with my two bodyguards," Sanders recalled. "We get out of the car and people are lined up outside the place to get in. The sidewalk is packed from the building to the street in both directions with beautiful people, the *most* beautiful. I'm thinkin', 'We won't be goin' there, obviously, 'cause we'll never get in.' My driver says, 'Wait here.' He goes to the door, talks to the guy there, and next thing you know it's like the Red Sea partin'. I not only get ushered right in but also right past all the rich and famous people who are already seated at tables on the floor, then led to this private balcony above the dance floor that I have all to myself."

Below was one of the strangest scenes Sanders had ever experienced. "There are all these movie stars and music stars," he recalled, "but there are also all these gangsters. I mean, wall-to-wall gangsters. And some of 'em looked pretty damn scary. I turn to one of my bodyguards—this guy who had told me he had been shot six times before he was twenty—and I say, 'Guys, you don't seem to be armed. How do I know I'm not going to get whacked when I try to walk out of here?' And the guy, my four-hundred-fifty-pound guy, tells me, 'Well, it's because of who your bodyguards are.' Then he tells me, 'Also, because of who your bodyguards are, you can have any woman in here if you want.' It was right at the beginning of my relationship with Lorn [Lee, the woman he would marry], so I could only look, but it told me one heck of a lot about how far L.A. is from Louisiana."

The part of the job that Sanders would come to dislike most was dealing with the Los Angeles press. "L.A. is the only place I've tried a case where public perception, what's happenin' in the media, seems more important than what happens in the courtroom," he said. "And the media in L.A. follows the *Los Angeles Times* wherever it leads." The deluge of negative and biased reporting he had faced from the moment he filed the lawsuit began to wear on Sanders well before the case came to trial. "It's been a big enough drag to have a whole bunch of very good lawyers against us in this case," he said, "but to have the biggest newspaper in the state doin' triple backflips to try to influence the jury against us has made it much more difficult."

Sanders had no doubt the city's attorneys were leaking anything that might damage his case to the *Times* after the newspaper ran a story reporting that the Wallace Estate had tried to settle for as little as $18 million. Sanders refused to comment on that claim, but did say that none of the *Times* articles had included one crucial detail about every settlement discussion he'd had with the city: his client's demand that the LAPD devote its resources to solving her son's murder.

"What I need from this lawsuit is that the person or persons who murdered my son are brought to justice," Voletta Wallace told me in 2005. "What I need from this lawsuit is honesty. What I need from this lawsuit is to show that humans have integrity, that they're not cowards, show that they're not liars, show that they care about the truth." For Sanders, Voletta Wallace had become an island of calm amid the storm of secrets and lies her court claim had unleashed. "Let it all come out," she said. "There's nothing they can surprise me with anymore."

For the City of Los Angeles and its representatives, their defense had grown steadily more fierce and manipulative, in part owing to the increase in their legal team's firepower. "They got the case continued on bullshit, and at first we couldn't figure out why," Sanders recalled. "I thought it might be just to make it more expensive and time-consuming for us, but then I figured out that it was to buy time to bring in a big-time lawyer." Without Sanders's knowledge, the city attorney's office had gone to the Los Angeles City Council to obtain a $500,000 appropriation to hire "outside counsel." The lawyer chosen was Vincent Marella, a widely admired—and feared—business attorney whose list of professional honors and accolades was lengthy. Marella, a former U.S. attorney, had been the lead defense lawyer in the largest federal tax case in U.S. history and had represented an assortment of CEOs and CFOs of major corporations in securities fraud and antitrust cases.

"Up until Marella, we had several city attorney representatives that were seasoned and very good in their own way," Sanders recalled, "but their style, from the way they dressed to the way they tried a case, was consistent with a more bureaucratic approach. Vince, on the other hand, owned his own fine clothes men's shop, and he was cut from distinctly different cloth, like the custom-tailored shirts and suits he wore. He had done lots of stuff that was way outside the zone of what even the best attorney workin' for the city would have done."

It had pleased Sanders that his Southern accent and good-time grin initially made it difficult for a lot of people in L.A. to take him seriously. The Louisianan was always "fixin'" to do this or that. "Bein' underestimated was probably our biggest advantage at the beginning of the case," Sanders admitted with a sly smile. Unlike the comically pretentious Paul Paquette, the city's lead attorney up to that point, Marella had recognized that Sanders was no rube from the moment he showed up in court. "All of a sudden, we had a very smart, tactical sophisticate on our hands," said Sanders. "It was like we were playin' a different team."

Sanders was convinced that Marella had coached former LAPD chief Bernard Parks on how to avoid giving answers that offered any illumination when he was cross-examined by Sanders and Frank during his deposition. The LAPD's investigation "never pointed clearly at any one suspect," Parks said, but then conceded a moment later, "I think the closest speculation was that there was one suspect, and it was later found out that he was not involved. I remember it was Amir. And later found out, at least from our investigation, he was not involved."

Yet Parks managed to provide absolutely no information about *how* the LAPD had determined Amir Muhammad was not involved. "It was one nonanswer after another," Frank recalled. "When all else failed, he claimed that sharing this or that information would compromise the continuing investigation." Parks made himself personally vulnerable on only a single point during the deposition, claiming that he had not known about Russell Poole's "involvement" in the Mack-Muhammad theory of the Biggie Smalls murder until he read about it in the newspaper. Poole told Sanders and Frank that this was a lie and that he could prove it was, because it had been brought up in a meeting with Chief Parks where there were other witnesses.

Sanders and Frank got very little from questioning either David Mack or Amir Muhammad, a.k.a. Harry Billups, a.k.a. Harry Muhammad. The attorneys had made a decision to drop both men as defendants in the case, in part because neither had any money that was not well hidden, but mainly because, as Sanders said, "we were concerned the jurors would be terrified of them if they were sittin' in court." In spite of this decision, neither Mack nor Muhammad was willing to cooperate in any way with the Wallace side—which was not surprising, given that the plaintiffs' theory of the case was still that Muhammad had been the shooter in a murder Mack had helped to set up.

Mack's deposition was at least interesting, though more confusing than anything else. The former LAPD officer was questioned by Frank at the same federal penitentiary in Talladega, Alabama, where Phil Carson had met with him. Mack had been transferred there after being stabbed on the running track at the prison in Illinois where he had begun his fourteen-year sentence for bank robbery. According to his attorney, a group of Hispanic prisoners had attacked Mack after they saw accounts in print and on television that described his career as a police officer and his association with Rafael Perez. According to the attorney, the prisoner who punctured Mack's lung with a sharp object was upset to learn that Mack and Perez had preyed on gang members in Los Angeles' Rampart District.

In Talladega, Mack answered a number of Frank's questions but responded to most by pleading the Fifth Amendment. Mack of course denied having been involved in the murder of Notorious B.I.G. or possessing any knowledge of Amir Muhammad's involvement in the crime. He also denied attending any Death Row Records social functions or any other affair where Suge Knight was present, contradicting multiple witnesses who claimed to have seen him with Suge at Death Row parties.

Obviously, none of that was surprising, said Frank, whose main memory of the deposition was how "physically intimidating" he found the former LAPD officer to be. Some of Mack's denials, though, left Frank dumbfounded. He denied ever having been interviewed by LAPD Robbery-Homicide Division detectives Brian Tyndall and Greg Grant, which amounted to an accusation that the two had fraudulently created their notes and tapes of that interview, part of the evidence that had helped convict Mack in court. Mack also denied that any police radios had been found when his home was searched after his arrest for bank robbery, though one had been and was logged into evidence at the time.

Odder still was Mack's claim that he was not a close friend of Amir Muhammad. Yes, Amir was his children's godfather, Mack said, but that was because Amir had asked to be. Yes, Amir had visited him once in prison, Mack conceded, but then refused to answer why, if they were not close friends, the man who had been his college roommate would make such a visit. He also refused to disclose what they had spoken about during that visit. He was a practicing Muslim, Mack said, but declined to say how or when he had become one, or whether Amir Muhammad had something to do with it. Mack acknowledged owning a black Chevy Impala in March 1997, but insisted it was never out of his possession for any "significant" period of time. When he was asked if Amir Muhammad had ever borrowed his Impala, Mack was cagey, saying that if Amir had driven the car, he was unaware of it.

Mack said he was unsure about where he had been between midnight and 4 a.m. on March 9, 1997, the date of the Notorious B.I.G. murder, and said he did not know where Amir Muhammad had been then, either.

By far the most revealing aspect of the deposition was Mack's assertion of his right to refuse answering questions that might incriminate him. It was no surprise that he pleaded the Fifth to avoid answering any questions connected to the Bank of America robbery. Mack's more telling Fifth Amendment claims, though, came when he refused to answer whether attorney Donald Re had represented him in his trial on the bank robbery charges. Re *was* Mack's defense lawyer in that case, and there was no risk of self-incrimination in saying so. At the time, attorneys who watched the trial had wondered how Mack could afford one of the most expensive attorneys in L.A. The defendant may have stolen more than $722,000 in the Bank of America robbery, but it was difficult to believe he could access that money from jail, and there was no way a lawyer as smart as Re would risk being paid with stolen funds. What Mack was concerned about became clear only when Frank asked the next question: Had Re been paid for his services with funds provided by Suge Knight? He was refusing to answer based on his Fifth Amendment right to avoid self-incrimination, Mack replied.

Amir Muhammad, who was deposed at his attorney's office in Orange County under what was still his legal name, Harry Billups, had split the difference on the question of how close he was to Mack. They were "pretty good friends," Muhammad said. "Not best friends, but good friends." He always had been and still was closer to Mack's wife, Carla, than he was to David, Muhammad added. He contradicted his friend on whose idea it had been for him to become godfather to the Mack children: "He asked me to be godfather." You didn't ask him, he asked you? Frank pressed. "Yes," Muhammad answered. Beyond this, however, the man denied everything and gave up nothing.

There was a jarring contrast, Frank recalled, between Muhammad's appearance and the way he tried to present himself. "From the moment he walked into the room I was afraid of him," Frank said. Muscled up, with a shaved head and a flat expression, Muhammad exuded menace, as Frank remembered him. "You felt this was someone capable of serious violence every time you looked him in the eye." Muhammad, though, was consistent throughout the deposition in portraying himself as an innocent bystander who was stunned and confused by how he had been drawn into this whole sordid mess.

"I'm a mortgage broker," he said several times in answer to Frank's questions, as if that alone were proof that he could not possibly have been involved in murder.

Sergio Robleto, though, was already poking holes in Muhammad's image. The man's criminal history, Robleto had learned, went back at least to his days as an athlete at the University of Oregon. In 1980, as Harry Billups, Muhammad had been arrested in three different Oregon cities for theft of services—skipping out on restaurant or bar bills. More serious was the record Muhammad had accumulated in California during the 1990s. State records showed a man almost constantly on the move, with addresses in an assortment of Southern California cities under at least four different names, regularly using driver's licenses and other identification that had been falsely obtained. Most troubling were the incidents stemming from Muhammad's relationship with a woman named Angelique Mitchell. He had been arrested in Anaheim in 1993 for infliction of corporal injury on a spouse/cohabitant after an altercation with Mitchell. That charge was ultimately dismissed by the Orange County district attorney's office on the grounds of "furtherance of justice." But Muhammad had been arrested again in 1994, this time in Fullerton, after Mitchell accused him of beating her in front of her children. The charges of assault, battery, infliction of corporal injury on a spouse/cohabitant, and willful cruelty to a child were again dismissed (and again as furtherance of justice), but only after Muhammad had pleaded guilty to trespass with refusal to leave a property and received a sentence of sixty days in jail, along with twenty-four months of probation.

The most significant incident involving Mitchell, though, had taken place on October 21, 1998, seventeen months after the Notorious B.I.G. murder, when Muhammad had been arrested in the city of Chino for brandishing a firearm.

Mitchell had called the Chino police to say that Muhammad showed up without warning at her workplace, a Department of Motor Vehicles office in Pomona. After he saw her climb into a Blazer SUV with her new boyfriend, Mitchell said, Muhammad followed the couple onto the freeway in his black BMW, a vehicle that was the basis of the lease fraud charges that had recently been filed against him in Los Angeles. After tailing them for some distance, the BMW sped up alongside the Blazer, and Muhammad pointed a pistol at them through his open window, Mitchell said. When the Chino police pulled Muhammad over, they found a semiautomatic Beretta loaded with an eight-round clip in his vehicle. Muhammad denied pointing the pistol at the couple, then explained that he was in the process of moving and had forgotten the Beretta was in his car. After providing the police with a falsely obtained California driver's license in the name of "Harry Muhammad" that bore an address in Fontana, California, he was cited for carrying a concealed weapon and released.

Six days later, Mitchell and her boyfriend were dead from gunshot wounds to the head. The San Bernardino County coroner's office ruled the deaths a murder-suicide.

"The coroner's verdict was based on one eyewitness, a cop who told this crazy story about how the couple jumped out onto the front porch of this house and the murder-suicide happened right in front of him," Sanders recalled. "It just didn't sound right."

Robleto, though, had not been able to find anything that tied Muhammad to the killings, other than their proximity in time to the firearm-brandishing incident. "The crime wasn't well investigated, but there was nothing you could really point to," he explained. "It was one guy's word, and there was nothing solid to challenge it with."

Still, Sanders said, "Sergio had found enough for us to know that we could put Muhammad on the stand and let the jury get a real good look at what a bad guy he was. I was especially lookin' forward to askin' him why he needed all those phony driver's licenses."

CHAPTER EIGHT

As the trial date loomed, Robleto, like Sanders and Frank, was working on so many fronts that it left him constantly frazzled. Part of what made his work so exhausting, he said, was that "a number of the witnesses coming forward were Suge Knight plants, sent our way to set us up for failure. Weeding them out became a big part of my job." What most troubled the investigator, though, was his growing disillusionment with the police department to which he had devoted most of his adult life.

"The lack of connections that had been made," Robleto said, "the lack of effort to make those connections—I kept bumping against it again and again. It pained me to say it, but I was literally forced to the conclusion that the Los Angeles Police Department did not want to solve the murder of Christopher Wallace."

Discrediting Russell Poole, Robleto had found, was the thrust of the "so-called investigation" that the LAPD had done since the detective's resignation. "The deeper I looked, the more obvious it was that the detectives assigned to the case weren't running the case. The city attorneys, Paquette and Vincent, they were the ones in charge. The detectives were actually asking Paquette what they could do. That was a big thing to me, because no one should be interfering with police investigators."

Even more disturbing to Robleto, though, was the way the Blue Wall had encircled the Notorious B.I.G. case and was "refusing to let any light in or out." Only a couple of police officers, both of low rank, had been willing to talk to him about the cops working for Suge Knight and Death Row Records. "One told me there were over thirty officers that worked for Death Row on a list," Robleto recalled. "He said that one of his command officers had literally hidden it from the police department's investigators." Even that officer would talk only with a promise that his anonymity would be protected. Most of the cops Robleto tried to speak with, including those who had worked with and for him, not only refused to talk but treated him as if he were a traitor to the LAPD. "One of the deputy chiefs came up to me pointing his finger right between my eyes. He said, 'You're giving Russell Poole credibility. Stop it!'"

Experiences such as that only deepened the respect he felt for his former detective, Robleto said. "I saw how everybody had aligned themselves against Russ. And I knew Russ. He couldn't back off from something he knew was right. His integrity was four inches before his nose. And he was despised for it when he should have been admired."

Robleto was simultaneously shocked and thrilled when he found a search warrant that had been written in 1999, shortly after Poole's resignation from the department. The author, a Robbery-Homicide Division detective named Buford Watts, had laid out the suspicions that Suge Knight was responsible for coordinating the hit on Biggie. "This affidavit was written to remain confidential, and the LAPD didn't want us to have it," Robleto said, "because it strongly corroborated what Russ had been saying." What made the affidavit so significant was that a good deal of it had been based on statements made by an informant who had been provided to the LAPD by FBI agents working in the San Francisco Bay Area. "Confidential and reliable" was how the man had been described by the feds, who had closed a number of major cases with the informant's help. After a good deal of searching, Robleto was eventually able to find this "confidential and reliable informant." His name was Mario Ha'mmonds.

Ha'mmonds, a former partner in a small rap label called Lock Records, had a long and complicated history of both criminal conduct and cooperation with the authorities. He was presently locked up in San Quentin, where Robleto, accompanied by Richard Valdemar, went to check him out. "I found him extremely credible," Robleto said. "He was a pretty heavy dude. He knew all the gangsters and who they were related to. He was a treasure house of information."

Robleto phoned Sanders and Frank and told them they needed to get themselves up to the Bay Area to depose this guy on videotape. When the attorneys arrived at San Quentin, they found themselves face-to-face with a hulking figure who wore graying dreadlocks and black horn-rim glasses with his prison blues. He was fingering prayer beads and seated in a wheelchair. When the lawyers asked why the wheelchair, Ha'mmonds said he was being treated for a broken neck and liver cancer, among other ailments, and did not believe he was long for this world.

Nevertheless, he remained a man who could take care of himself; Ha'mmonds had recently been transferred from the Marin County Jail following a bloody battle with another inmate. This man had attacked him with a pen, Ha'mmonds said, after overhearing a phone conversation involving the Biggie Smalls case. Even from his wheelchair Ha'mmonds had managed to inflict what the Marin County Sheriff's Department described as "great bodily harm" on his assailant.

"Music, records, film—crime," Ha'mmonds replied to a question about what kinds of businesses he had been involved in. The man seemed anything but ashamed that he had spent twenty-six of his forty-nine years behind bars. An Oakland native, Ha'mmonds was OG in a fundamental sense, having joined the Black Guerrilla Family while incarcerated in his early twenties. What really had given Ha'mmonds status in the gangster rap world, though, was the time he had spent as an enforcer for the most powerful drug lord in Northern California, Felix Mitchell. He had dropped out of the BGF in 1987, Ha'mmonds said, when he joined a Nation of Islam splinter group known as the Five Percenters,*

---

* The Five-Percent Nation is an offshoot of the Nation of Islam that believes white men are devils and black men are gods.

which anointed him "a Muslim who will commit crimes in the name of Allah," as Ha'mmonds explained it. Ha'mmonds had quit the Five Percenters, he said, to become an Orthodox Sunni Muslim in 1990, around the same time he decided to inform on his fellow gang members ("debrief," he called it) in order to escape the suffocating confines of the super-maximum-security prison at Pelican Bay and return to a mainline institution. Most of the information he provided to the government involved "when we had dudes killed or we killed ourselves," Ha'mmonds told Sanders and Frank.

He had worked ever since, Ha'mmonds said, as what he liked to call an "agent provocateur" and had been well paid for assisting the government in various investigations, in particular those involving Suge Knight and Death Row Records.

Ha'mmonds said he had been introduced to Knight by Tupac Shakur. He and Pac had known each other since the late 1980s, when the future rap legend was a skinny, scared teenager living in Marin City and working as a dancer with Digital Underground. The two met up in Las Vegas for the Holyfield-Bowe heavyweight title fight in November 1995, Ha'mmonds said, and were gambling with a group that included Knight, Snoop Dogg, and several members of the Dogg Pound at Caesars Palace before adjourning to the VIP room at Suge's 662 Club. One night, Suge arranged for the two of them to be alone in that room, Ha'mmonds recalled: "Knight said, 'You're from up north, right, man? You fuck with Felix and them, right?' I said, 'Yeah.' And he mentioned Christopher Wallace—Biggie Smalls—and he say, 'You know, that fat punk is giving me a lot of lip and lot of shit on the East Coast. You think you can handle it?' By 'handle it' meaning, 'Can you arrange to do—assassinate—Christopher Wallace, Biggie Smalls?' I told him no." Suge seemed very disappointed, Ha'mmonds recalled: "He say, 'Aww, I thought you was hard, man.'"

In spite of this exchange, he was still welcome to hang with Suge and his crew, Ha'mmonds said. During a video shoot in L.A., Knight had told him that there was no need to worry about drug busts and such while on location, "'cause we got LAPD." It was in this period that he met David Mack, whom he understood to be a member of Suge's security team, Ha'mmonds said. "I don't trust cops, regardless of how cool they is," Ha'mmonds told Sanders and Frank, and said he avoided Mack. But he felt an immediate connection with another man he met at one of Suge's parties in Las Vegas, Amir Muhammad. He was impressed, Ha'mmonds said, that Muhammad had greeted him in fluent Arabic.

Suge Knight and Mario Ha'mmonds spent a good deal more time together in the late 1990s at the California Men's Colony in San Luis Obispo, where they were housed on the same cell block, living just ten feet apart. Both the LAPD and the FBI had started using Ha'mmonds to collect intelligence after learning that he was close to Suge—it was possible they were responsible for where he had been assigned at the prison in the first place. Ha'mmonds said of their first few days on the block together, "Me and Suge reacquainted ourselves from our little escapades in Las Vegas and Los Angeles, and we reminisced and laughed and jived and bullshitted about it."

Their relationship grew more serious, though, Ha'mmonds said, when Suge began to rely on him for physical protection. Suge had heard that the Rolling Sixties Crips wanted him dead, but at this time Knight "wouldn't even trust his own Bloods associates," Ha'mmonds explained, "because a lot of them wanted to do something to him there as well." Suge turned to the Muslims and to brothers who either were or had been members of the BGF, Ha'mmonds said: "He made sure we had money on our books, made sure that our families was taken care of." Over time, Suge began to rely on him in almost every detail of daily life in prison. Ha'mmonds recalled, "I would get people to run his errands for him . . . to run his weed over to different quads, make sure the officer was bringing us what he needed." Since Suge could barely read or write, Ha'mmonds said, "I used to sign for his packages," and he spent evenings reading aloud to Knight in the prison yard's bleachers.

The murder of Notorious B.I.G. had taken place not long before Knight was moved to the Men's Colony, and Ha'mmonds recalled that

Suge hadn't needed much time after his arrival to take credit for the killing. "He said, 'My people handled the business. They took care of him . . . and he took it like a fat bitch.' He started laughing, and he said, 'We just missed Puffy.'" At first, Suge maintained that Biggie's murder was retaliation for the Tupac killing, recalled Ha'mmonds, who told Sanders and Frank he had begun to doubt this story when people associated with the Bay Area rappers Too Short and E-40 offered him money to assassinate Knight, insisting it was Suge who had arranged Tupac's murder.

"They asked me, Why am I hanging out with this dude when you know he killed homeboy?" Ha'mmonds recalled.

Two of the names Suge had mentioned in connection with the murder were Reg and Big Sykes (presumably Death Row director of security Reggie Wright Jr. and Bloods gang member Devon Sykes), Ha'mmonds said. Eventually Suge would name two other members of the team, Ha'mmonds recalled: David Mack and Amir Muhammad. Suge told him that all four had helped him arrange the murder by phone while he was locked up in the county jail in Los Angeles, and he gradually offered details about how the killing had been accomplished: two women who had infiltrated the Bad Boy Records camp provided information about when and where Biggie and Puffy would be exposed, and his team had coordinated events on the night of the murder by using burner cell phones.

Suge never did tell him who exactly pulled the trigger, Ha'mmonds said. He did, however, ultimately reveal that his story about the Biggie killing being payback for Tupac's murder was "a smoke screen." Shortly before Suge was transferred to Mule Creek State Prison he told Ha'mmonds, "Later on, down the line, you'll see the big picture. It's about money." Suge also told him that he had no concern about being charged with Biggie's death, Ha'mmonds said. "He told me this out of his own mouth, that because LAPD was involved, that this murder would never be solved, and that 'If anybody says anything against me, I can find out.'"

For Sanders and Frank, Ha'mmonds's pretrial testimony was about as good as it could get. Still, they knew the man would pose problems as a witness. He was at once a snitch and a career criminal who by his own admission had been involved in other murders. Of greater concern was that, while LAPD records indicated Ha'mmonds had passed along the information about Big Sykes and Reggie Wright Jr. being involved in the Notorious B.I.G. assassination, there was no mention of Mack or Muhammad in those documents. When Sanders asked about this, Ha'mmonds explained that the moment he had brought up Mack and Muhammad in his meetings with LAPD detectives, he was told, "We don't need to talk about that." Later, Ha'mmonds said, he came to believe that whatever he told the LAPD was somehow being passed on to Suge Knight. At his two most recent court appearances, Ha'mmonds said, "people from Knight's camp" had taken seats in the gallery, and both of them had made slashing motions across their throats when he looked at them.

What put teeth in Ha'mmonds's claims were the lengths to which the LAPD had gone to hide him from the Wallace Estate's attorneys. Not only had the police department attempted to withhold documents generated by its interviews with Ha'mmonds, but when it finally did turn these over, the informant's name was blacked out. "The city and the LAPD clearly understood how damaging Ha'mmonds's testimony could be to them," Frank observed. He and Sanders might never have found their way to the informant, Frank said, if not for the fact that, with Robleto's help, they discovered a single obscure reference in the materials the LAPD surrendered to them. The lawyers threatened to seek a court order if every bit of information relating to Ha'mmonds was not turned over at once. This resulted in the production of documents that revealed the biggest danger the informant posed to the LAPD: the department itself had vouched for his integrity when it used his testimony to obtain search warrants in its investigation of Suge Knight for the murder of Notorious B.I.G.

During his interrogation by the city's attorneys, Ha'mmonds put it this way: "I am an honest individual. Even though I'm a criminal, I do not lie. My credibility . . . must be good, because I've made a livelihood out of this. People are in prison . . . locked up from some of the information that I have contributed to government agencies."

"The LAPD has to be asking themselves how they're going to call him a liar now," Sanders said, "when they've already called him a credible witness."

Finding Mario Ha'mmonds was a breakthrough Sanders and Frank desperately needed. The disappearance of Mike Robinson and the inability to locate Kendrick Knox were major blows to their case, the lawyers knew. These were made even more significant by a key ruling against them by Judge Cooper about how the trial should be structured.

Cooper had decided to break the proceedings into three parts, and the first hurdle the plaintiffs had to get over would be the highest. On the one hand, Sanders and Frank knew they possessed overwhelming evidence that the LAPD had alternately neglected and obstructed an investigation into the possible involvement of LAPD officers associated with Death Row Records in the murder of Notorious B.I.G. But "you can't sue someone for the failure to fully investigate a crime," Frank explained. To win their civil rights lawsuit, the attorneys would have to prove that the LAPD was guilty of a "pattern and practice" that had resulted in the rapper's death. And to do that, Judge Cooper had decided, they would first have to convince the jury that David Mack had been involved in Biggie's slaying. Only if they were successful in that, Cooper had ruled, would Sanders and Frank be permitted to make the case for an LAPD cover-up.

On the other hand, they wouldn't be held to the "proof beyond reasonable doubt" standard of a criminal trial, and would have to convince a jury only that it was more likely than not that Mack and his friend Amir Muhammad were involved in the murder. Mario Ha'mmonds and Eugene Deal, whom they intended to call to the stand as their final two witnesses, would provide plenty of evidence to persuade a jury that it needed to hear the rest of their case, Sanders and Frank believed.

Robleto, though, knew that the two lawyers were more apprehensive about how their witnesses would perform than they were letting on. "As the trial date approached, everybody was afraid," the investigator recalled. "All the witnesses for our side, I could tell they were starting to flinch. I had a law enforcement friend who was a good, stand-up guy, but he started refusing to talk to me. I had to tell Perry I didn't think we could put him on the stand."

How precarious their case was Sanders and Frank would learn when the first important witness the attorneys intended to call at trial, former Death Row Records bodyguard Kevin Hackie, began to wobble. Robleto had told the attorneys that he found Hackie "quite credible," especially in his descriptions of seeing David Mack and his former LAPD partner Rafael Perez at Death Row Records parties. Also, Robleto said, he believed Hackie's anger at the LAPD and other law enforcement agencies that had broken their word to him about providing protection from Suge Knight and the Bloods gang would come through powerfully on the witness stand. The day before Hackie was to be called to testify, though, Sanders and Frank learned via the *Los Angeles Times* that this key witness had gone sideways. "Witness in B.I.G. Case Says His Memory's Bad," read the headline on the Chuck Philips article.

"I will be in court to testify," Hackie had told the reporter in an interview at his attorney's office in Torrance, "but it is a matter of record that I am stressed out and have been on medication for the past five years. My memory is bad. I'm going to answer questions to the best of my knowledge what I remember. But this whole thing has put me over the edge. I am so stressed. I probably won't even remember our conversation tomorrow."

Philips did not report that Hackie had said what "stressed" him was his fear of Knight, the Bloods gang, and the Los Angeles Police Department. Sanders and Frank were able to get the former bodyguard to say all this when he began his testimony the next day. Still, the newspaper called his performance in court "erratic" and emphasized the bodyguard's repudiation of his previous sworn testimony that David Mack had worked in a "covert capacity" for Death Row Records and that Mack had been given special access to "numerous Death Row functions" reserved for Suge Knight's closest associates.

"That was a nasty day in court with Kevin Hackie," Frank recalled, "to have a witness turn on you like that. And then there was Chuck Philips, sitting in the back of the courtroom with a smug expression."

Sanders was so infuriated by the *Times'* reporting that he held a press conference in the hallway outside the courtroom on the morning of the trial's second day. When these proceedings were concluded, Sanders promised that "all evidence gathered, without exception, will be donated to a local public library so the public will be able to access this information without having to rely on the *L.A. Times'* spin about what these volumes contain."

Robleto, though, was critical of Sanders's and Frank's failure to give Hackie greater assurance that he would come to no harm. "He was concerned about safety, wanted certain things done to protect him, and was pissed off when it wasn't," Robleto said. "He was afraid. I think they should have done more to protect him."

For their part, Sanders and Frank were peeved by what they perceived as their investigator's hesitation to interview witnesses who had never been contacted by the LAPD. "I was reluctant because I could be considered to be interfering with a police investigation," Robleto explained.

Nevertheless, Sanders and Frank were counting on Robleto to be perhaps their most important witness at trial, and were confident he could handle that responsibility. "From his work on cold cases in particular, Sergio could perform a complete autopsy of a police investigation," Frank observed. "Sergio is such a pro at that. He can take a case apart with such insight. We knew he was going to impress the hell out of the jury, and we were pretty sure the city's attorneys could never put a dent in him."

Robleto would never take the stand, however, because of what was about to happen over the next seven days

CHAPTER NINE

The instigator of it all was Xavier Hermosillo. A longtime Los Angeles social activist and radio host, Hermosillo was also perhaps the best-connected and most influential civilian employee of the LAPD. He had sat in judgment of more disciplinary complaints against police officers than any other person in Los Angeles. Board of Rights hearings, as these proceedings were known, were presided over by tribunals made up of two members of the department's command staff—almost always captains—and a single civilian who was employed on a contract basis. Hermosillo had been selected for his position because he was not only an outspoken critic of police abuses in Los Angeles's Hispanic communities, but also a man with a criminal justice degree who felt real sympathy for the difficulty of police work and genuine admiration for those who did it well.

He was "a homeboy from the housing project," Hermosillo said, who had known a good many of the LAPD's black and Latino officers since childhood. "Having grown up with these guys, I knew a lot about who were the good ones and who were the bad ones." Only by serving on LAPD Board of Rights tribunals, though, had Hermosillo come to know the unscrupulous tactics of Bernard Parks.

Hermosillo was personally responsible for the fact that Parks was not selected as LAPD chief after the resignation of Daryl Gates in 1992. Because of his position as a hearing officer, and because he had become the confidant of a number of officers disturbed about the abuse of power by certain senior LAPD commanders, Hermosillo was made aware of several instances in which Parks had misused his authority.

Two of these were "shocking examples" of Parks's disregard for propriety, Hermosillo said. The first involved the case of a serial rapist on the USC campus. Hermosillo had followed the investigation from afar and knew that the victims were all young white woman and that the perpetrator was a black male. "But there were no real details about the guy," Hermosillo recalled, "because he'd worn a mask. So it went unsolved for quite a while." Finally the rapist was literally caught in the act. "They arrested him when he was right on top of this girl," Hermosillo said, "then found his burglary tools in the backpack he had with him." The rapist turned out to be a relative of Bernard Parks.*

Hermosillo wasn't bothered by the fact that word of the family connection between the LAPD's then–deputy chief Parks and the USC rapist had been squelched so thoroughly that not a single reference ever appeared in news accounts. "That, I could understand," he said. What offended him was that Parks had shown up at the LAPD's Southwest Division headquarters at about 2 a.m. in the hours after the rapist's arrest to use a provision of the city code that permitted anyone holding the rank of deputy chief or above to take personal custody of a criminal suspect. "Just hours after they pull this guy off the girl he was raping, Bernie walks him back out onto the street, which I found absolutely outrageous," Hermosillo said. "Then the guy disappears." The young man would ultimately be recaptured, convicted of the rapes, and sentenced to decades in prison, but "who knows what else he might have done in the time he was loose," Hermosillo said.

---

* Hermosillo described a specific family relationship between the rapist and Parks that was confirmed by two other persons. Only one of the three recalled the name of the rapist; because the Hermosillo complaint and the documents that supported it were turned over to the LAPD's Internal Affairs Division, and because what is now the Professional Standards Division refuses to release it without a court subpoena, I've omitted the name and exact relationship.

The second instance of Parks's abuse of his position that would impel Hermosillo to act against him involved the deputy chief's daughter Michelle. Hermosillo's knowledge of the incident had come through his friend Al Rubalcalva, an LAPD Internal Affairs Division sergeant who was also the vice president of the Latin American Law Enforcement Officers Association. It was a messy, complicated story, Rubalcalva explained.

Michelle Parks was separated from her husband and living with a new boyfriend, but, according to the estranged husband, she had been lending him her automobile on a regular basis while their divorce was pending. One summer evening, the husband showed up at the house to pick up the car while the boyfriend was with her, and Michelle Parks stepped out onto the front porch to shout that the husband was stealing her car. The husband jumped behind the wheel of the car and drove off, with the boyfriend in pursuit in his own vehicle. The chase ran all through South-Central Los Angeles before the husband escaped.

Two days later, though, the husband was arrested while driving the car in Wilshire Division, Rubalcalva continued. Informed that the vehicle had been reported stolen by its owner, Michelle Parks, the estranged husband said, first, that the car was borrowed, and, second, that Michelle was his wife. He then described the car chase that had taken place two nights earlier, a story that included a startling claim: Michelle's boyfriend had fired a shotgun at him several times during the pursuit, and the husband believed that one of those blasts had hit some innocent bystanders at a bus stop on the corner of Crenshaw and Adams boulevards. The Wilshire detectives reviewed the police reports filed in Southwest Division on the night in question, and indeed found one involving a drive-by shooting at Crenshaw and Adams. They notified Southwest Division detectives, who promptly arrested Michelle Parks's boyfriend.

That was when Bernard Parks became involved. Not long after the boyfriend's arrest, Parks had shown up at Southwest Division to meet privately with Alan Kerstein, the commander of detectives in the division, who was also his longtime friend and protégé. Almost immediately, Michelle Parks's boyfriend was released from custody on the basis of what Rubalcalva called a "concocted story" that he was chasing an armed burglar and had fired the shotgun in self-defense. Parks's wife's brother Cedric Wilder, a Southwest Division detective, was also involved in "the so-called investigation" of the incident, Hermosillo remembered.

Rubalcalva had learned of the case only because the detective adjutant at Southwest Division had phoned, furious, to describe what had taken place and to give him the relevant report numbers. "I pulled the reports," Rubalcalva recalled, "and there it all was. I gave the reports to Xavier, and he filed the complaint."

Before filing the complaint against him, Hermosillo remembered, he had paid a visit to Parks at his office in LAPD headquarters. "I said, 'Look, I've seen this, I've seen that.' He says, 'Ignore it.' I say, 'Bernie, I can't support you.' He looks at me and says, 'I don't need your support. I'm gonna be the next chief of police.'"

Hermosillo's formal complaint against Parks for his actions involving his rapist relative and his daughter's boyfriend had forced the LAPD to open an investigation. He and Hermosillo both believed "Bernie would be destroyed" by what was revealed in the reports that had accompanied the complaint against Parks, Rubalcalva said, "but, basically, nothing happened. The people I worked with in Internal Affairs thought it was their job to bury this thing. In the end, I was the only one punished, because everyone knew I had given Xavier the reports. Basically, my career was frozen. I retired a few months later."

At least the investigation his complaint launched prevented Parks from being considered for the position of LAPD chief, Hermosillo said. The officers running the Parks investigation "did everything they could to mess with me," explained Hermosillo. "So I got a lawyer, and we answered by setting up meetings and canceling them. They always wanted to meet with me in hotels or some other off-site place, so I was legitimately concerned about my safety, but I also wanted to drag the thing out, to block Bernie becoming chief."

Hermosillo by then was supporting the leading Hispanic candidate, Lee Baca,* "but the fix was in: the people appointed to the selection committee all were going to pick a black chief, period," he said. "So they chose Willie Williams, which I know was a dagger in Bernie's chest."

Parks would not replace Williams until five years later. "Because Willie Williams was such a joke, Bernie considered himself the first black chief and became ever more arrogant," recalled Hermosillo. "He and I by then had a very contentious relationship, but he couldn't touch me and he knew it." Parks's standard rebuke to any white officials or politicians who challenged him was to accuse them of racism, but Hermosillo was a major figure in the largest minority group in California, "so he couldn't try that stuff on me."

Also, Hermosillo had won the support of many of the LAPD's African American cops because of how he handled the case brought against a black rookie officer he considered to be "the victim of a training officer who hung him out to dry." For reasons Hermosillo could never learn, "Bernie wanted this kid gone, and the two captains who sat with me on the board knew it. That apparently was why they thought they could get away with the shit they tried. Every time we were meeting alone, they would refer to the kid as a 'nigger.' This one captain in particular was a dirty, rotten, racist bastard. He'd say things like, 'We're gonna nail that nigger boy.'"

When he couldn't take it anymore, Hermosillo announced he was halting the proceedings, then walked out of the room and straight to the city attorney's office. "I told him I wouldn't sit in a room with these two captains who keep calling the defendant a nigger," he said. An investigation was launched, and both captains received suspensions and demotions. Hermosillo's resulting notoriety made it impossible for the LAPD to refuse to renew his contract as hearing officer.

* Baca was elected Los Angeles County sheriff in 1998 and in 2017 was sentenced to three years in state prison for perjury and obstruction of justice while in office.

"And so I stayed in a position to see again and again what a villain Bernie Parks is," Hermosillo said. A case that especially rankled him involved Parks's attempt to fire an officer who was less than sixty days from qualifying for his twenty-year pension. "He was a good police officer," Hermosillo recalled, "and his wife was a great one. It was actually a photograph of her that they used on LAPD recruiting posters. They had three kids together, all developmentally disabled, so they were dealing with a whole lot. One day the wife calls and says she's losing it. She's home alone with the three kids, who are out of control and throwing stuff, and she's sobbing. So the husband drives to their house, helps get her and the kids calmed down, then goes back to work. But he'd left the division he was assigned to and driven into another one, which could technically be considered abandoning his post. And Bernie, who had something against this guy, wanted him fired for it.

"One of the two captains on the board hearing his case was Bernie's boy, so there was no reasoning with him. He was gonna vote guilty and that was that. The other captain told me he had to vote to convict because Bernie had told him there would be no promotion otherwise. By then I was used to hearing that. Over and over captains would tell me, 'Hey, I got a call from the sixth-floor corner office—the old man doesn't like this guy.'"

This particular case had gotten under Hermosillo's skin, however. "The second captain on the board was basically a decent guy and was torn," he recalled. "At one point he actually admitted to me that he knew he was choosing between his career and doing the right thing." Hermosillo, unable to accept the possibility of a conviction in the case, finally went directly to Parks and threatened to go to the media "with what I knew about him." When the Board of Rights hearing reconvened, "this captain tells me he just got a call from the chief's office," Hermosillo remembered. "I said, 'He didn't fire you, did he?' He laughed and told me, 'I just got a promotion.' I told him, 'I think you owe me ten percent of your raise,' and he said, 'I probably do.'

"So now I not only know how dirty Bernie is, I also know how afraid he is of being exposed."

In December 2000, Hermosillo had joined the Board of Rights panel that would conduct the fourth hearing of the charges against LAPD sergeant Paul Byrnes. Sergeant Byrnes was among the many officers from the LAPD's Rampart Division accused of misconduct by Rafael Perez. In the late 1990s, Byrnes had been a supervisor of the Rampart Community Resources Against Street Hoodlums (CRASH) unit. After Perez was charged with stealing large quantities of cocaine that had been booked into evidence at the LAPD's Property Division, he had negotiated a deal based on his claims that he could name other corrupt CRASH team members and provide evidence against them. Paul Byrnes was implicated by Perez in an incident involving Gabriel Aguirre, a gang member who was wanted on suspicion of assault with a deadly weapon, and who was believed to have been involved in more than one murder. Perez and three other CRASH officers had found Aguirre sleeping in an abandoned apartment, and in the process of arresting the man had given him a severe beating, according to Perez. When their supervisor, Sergeant Byrnes, arrived on the scene, Perez said, he ordered the CRASH team to pour some beer on a nearby fire escape in order to support their story that Aguirre's injuries were caused when he slipped and fell attempting to flee.

The three CRASH officers charged in the case were all convicted based on testimony by Perez and Aguirre. Byrnes, however, was not charged criminally. The LAPD did file administrative charges against him, though, and relieved the sergeant of duty. By the time he came before the hearing panel that included Xavier Hermosillo, Byrnes had already been acquitted by three previous Boards of Rights.

Cliff Armas of the LAPD's Officer Representation Section was assigned to assist Byrnes in his defense and had performed an independent investigation that poked a number of holes in Perez's story. "What happened was that Perez and a couple of these other guys found Aguirre in that apartment and were standing around talking about whether they should beat the shit out of him," Armas recalled. "They hadn't handcuffed him yet, and while they were talking the guy jumps up and runs out onto the balcony and climbs onto the fire escape. When he got down to the bottom floor, though, there were two other officers waiting. There was a struggle, and he was thrown up against a wall, where his head put a hole in the plaster. By the time Byrnes showed up, Perez and the others all had this story that the guy hurt himself when he tried to escape and fell. Byrnes didn't speak Spanish, so he used Perez as his translator when he questioned witnesses at the scene about what happened. And Perez tells him the witnesses are saying nothing happened, they didn't see anything, or they agree with the story he and the others are telling. So Byrnes buys it. That's all he did wrong."

Byrnes would be tried a fourth time, though, "because Bernie Parks wanted him to be," as Hermosillo put it. By then, the sergeant had been suspended without pay for more than two years. Once again, Rafael Perez would be the main witness against him. Hermosillo had already listened to Perez testify in "seven or eight previous cases" and knew the man was unreliable. "While he testified I would sit with my laptop and type and I would hear something and I don't believe it," Hermosillo recalled. "Within fifteen minutes he would contradict himself. I'd point it out and he'd say, 'Oh, you heard me wrong.' So I'd go to the court reporter and have her read his testimony back. Then he'd just say it didn't matter."

"Slick and slimy" was how Hermosillo described Perez: "He had this smug attitude. He was cocky and combative at the same time. He loved being the center of attention." Hermosillo had gradually grown dismayed at how determined the LAPD seemed to be to protect Perez. For instance, none of the cases involving Perez were held at the magnificent Bradbury Building on Broadway in downtown L.A. where Boards of Rights were ordinarily convened, Hermosillo remembered: "The hearings with Perez were held all over the place. I'd leave my house with no idea where the hearing was gonna be. I'd get a call on my cell phone while in transit directing me to this or that address. Then Perez would arrive like some head of state, with a security detail that large, all officers from Metro Division, who'd make the other cops on the scene put their guns away. When he'd change clothes, from his prison garb to a suit, it was like a ceremony." By the time of the Byrnes hearing, Hermosillo had heard from other prisoners housed with Perez about how he received special treatment and extra privileges from his jailers. "One guy told us how they would bring the *L.A. Times* first thing in the morning, and give him a pair of scissors so he could cut out any articles that he thought might reflect badly on him."

Perez had testified in the Byrnes case at a downtown hotel. "We weren't allowed to go into the room where the hearing was held until he was in place," Hermosillo recalled. "When we walked into the room, that smile on his face. This guy reveled in his lies."

The rest of the Byrnes hearing would be held in the basement of the Men's Central Jail in downtown Los Angeles, "the first and the last time I've ever seen that," Hermosillo said. The location seemed to have been selected because of two witnesses who had been discovered and delivered by Cliff Armas. These were a pair of prison inmates named Kenneth Boagni and Felipe Sanchez, each of whom had been held with Perez at the special jail facility in Lynwood used to house accused criminals who either were police officers themselves or had close relatives who were cops.

In September 2000, Armas had read one of the few *Los Angeles Times* articles that suggested reason to doubt Perez's credibility. Another jailed ex-LAPD officer, Hank Rodriquez, had told investigators that while he was in a cell next to Perez's, he had heard the former detective boast repeatedly about his ability to inflict harm on those who challenged or criticized him. "If someone pisses me off, I'll throw their name into a hat and they'll get investigated—innocent or not," Perez had told his cellmate, according to Rodriquez, who said that Perez had adopted "a gang-member type of attitude" while locked up and regularly broke into rap tunes in which he savored having become the most powerful person in Los Angeles and boasted of his book and movie deals. The *Times* article included a claim by LAPD commander Dan Schatz that, although Rodriquez had made his allegations more than five months earlier, they were only now coming out because his statement was "misplaced" by investigators from the Rampart Task Force.

Armas arranged a visit with Hank Rodriquez the next day. "He told me how he had heard Perez boasting about how he made up most of what he was claiming, to get a deal on his case," Armas remembered. "What impressed me about Rodriquez was that he only told me what he had heard and said it wasn't that much. But there was a guy who knew a lot more, he said, and that was somebody who had been Perez's cellie at Lynwood. Rodriquez said the two were really tight and talked a lot to each other. He said the guy's brother was a sheriff's lieutenant and that his name was Kenneth Boagni. If I could get Boagni to talk, Rodriquez said, he could tell me a lot."

The next day, Armas drove southeast through the coruscating heat of the Colorado and Sonora deserts to Calipatria State Prison, in the southeast corner of California, near the Mexico border, to meet with Boagni. Though the crime that had gotten him locked up was burglary, Boagni was serving a sentence of forty years to life under the state's three strikes law.

"With nothing to offer in terms of helping with his sentence, I had the full expectation of him telling me that he didn't want to talk," Armas recalled, "but to my surprise he more or less opened up. He told me that almost everything Perez was saying was made up, that it was all a gag. He said the district attorney's office would bring Perez stacks and stacks of arrest reports and that Perez would take them into his cell and start dividing them into three piles that he called 'the Good, the Bad, and the Ugly.' The first was arrests that were truly good, and the second was arrests that were bad. The 'Ugly' pile was for good arrests where Perez made up lies that turned them into bad arrests, because he wanted to fuck one or more of the other officers involved."

Knowing that he now had at least one strong witness who could impugn Perez, Armas began to look for corroboration. That was what had led him to Felipe Sanchez, another inmate who had been locked up with Perez at the Lynwood jail. Sanchez was now incarcerated at High Desert State Prison in Susanville, south of the Oregon border. "Sanchez told me a story that was very similar to the one I had heard from Boagni," Armas recalled. "He said he was angry at Perez because his brother was a sergeant on the Pasadena police and was a good cop, and that he knew Perez could have done to him what he was doing to others. Sanchez said he had made detailed notes of the stuff Perez told him and that he had offered them to the *L.A. Times* but had been told the *Times* wouldn't publish them and didn't want to talk to him." Two LAPD Metro officers who had been assigned to the Rampart Task Force, however, already *had* spoken to Sanchez about Perez. "I only knew that because Sanchez told me," Armas recalled. "The task force was hiding the fact that they'd interviewed him and that while he was in the same pod with Perez at Lynwood he'd offered to wear a wire to get Perez to admit what he was doing. Not only did the task force guys turn that down, Manny Hernandez told them not to talk to Sanchez anymore and not to create any notes or reports of their conversations with the guy." "Manny" was Lieutenant Emmanuel Hernandez, the Bernard Parks acolyte who Russell Poole claimed had threatened him and blocked his investigation back in 1998–99.

The day before the Byrnes hearing, Armas would requisition a plane from LAPD Air Support to fly first to Susanville to pick up Felipe Sanchez, then to Calipatria to collect Kenneth Boagni, whom he considered his side's two most important witnesses.

"Boagni and Sanchez had been housed with Perez two years apart," Hermosillo noted. "Plus, Boagni was black and Sanchez was Latino, and they were inmates in prisons in the far south and the far north of California, so we knew these guys didn't know each other. That's what made how identical their testimony was so convincing."

In the basement of the county jail, Boagni testified at length about all the times "P-Dawg" had boasted of punishing cops he didn't

like—especially those who "disrespected" him—by making up stories that destroyed their careers and their lives. He still considered
P-Dawg a friend, Boagni went on, and felt bad about "stabbing him
in the back," but knew for a fact that Perez had falsely accused any
number of fellow officers, including Sergeant Byrnes, of crimes they
had not committed.

The hearing's central drama did not begin to unfold, though,
until Boagni began to talk about what Perez had told him of his
involvement, and David Mack's, in the murder of the rapper Biggie
Smalls. The LAPD's representatives, Lieutenant Fabian Lizarraga and
Sergeant Gary Farmer, immediately objected that Boagni was about
to compromise an ongoing investigation. Farmer actually leaped to
his feet and shouted out his objection. It was overruled. Just moments
later, Hermosillo followed up with a question about whether Boagni
had been in contact with anyone connected to Perez since he'd seen
him at the Lynwood jail. Boagni began to answer that he had been
visited by two LAPD detectives who warned him against testifying
about what he had heard from Perez, but Sergeant Farmer again
leaped to his feet and cut the witness off. "I remember Farmer shouting at him, 'Shut your mouth! You were told not to talk about that. It
has nothing to do with this case,'" Hermosillo said.

Boagni went silent for a few moments, "then says, 'I'm done. Let
me out of here. I just wanted to fly on a private plane and it was hot
down there,'" Hermosillo recalled. "He stood up and said, 'I don't
wanna die.' I asked him, 'Whattaya mean, you don't wanna die?' And
Boagni says, 'I shoulda listened to those detectives.'"

He and the two captains sitting with him on the hearing panel,
Kenneth Hale and Earl Paysinger, called a recess, Hermosillo remembered, then, "Earl and I went to talk to Boagni off to the side." The two
hearing panel members had known each other since Paysinger was a
star high school athlete and Hermosillo was a teenage sportswriter. "I
knew Earl was straight," Hermosillo said. "So we try to talk to Boagni
and he just says, 'No, I don't wanna die. I should have listened to those
guys when they came to see me.' Earl shifts course and tells Boagni

he looks athletic, and asks if he ever played sports. He tells us that he was a baseball player, that he signed with the Houston Astros for a fifty-thousand-dollar bonus back when that was real money, but blew everything on drugs. He tells us he's got a brother who was one of the best high school basketball players in L.A. history and who's now a lieutenant on the Sheriff's Department, and a sister who's a doctor. 'I'm the fuckup of the family,' he says, and you could tell this guy felt really bad about that. We get him talking about Perez, and then we ask him about the two cops who came to see him, and eventually we get him to agree to tell us the story on the record."

He had thought at first that the two LAPD officers who visited him at Calipatria were detectives investigating the Biggie murder, Boagni said, which was why he had been startled when they began making it very clear to him that any testimony he wanted to give about Rafael Perez would not be welcome. "Boagni tells us that the LAPD investigators were telling him, 'Look you don't really recall what Perez was saying. You were probably high, weren't you?'" Hermosillo recalled. Then the two began to warn that he would put his life at risk if he went against Perez, Boagni said. "They told him that Perez had friends in prison who would 'shank' him if he talked," Hermosillo remembered. "I was sitting there thinking, 'I can't believe it. I can't believe these guys would think they could get away with something like this. But I had a gut feeling Boagni was telling the truth. You listen to enough testimony, you get real good at separating the liars from the ones who are telling the truth. And I felt pretty sure Boagni was one of the ones who tell the truth."

Unfortunately, Boagni was unable to provide the names of the two LAPD officers he said had come to Calipatria to threaten him. "He did give very good physical descriptions of them, though," Hermosillo recalled. "One was a short, stocky guy with a bushy head of hair, and the other was a tall, slender guy who, Boagni said, looked like he might have been a basketball player." Armas, listening, decided to wait to present the copy of the visitors' log he had made at Calipatria that showed Boagni's visitors had been two

Metro officers assigned to the Rampart Task Force, Thomas Wich and Vincent Vicari.

Sanchez followed Boagni to the stand, carrying a small cardboard folder like the ones Hermosillo remembered being sold at Sav-on in the 1960s. "We start to ask him some of the same questions we asked Boagni," recalled Hermosillo, who noticed that the department reps were looking "real uneasy." Sergeant Farmer began to object repeatedly, interrupting Sanchez's testimony again and again. Gradually, though, Sanchez got out a story that included his memories of how Perez had bragged about being on the scene with his friend "Mack Attack" on the night Biggie Smalls was shot to death. "He said Perez bragged that he was part of it," Hermosillo remembered.

Lieutenant Lizarraga let his sergeant handle the department's questioning of the witness. "Within seconds Farmer is asking Sanchez, 'What's the real reason you flew down here? Did you cut a deal for early parole?'" Hermosillo recalled. "And Sanchez says, 'Fuck you, asshole. I got four months to go. I been a model prisoner. I been on a fire-suppression crew. I'm a good man. I'll never go back to prison again.' Then he asks, 'Are you from the guys who visited me in prison?' And you could have heard a pin drop. Earl, sitting right next to me, whispers, 'Oh my.'"

The two LAPD "investigators" who had visited him at Susanville had blatantly threatened him, Sanchez said. "He told us they said, 'Don't go to L.A., or your life will be short,'" Hermosillo remembered. "They told him that same thing about getting 'shanked' by Perez's friends." Sergeant Farmer began to object so vociferously "that we threatened to have him removed," Hermosillo recalled. "And Sanchez tells us, 'When those assholes said if I came and testified I'd get killed, I told them to fuck themselves.' I asked if he remembered anything about the names of these two officers and Sanchez turns to Farmer, who's been told to sit there and be quiet, and says, 'Hey, you know who they were. You tell him.'"

When Farmer kept silent, Sanchez opened the cardboard folder on his lap, exposing the slice he had made in the seam to create a small pocket. "He reaches in and pulls out a couple of little papers," Hermosillo recalled. "He says these are the notes he made when he was locked up with Rafael. He handed them to me and I'd never seen handwriting so small. Sanchez says, 'Once those guys threatened me, I figured I better hang on to these, and keep 'em hidden.' Then he pulls out two more pieces of paper from the little pocket he'd made in the notebook. He tells us, 'After they left, I asked who those two fucks were,' and that the guard answered by handing him two business cards. When Sanchez showed them to us, I froze. I couldn't breathe."

The cards bore the names of Rampart Task Force members Michael Gannon and Bill Brockway.

"Ken Hale could not believe it," Hermosillo remembered. "He said, 'I've been on this department most of my life and I fucking cannot believe this.'"

After conferring, he and captains Hale and Paysinger announced that they were sending formal complaints against the four detectives who had visited Boagni and Sanchez in prison to the LAPD's Internal Affairs Division, demanding a full investigation. According to Armas, "There was no investigation whatsoever. I kept waiting to be interviewed by IA, but I never was. Eventually I obtain the final report of the 'investigation,' and it's three pages of nothing. The IA investigators hadn't interviewed so much as a single witness. The complaints against those four guys had been dismissed, no surprise. But what got to me was the rationale they had used for saying the allegations against them were not sustained. It was basically that serving on the Rampart Task Force had been a high honor accorded to the best of the best, who had put in long, grueling hours, and the department needed to show its appreciation and gratitude for their service."

By the time the Byrnes Board of Rights hearing ended, Xavier Hermosillo said, "I knew I was sitting on something explosive. I just had no idea what I would do with it."

Incendiary as what he had heard from Boagni and Sanchez was, Hermosillo said, the most shocking moment of the hearing was still to come. It would arrive in the form of an eight-by-ten-inch photograph that was offered as evidence for purposes of showing the relationship between, and the affiliations of, Rafael Perez and David Mack. In the photograph, Mack and Perez were wearing bright red suits, red shirts, red ties, and red bowler hats. "These guys were literally announcing that they were Bloods gang members," Hermosillo observed. It wasn't Perez or Mack who riveted his attention, though, Hermosillo said, so much as the woman standing between them, wearing a red dress with a red ribbon in her hair. "There was something kind of familiar about her," he recalled. "I asked Ken Hale why that was. He takes a look and says, 'Oh my God, do you know who that is?'" Before Hale even said the words, Hermosillo knew the answer. It was LAPD Chief Bernard Parks's daughter Michelle.

"There'd been rumors going around for a long time that Michelle Parks was a drug mule for the Bloods gang," Armas recalled.

They were more than rumors.

In late 1997, when he took a call from his closest contact in the Las Vegas Police Department's Narcotics Division, Shelby Braverman, an undercover detective in the LAPD's Harbor Division, had not the faintest idea that what he was about to hear would destroy his career and shatter his life.

According to the Vegas detective, he and his colleagues in Narcotics Division had developed information that a considerable quantity of heroin and cocaine was being brought into the city from L.A. in automobiles driven by a woman named Michelle Lynette Parks, whom he described as a major drug mule for the Bloods street gang. He and the other narco guys in Vegas had been startled to discover, Braverman's friend said, that, first, this Michelle Parks was a "clerk/typist" in the Los Angeles Police Department's Pacific Division and that, second and even more astounding, she was the daughter of LAPD chief Bernard Parks.

Braverman had agreed to do some "nosing around" into the nature of Michelle Parks's position at the LAPD. "I hadn't even known Parks had a daughter, let alone that she worked for the department," Braverman recalled. "After I did some investigating, I became concerned that she was working in a part of the LAPD that gave her access to a lot of confidential files. She could get information about who was under investigation, what the evidence was, who the witnesses were, and so on." If she *was* working for the Bloods, Braverman realized, Michelle Parks was in a position to provide them with information that could not only protect gang members from apprehension, but endanger the lives of those prepared to testify against them.

Braverman took his concerns to his senior supervisor, Richard Ginelli, a storied veteran cop who had been working narcotics for nearly a quarter century. "I was his number one boy, because I was the best-producing undercover in the department for heroin," Braverman explained. "We were close, I thought."

When he told Ginelli what he had learned, Braverman said, his boss's reaction took him aback. "He told me that this was over my head and way too hot for me to handle," Braverman remembered. "He said he'd go directly to Chief Parks himself." What Braverman didn't know was that Ginelli was Parks's former patrol partner and one of the chief's closest allies within the entire LAPD.

Ginelli "told me to keep my mouth shut about what I had learned," Braverman said. But he wasn't really troubled by this, because he believed his boss had gone to Chief Parks as promised and that action had been taken: In November 1997, Michelle Parks was placed on medical leave from her LAPD job. She was collecting disability pay, but no longer had access to sensitive police records.

What changed his mind about Ginelli, Braverman said, was hearing from the hooker he considered his best informant. The woman told him that Ginelli had started picking her up on the weekends to share sex and heroin stolen from the Harbor Division evidence locker. "She thought she had Ginelli by the balls and threatened to tell me what he was up to—basically she tried to blackmail him," Braverman recalled. "She told me he said that if she ever said anything to me, he'd kill her and kill me. She was so terrified that she told me anyway, because she wanted my protection."

Worried now, Braverman went to another supervisor, the man between himself and Ginelli in the hierarchy of the Harbor Division's narcotics unit. "He was very unhappy to get this information," Braverman recalled. "But I wasn't trying to get Ginelli arrested or anything like that. I thought maybe they could force him to retire and get some help." The second supervisor, though, went directly to Ginelli with what Braverman had said. And Ginelli took that straight to Chief Parks.

As those above him began to plot the best course for dealing with Braverman, Michelle Parks was making news. On June 25, 1998, she and an accomplice named Reginald Gaithwright had been arrested in Las Vegas while allegedly trying to sell twenty grams of cocaine to an undercover police officer. The two had been stopped because they were the occupants of a "suspect car," according to narcotics cops in Las Vegas. Michelle Parks, who was at the wheel, had informed them immediately that she was the daughter of the LAPD's Chief Parks. The *Los Angeles Times* did not report that arrest until September, right around the time that Braverman began to feel pressure from the LAPD to keep what he knew to himself.

What made Braverman vulnerable was a contentious divorce that was followed by a vicious custody battle. Tensions had escalated to a point where Braverman's ex-wife filed for a restraining order against him. Braverman elected not to fight it. "For one thing, I didn't have the money to pay a lawyer, and for another I didn't give a shit if I had to stay away from her." The judge handling the custody case helped negotiate an agreement that from this point forward, Braverman and his ex-wife would exchange their son in the lobby of the LAPD's Harbor Division. "I thought it protected me, so I was fine with it," Braverman said.

In retrospect, he realized he had been far too sure of himself, and of the LAPD, said Braverman. He didn't see the handwriting on the wall even when he was advised by his direct supervisor—the same one he had spoken to about Ginelli—that he might be violating the law by carrying a gun while under a restraining order. "I came straight to you when the restraining order was filed, and you told me not to worry about it," Braverman retorted; there was a record of the conversation.

A short time later, Cliff Ruff, president of the LAPD officers' union, the Police Protective League, informed Braverman that he had been approached at a departmental function by Chief Parks himself, who asked what he knew about "this Braverman guy." The chief had opined that Braverman knew things he shouldn't know and wasn't being as careful as he should with the information, then had proposed a solution to "the problem," Ruff said: Braverman could go on inactive duty for the next six months, until he reached the twenty-year mark as a police officer and qualified for his pension. All he had to do in exchange was keep his mouth shut.

"I told Cliff Ruff to tell Parks to go fuck himself," Braverman recalled. "I was still a police officer, and proud of it. Ruff told me, 'I won't tell him to go fuck himself, but I will say you refused his offer.'"

A week later, Braverman walked into the lobby of the LAPD's Harbor Division to collect his son in the scheduled custody exchange when he was surrounded by "fifteen to twenty guys in SWAT gear, all with guns pointed at me, telling me to get on the ground."

No one would tell him what he was being arrested for, Braverman recalled, as he was driven to the LAPD jail downtown, where misdemeanor suspects were typically locked up. Placed in a single cell, he was held for two days without food or water, "with no idea why I was there," Braverman recalled. "They pulled me out only once and told me to strip. I said no. They pulled out a Taser and threatened to use it on me. So I stripped."

Finally, Braverman was informed that he had been placed under arrest for violating a court order—the restraining order his wife had taken out—by carrying a firearm. Braverman again pointed out that he'd informed his supervisor of the restraining order and had been told not to worry about it. "They told me, 'Some new information has come to our attention.' It turned out there were federal 'consanguinity guidelines' that covered someone accused of domestic violence, and that a fight I'd had with my ex-brother-in-law placed me under them."

In short order, Braverman found himself facing 160 felony counts, one for every day he'd carried a gun on the job since the restraining order was filed. Though separated from them, Braverman was locked up in a pod of the jail where criminal suspects with law enforcement backgrounds were held. One of them was Rafael Perez, just about to negotiate the deal that would launch the Rampart Scandal. Perez was of interest to him then, Braverman said, only because of what he had heard from another LAPD narcotics detective: this detective and his colleagues had found evidence that Michelle Parks was both dating Perez and running his stolen drugs; it was Perez, the detective said, who had posted the $100,000 bond that bailed the chief's daughter out of jail in Las Vegas after her arrest there in June 1998.

Before he ever had the opportunity to speak to Perez and to ask about Michelle Parks, Braverman was moved into an isolation unit—solitary confinement—where he would spend nearly an entire year awaiting trial. During that time, Braverman was advised by fellow LAPD detective Jeff Pailet of just how politicized the Michelle Parks investigation had become. Pailet described how the career of a friend, LAPD Internal Affairs Division investigator Sergeant John Cook, had nearly been ruined by his assignment to investigate the association between Chief Parks's daughter and Reginald Gaithwright. "He'd found stuff he wasn't supposed to find," Pailet would say nearly two decades later. "He never told me what exactly that was." Cook, still choosing his words carefully nineteen years afterward, would acknowledge only that he had conducted a face-to-face interview of Michelle Parks in which he had challenged her "evasive" replies to his questions. Just days later, Cook said, he was informed that he had been removed from the case. This wasn't retaliation, Cook remembered being told by his supervisor, but "a matter of your career survival."

Shelby Braverman would survive as well, though just barely. He agreed to accept conviction on a single felony count, with a promise he would not serve any prison time. The LAPD also agreed to let Braverman retire "in lieu of dismissal" and collect his twenty-year pension.

Two events had saved him from utter ruin. One was the decision by the district attorney in Las Vegas not to prosecute the narcotics case against Michelle Parks. The other was the September 30, 1999, arrest of Richard Ginelli for pilfering heroin held as evidence at the LAPD's Harbor Division. In the *Los Angeles Times* story about Ginelli's arrest, published the next day, Bernard Parks had emphasized that this "singular event" was in no way connected to the Rampart Scandal that had only recently begun capturing local headlines. Braverman was one of the very few who knew this was not true.

"They broke me," said Braverman, who by the time he spoke those words had remarried and fathered two more children, "and I never breathed a word about any of this to anyone. I didn't even tell my wife. For almost twenty years I kept it to myself. I was that afraid of what might happen to my family. Because I know like few others do just what these people are capable of."

Hermosillo remembered holding the photo of Chief Parks's daughter with Perez and Mack in his hands and signing his initials on the back of it. He believed Hight and Paysinger had initialed it also, Hermosillo said, but could not say what happened to the photo after it was passed to Lieutenant Lizarraga and Sergeant Farmer. "All I know is that it disappeared," he said.

Hermosillo, along with Hale and Paysinger, would agree unanimously to find Paul Byrnes not guilty for the fourth time. This provided perhaps some relief, though nothing like comfort, to Sergeant Byrnes. By then Byrnes was a broken man, financially ruined, drinking too much, and addicted to painkillers. He was returned to active duty, but placed on what in the LAPD was called "freeway therapy," assigned to Devonshire, the departmental division farthest from his home, ensuring that he would spend hours each day commuting to and from work. Byrnes hung on for another four years, until April 29, 2004, when he died of a prescription drug overdose that was officially "accidental." "The LAPD and Bernie Parks caused the death of Paul Byrnes," said Hermosillo, who attended the sergeant's funeral at St. Finbar Catholic Church in Burbank.

Armas was there also. "The department, under Parks, wouldn't have anything to do with coordinating his funeral," Armas remembered. "So I made up a death and funeral notice to distribute throughout the rank and file. I was called in and informed that what I'd written made it look like Byrnes had died in the line of duty and that I couldn't pass it out. So I made up another notice and sent it. When I asked for a motorcycle escort, the LAPD told me no, so I had to go to the Burbank P.D., and they came through."

The City of Los Angeles would eventually concede how unfairly Byrnes had been treated, agreeing to pay his family $675,000 for the "unreasonable harm" that had been caused to the sergeant by the police department's backing of the testimony of Rafael Perez. "Paul Byrnes was one of the biggest victims of the whole Rampart mess," the chief attorney for the Police Protective League would tell the *Los Angeles Times.* Councilman Dennis Zine, a former police union official, told the *Times* that Byrnes had been "swept away in that cloud, but the investigation proved he didn't do anything."

Maybe, hopefully, Xavier Hermosillo said, the Byrnes family had found some consolation in reading that. Armas doubted it.

He had known Xavier Hermosillo for years, Sergio Robleto said. "We were not close, but he was somebody you never forget, very strong-willed and opinionated. If he believes somebody is doing an injustice to somebody else, he can't keep his mouth shut about it."

Hermosillo, though, understood that in this instance keeping his mouth shut was probably the wise course. Hermosillo earned most of his income running a crisis management and communications company that made him privy to a good deal of sensitive information that was shared with him by government and corporate clients. "Trust is everything," he said. "People have to know I can keep a secret."

At the same time, he was concerned about the safety of Kenneth Boagni and Felipe Sanchez, Hermosillo said. "Sanchez tried to act like he wasn't scared, but Boagni made no secret of it," Hermosillo recalled. "The last thing he said to me as he left the hearing room that day was, 'You're gonna take care of me, right?' So I was thinking about whether I would put him at risk if I told somebody from outside the department about his testimony. Then again, I wondered if going public might keep him safer. I was weighing it back and forth."

Following the progress of the Notorious B.I.G. wrongful death lawsuit in the *Los Angeles Times* was what finally pushed him forward to a decision, Hermosillo said: "I read that Perry Sanders was asking for evidence that cops had been involved in Biggie's murder, and that Don Vincent was telling him there was no evidence, and that the judge was telling Perry she might have to dismiss the case if he couldn't show her some. That pissed me off. I knew Vincent and thought he was a total asshole. The bigger thing, though, is that I'm a father of five, and if something like that happened to one of my kids and somebody out there knew something important about it, I'd want them to step up for the truth."

What finally convinced him he needed to go public, Hermosillo said, was seeing Voletta Wallace on television: "I saw her pain in trying to get to the truth of what happened to her son. I was raised by a very strong mother, and all of a sudden I began to realize I might be the only person who had the ability to bring some light to the missing evidence."

Before acting, though, Hermosillo paid a visit to the man he called his mentor, someone he would identify only as "a business guru, genius, super-successful entrepreneur." The mentor arranged for an appointment with what he said was the top criminal defense firm in L.A., Hermosillo recalled. "I explained my concerns to the lawyers there, and they explained to me both my obligations to secrecy and my options to do the right thing. Feeling a little smarter and more

Russell Poole (3rd from right) and Sergio Robleto (far right), posing with the then-LAPD Chief Willie Williams (center) and detectives from LAPD South Bureau Homicide.

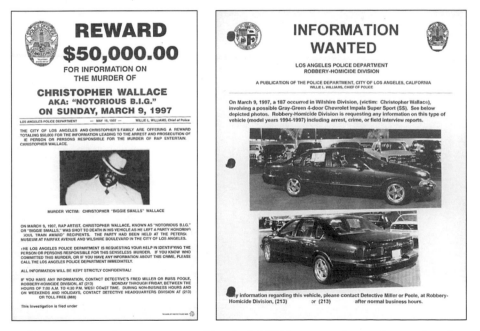

First two reward posters prepared by the LAPD in connection to the murder of Christopher Wallace, aka the Notorious B.I.G. The one on the right was distributed before Poole and his partner Fred Miller determined that the Impala driven by the killer was black, not green.

Perry Sanders Jr. (left) and Robert Frank (right), the lead attorneys for Voletta Wallace and the other heirs of Christopher Wallace in the wrongful death lawsuit filed against the City of Los Angeles.

Judge Florence-Marie Cooper, who presided over the Wallace v. Los Angeles lawsuit for seven years and made the mistrial ruling in 2005.

Voletta Wallace with a wax statue of her son, Notorious B.I.G. (top), speaking to reporters outside the federal courthouse in Los Angeles (bottom left), and posing with Biggie's son C.J. Wallace (bottom right).

Former LAPD officer David Mack (above) and his friend Amir Muhammed, aka Harry Billups, aka Harry Muhammed (below left), accused in the Wallace v. Los Angeles lawsuit of conspiring to murder Notorious B.I.G. To the right of Muhammed is the sketch of the killer made with the help of witnesses riding with Biggie when he was shot to death.

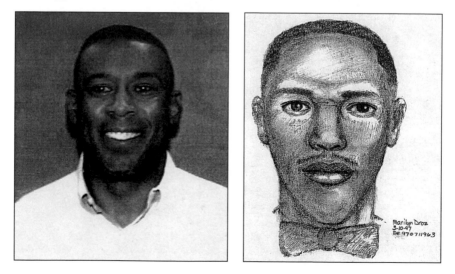

Former LAPD Deputy Chief Michael Berkow, accused by former FBI agent Phil Carson and others of conspiring with disgraced *Los Angeles Times* reporter Chuck Philips to derail the federal investigation of the murder of Notorious B.I.G.

Sergio Robleto, the former head of LAPD South Bureau Homicide who became the lead investigator for Biggie's family in the Wallace v. Los Angeles lawsuit.

Biggie's mother Voletta Wallace and his widow Faith Evans, who grew closer to one another after the murder.

Former Death Row Records bodyguard Kevin Hackie, whose changing story complicated Wallace v. Los Angeles.

Marion "Suge" Knight, former head of Death Row Records suspected of arranging the assassination of Notorious B.I.G. Shown here while in custody at the Los Angeles County Men's Central Jail.

Biggie with Bad Boy Entertainment head Sean "Puffy" Combs, whose failure to help solve the murder of Notorious B.I.G. frustrated the attorneys prosecuting the Wallace v. Los Angeles lawsuit.

Rafael Perez, the dirtiest of the LAPD's dirty cops, fabricator of the Rampart Scandal, accused by Kevin Boagni and Felipe Sanchez, among others, of involvement in the Notorious B.I.G. murder.

Bernard Parks, the former LAPD chief alleged to have covered up the employment of LAPD officers by Death Row Records, protected Rafael Perez and his false narrative of the Rampart Scandal, and stymied Russell Poole's investigation of the Notorious B.I.G. murder; perhaps no man in the history of Los Angeles will go to his grave with more secrets than Parks.

Gerald Chaleff, the former Los Angeles defense attorney who became
an LAPD deputy chief and gave the court testimony that blocked the
release of evidence in the Notorious B.I.G. murder investigation that
remains hidden in the bowels of the federal courthouse in Los Angeles.

Chuck Philips, the disgraced former *Los Angeles Times* reporter accused
by Phil Carson and others of serving as the conduit of the LAPD's disinformation campaign during the Wallace v. Los Angeles lawsuit.

comfortable with trying to do the right thing, I made a concerted effort to get as much info and detail about the whereabouts of all the missing evidence as I could."

Mostly, Hermosillo said, he called in favors from old friends on the LAPD. "And within a day I pretty much had solid info that where the documents were located was in the locked file cabinet in RHD behind Steve Katz's desk—[to] which I was told only he had the key—and possibly also in a hidden compartment in his desk."

Phil Carson would question whether Hermosillo had accomplished this on his own. Carson, too, knew where Katz had concealed "the Boagni evidence" and had prevailed upon the one person among the LAPD command staff he believed could be trusted to do the right thing. "I asked him to make sure that word of where the stuff was hidden got to Perry Sanders," Carson said.

It was a person holding the rank of LAPD sergeant, though, not someone of higher rank, who told him where Katz was keeping the documents locked up, said Hermosillo. He doubted but did not dismiss the possibility that there was a connection to Carson.

Whoever was involved in arming him with the information, it was Hermosillo who placed the phone call to Perry Sanders's law office on June 23, 2005.

Sanders and Hermosillo had actually met face-to-face several months earlier. "For me it was a get-acquainted meeting," Hermosillo recalled. "I was still trying to decide how much I could or should tell him, because he sounded like one of those Louisiana good-old-boy lawyers, and I needed to know if I could trust him." Sanders's main memory of that meeting was the setting, a huge, muraled Mexican restaurant in Lynwood that had just been opened by Hermosillo's friend Martin Garcia. "I walk in and Xavier is the only one in the place except for the owner," Sanders recalled. "He's sitting at a table right in the middle of the place, and he's a big man. The owner is fawning all over him and bringin' out special dishes. It was like goin' to meet a king." Sanders had owned a number of restaurants, including two Mexican eateries, "so I was mainly interested in the food, which was great. And Xavier didn't really tell me much. It was more like he was askin' the questions and I was answerin' them. He did say somethin' about that there might be some Internal Affairs investigations I didn't know about, but there was no detail."

Hermosillo was ready to share the details when he phoned Sanders's law office on June 23. He knew he was about to "unleash the dogs," Hermosillo said, but even he couldn't imagine how convulsive the drama of the next fourteen days would be.

"After he talked to Xavier, Perry phoned me and said, 'I'm gonna have this guy call you," Robleto recalled. "Vet him for me.'" Hermosillo was startled when the person who answered his call to the number Sanders had given him turned out to be Robleto. The admiration the investigator had expressed for him was mutual, Hermosillo said: "Sergio is one of the brightest, classiest guys I've ever been around, and the greatest homicide investigator ever." Determined to protect his anonymity, though, Hermosillo decided to disguise his voice the moment he realized he was talking to someone who knew him. "An accent, a change in pitch, a little slurring here and there," Hermosillo said.

"It worked," Robleto recalled. "I had no idea it was him. He told me about the Boagni testimony at that Board of Rights hearing and told me that not only he but both of the captains on the panel with him had found Boagni credible." Robleto decided he needed to speak to Boagni personally and drove four hours southeast through the glimmering desert to Calipatria Prison, literally the lowest place in North America, more than 180 feet below sea level, where the furnace blast of heat sucked the breath out of visitors. By the time Robleto arrived, a full-scale riot had erupted and the prison was locked down. "I knew I had to talk to Boagni that day," Robleto said, "but I didn't see how I could. Remember, the trial was still going on, everything was in full swing." After the rioting inmates were forced back into their cells, he was able to persuade prison officials to let him speak to Boagni by phone, Robleto said, "and he relayed the same story that Xavier had told me. So I get on the phone with Perry and tell him the stories match. He had me fill out a declaration that he presented to the judge. When the judge read it, she was really upset. I mean *really* upset. If what I had written was true, it would mean that a lot of what the city had claimed was not true."

After a plea from Sanders in open court that the LAPD's Robbery-Homicide Division be searched for any and all documents relating to Kenneth Boagni, Judge Cooper seemed disposed to agree. First, though, she issued a subpoena for Xavier Hermosillo (Robleto had used his phone number to identify Hermosillo) and dispatched two U.S. marshals to serve it at his home in San Pedro, then bring him directly to her chambers.

"I hear a loud knock, look through the peephole to see who's banging on my front door, see these two mammoth guys wearing guns and vests," Hermosillo recalled. "Then I see their U.S. marshals' badges, so I open the door. The moment I do, they hand me a subpoena. I'm thinking, 'Nobody said anything about a subpoena.' Then they tell me I need to come with them to see Judge Florence Cooper."

At the federal courthouse, one of the marshals led him to Judge Cooper's chambers. "No one else was in the room with us after the marshal left," Hermosillo recalled. "The judge said she was led to believe I knew something about evidence connected to a police discipline case that may have been 'placed' somewhere at LAPD and asked me what I knew and why." After he briefed her on that evidence and how he had come to know about it, the judge, who had been making notes the entire time, asked if Hermosillo knew the precise location of "these missing items."

"I told her I had it on good authority that they were hidden in Steve Katz's personal file cabinet and possibly in a hidden compartment in his office desk at RHD. She asked me how I knew that, and I told her I had a lot of friends in the department who had worked certain cases and certain areas and were in a position to know."

Cooper then asked about his interest in the Wallace case, Hermosillo recalled, "and I told her that among the missing documents were the results of an internal investigation that my fellow board members and I had initiated after learning that Rampart Task Force detectives visited two former cellmates of Rafael Perez at state prisons, attempting to dissuade them from testifying by asserting Rafael Perez had friends at those prisons who would 'shank' them.

"I then saw her press a button on her phone and ask a fellow on the other end to come into her office. A marshal walked in, she handed him some documents, which I believed included notes from my statements, and said, 'Here you go. Go lock down Robbery-Homicide and you should find these documents in "his"—she pointed to something on the paper on top—file cabinet and hidden compartment in his desk.'"

"And of course we all know what they found," Robleto said, "all the records of the lengthy investigation—attempted suppression would be more like it—of Boagni's claims that the LAPD had made. All if it right in the drawers of Steve Katz."

For him, Robleto said, "this was a really sad day, the saddest moment of the whole case. I'd been an LAPD cop for many years. I had been proud to be a member of the department. But now I was just stunned. The lengths people in the department had been willing to go to keep the evidence hidden that would vindicate Russ Poole—I felt this combination of amazement and sorrow when I realized it. The LAPD had actually spent more time trying to avoid any appearance of this information than they ever did trying to solve the murder case itself."

That was apparent to Judge Cooper when she got a look at what had been recovered from the Robbery-Homicide Division. Along with the tape recordings of interviews of Boagni by the LAPD that had been conducted on December 8, 2000, and May 3, 2001, what Katz had secreted away included the message memo that Cliff Armas had sent alerting the detective to Boagni's information and also his own handwritten notes of his first interview with Boagni, on March 11, 2000 (nine months before Boagni's appearance at the Byrnes Board of Rights hearing); of his second, on October 11, 2000 (two months before the Byrnes hearing); and of his third, on March 9, 2001. In addition there were two "paraphrased" interviews of Boagni by Katz, three declarations about his conversations with Rafael Perez that Boagni had signed in November 2000, and a raft of other materials that demonstrated how seriously the LAPD had taken the threat Boagni posed both to the Christopher Wallace murder investigation/cover-up and to the Rampart Task Force's determination to validate Rafael Perez at all costs. The complaints filed against Task Force detectives Wich, Vicari, Gannon, and Brockway were also among Katz's hidden files, as was the "Intradepartmental Correspondence" describing the methods by which the LAPD's Internal Affairs Division had suppressed its own investigation of those complaints.

Rob Frank had taken particular pleasure in describing to Judge Cooper how, months earlier, he had conducted "the most important deposition to date" at Detective Katz's desk in RHD, a deposition in which Katz had assured him he had the complete investigative file of the Wallace case, even as the detective was sitting just inches from the drawers where he had concealed "all these materials from Mr. Boagni indicating that Rafael Perez confessed to [the Biggie] murder and his role and David Mack's role in the murder." Judge Cooper, her fury barely contained, granted Frank the immediate right to yet another deposition of Detective Katz.

For the plaintiffs, that question-and-answer session would improve their position considerably. Katz, it turned out, was a bad liar whose explanation for his failure to turn over the Boagni materials was as pathetic as it was tortured. He had remembered his Boagni file "as I was reviewing my chronological record Friday at court," said Katz, apparently oblivious to the fact that this had been the very moment when Perry Sanders was informing Judge Cooper of what he had heard from Xavier Hermosillo. Katz had promptly adjourned to his desk in the Robbery-Homicide Division, where he retrieved the file he "forgot was in there" and turned it over not to the U.S. marshals dispatched by the judge but to an investigator from the city attorney's office.

Katz first attempted to say that he hadn't considered Boagni an important witness, but then had to explain why he had interviewed the informant multiple times in prison, and also why he had, for the first and only time in his career, requisitioned an LAPD aircraft to make the trip to question a witness. Best by far, though, from Frank's point of view, was that Katz had spread the blame across a wide swath of the LAPD, explaining that he had shared the substance of his interviews of Boagni not only with members of the Rampart Task Force and the Internal Affairs Division, but also with his commanding officers. "The wider the net [that] can be thrown around people in the LAPD who knew about this stuff, the better for us, obviously," Frank said.

Katz knew he was cooked; within days he was removed from the Christopher Wallace murder investigation. By the end of the deposition the detective was trembling with rage. "He refused to shake my hand," recalled Frank, who, like Sanders, was certain they would make mincemeat of the detective when they cross-examined him in front of a jury. "I started telling my fiancée that if we won this case I was going to buy a big boat and call it the *Detective Katz*," Frank said.

Before Judge Cooper, Don Vincent would attempt to argue that Katz was guilty of nothing more than a memory lapse, having mislaid some of his files from the Christopher Wallace murder investigation. "But the only stuff in Katz's drawers was stuff implicating police—Mack and Perez," Sanders observed. "So no way that was an accident. And Judge Cooper was too smart not to see that." The city's attorneys then contended that there had been no actual request from Sanders and Frank for the documents in the Boagni file. The transcript of the Rule 26 conference that Sanders had insisted on back at the beginning of the case defeated that argument: Rob Frank had been meticulous in demanding "the entire universe of material in the LAPD's possession that related in any way to Biggie's murder, and any and all information they had where cops were potentially implicated," as Sanders put it.

On July 6, the judge declared a mistrial. She also announced before the packed courtroom that the City of Los Angeles would repay the plaintiffs' side every penny that had been spent preparing and presenting their evidence. The decision seemed to turn the entire case upside down in a single stroke.

Sanders and Frank were gratified by watching the *Los Angeles Times* absorb the new reality of the case. The newspaper's first story ran under the subhead "Three weeks into their civil case, lawyers for Notorious B.I.G.'s family have failed to prove an LAPD link to the star's 1997 slaying." That version did not even mention the lockdown of the LAPD's Robbery-Homicide Division and the discovery of the hidden tapes and documents until the fifth paragraph. By the third edition, printed later that day, however, the lead sentence of the story reflected what was already appearing in the *New York Daily News* and the *Washington Post*: "The LAPD deliberately hid witness statements tying corrupt police officers to the slaying of Notorious B.I.G., a federal judge said Thursday in granting a mistrial and potentially lucrative attorney fees to the rapper's family."

Sanders had no doubt the *Los Angeles Times* would continue to be as much his adversary as were the attorneys representing the city, "and maybe more so. But finally, for the first time, they were swinging at us from their heels and we were on our toes."

CHAPTER TEN

In the immediate aftermath of the mistrial, both the city's attorneys and the *Los Angeles Times* had gone silent on the subject of the Christopher Wallace wrongful death lawsuit. In part this was because for most of the next year the only issues before the court were the size of the sanctions against the city and the scope of discovery that would be permitted in a new trial. The plaintiffs would prevail on both.

While Sanders and Frank were demanding $1.3 million in sanctions, the city, hoping the court might split the difference, had countered that the amount should be less than a third of that. Judge Cooper ultimately decided on an award of $1.1 million. What seemed to the L.A. media an astoundingly large sum was less impressive to Sanders and Frank. The money covered their costs up to this point, but was well short of an amount that would provide the attorneys with a profit. And now, with the addition of Rafael Perez as a defendant, the scope of the case had been enormously expanded. The city would have to turn over every shred of evidence that related to the crimes and claims of Rafael Perez, Judge Cooper had ruled, but the city's attorneys were now using any delay tactics available to them, knowing that, for the other side, time was money. Sanders and Frank had brought four Los Angeles attorneys in to assist with the case—Dennis Chang and his associate Catherine Liu, Chris Brizzolara, and Bradley Gage—and would have to share with them the ultimate payday, if there was one.

Brizzolara and Gage in fact would be doing much if not most of the work on the case from that point forward. Both attorneys recognized from the start that they had joined a lawsuit unlike any they'd been part of before. Brizzolara had litigated dozens of civil rights cases and had worked with attorneys who had handled hundreds more. He believed he knew the lay of the land, but he'd never seen terrain like that created by *Wallace v. Los Angeles*. "I don't know of a single other civil case where a public entity has been sanctioned more than a million dollars for its conduct," he said. "There was an obvious case for obstruction of justice already on the table, but neither the FBI nor the U.S. attorney's office wanted to pick it up. It was not just an easy case to make—it had already been made. And it just kept growing as we found more and more stuff that the city and the police department had hidden from us."

Material obtained from a former cop named Bennie Keys, who had been locked up with David Mack at the Montebello City Jail after Mack's arrest for the Bank of America robbery, was especially significant. It was Keys who told the LAPD that, within minutes of arriving at the jail, Mack had informed the other prisoners he was a Mob Piru Blood and that they had better not fuck with him. Mack had also boasted that the $700,000 he retained from the bank robbery was "invested" in a way that would at least double his money by the time he got out of prison; that he could do eight years standing on his head and would be a rich man when he hit the streets again. It was Keys as well who reported that Mack had hired a Hispanic gang member to kill his ex-girlfriend and accomplice in the bank robbery, Errolyn Romero, after learning she had made a deal to testify against him.

All that was in the material the city and the LAPD had turned over in discovery. What the city had not turned over, however, was the statement by Keys in 1998 that Mack had told him that he was at the scene of the Biggie Smalls murder, implying he had been part of it. It was only when they obtained records of a lawsuit Keys had filed against the FBI for failing to put him in the witness protection

program, as promised, that Brizzolara and his colleagues learned of
what Mack had allegedly told Keys about the Biggie murder.

"We all knew there was more—probably a lot more—that the
city was keeping from us," Brizzolara recalled. "Figuring out what it
was became a big part of our job."

Gage, who had been the attorney in a good many cases involving
LAPD officers as either plaintiffs or defendants, was the one who suggested trying to obtain the LAPD's Training, Evaluation and Management System (TEAMS) reports on the various officers they suspected
of involvement with Death Row Records and the Biggie murder.
Sanders, who had never heard of TEAMS reports, was enthusiastic
when Gage explained that these were computer documents that listed
all the complaints of misconduct—and their resolutions—involving
LAPD officers. The average TEAMS report on a veteran officer was
at most two or three pages long, Gage said. The TEAMS reports on
David Mack and his friend Sammy Martin were each at least two
or three times that length. Gage was boggled, though, when he saw
the TEAMS report on Rafael Perez. "It was pages and pages long,"
the attorney remembered. "And the complaints against him were for
really bad shit. Some of those arose out of the Rampart Scandal, but
there were at least seventeen serious allegations that had been made
against Perez before Rampart. The LAPD had known for a long time
what a bad guy this was."

"Stunning stuff," Brizzolara called the Perez TEAMS report
(the details of which were placed under seal by the court). What most
amazed him after he spent a few months on the *Wallace v. Los Angeles*
case, though, Brizzolara said, was the role the *Los Angeles Times* had
played in distorting the public perception of what was taking place
in the courtroom. "I'd go to hearings, get up the next morning and
read the *L.A. Times,* and think, 'Were they at the same hearing I was?'"
recalled Brizzolara, who was learning a great deal about the sway the
newspaper held not only in Los Angeles but all across the country.
"I grew up in Oklahoma," he explained, "and I would get calls from
people there who read the *L.A. Times* articles reprinted in their local

newspaper. And it was very upsetting to me that people out there believed this stuff was true."

Gage said, "People that knew I was on this trial stopped talking to me"—because of the way the case was being presented in the newspaper. "The *Times* then had so much power and clout in L.A. that they could virtually control the narrative. And they did."

"What worried me—and I was pretty sure it was part of the city's strategy—was the impact on the potential jury pool," Brizzolara said. "Through Chuck Philips, the city was really poisoning the waters, and it was tough to combat."

The vastly changed and immensely larger lawsuit that resulted from Judge Cooper's declaration of a mistrial received almost no attention from the media in Los Angeles until November 2005, when *Rolling Stone* published "The Unsolved Murder of Notorious B.I.G." There were two especially newsworthy aspects of the article for the Los Angeles media. One was the blunt criticism of how the *Los Angeles Times* had reported on the Biggie Smalls murder and the resulting wrongful death lawsuit. The other was an argument that the mostly fictional Rampart Scandal, ginned up by Rafael Perez, had been used to camouflage the real scandal: a group of police officers in the employ of Death Row Records had become a de facto criminal gang responsible not only for the murder of Biggie Smalls, but also for the killings of a number of young black men, and for the depredation of the Rampart district. This latter point was acute in Los Angeles because before writing the *Rolling Stone* article I had written the book *LAbyrinth*, which had taken the city's media to task both for ignoring evidence of LAPD involvement in the Biggie murder and for giving unthinking credence to Perez's claims of corruption in the Rampart Division CRASH unit. *Rolling Stone*, though, created a chink in my argument when an editor removed a paragraph concerning the *Times* story that had first reported Russell Poole's theory of the Biggie murder. Marc Duvoisin recognized this as a chance to strike back and sent off a letter to the magazine stating that, because of my failure to mention that article, I had forfeited "any claim to be taken seriously." I replied that

I had acknowledged the *Times* 1999 article about Russell Poole "first in my book *LAbyrinth* and again in the article I submitted to *Rolling Stone*." The magazine's editors inserted a note stating, "This citation was cut for space from the final article."

Nevertheless, the back-and-forth permitted most of the L.A. media to reduce the story to a spat between a national magazine and the largest newspaper west of the Hudson River, without any actual consideration of the facts. The single exception was the city's second and much smaller daily newspaper, the *Los Angeles Daily News*, which printed a front-page story about the *Rolling Stone* article that focused mainly on the revelation of a link between the Rampart Scandal and the Notorious B.I.G. murder. Sanders, who for several years had shrugged off my contention that the murder and Rampart were connected, told the *Daily News* that he had changed his mind. "We had never focused on the Rampart aspect," he told the newspaper. "Now in hindsight, now that we've seen how things unfolded, that theory could make complete sense." The story's next paragraph read: "Sanders said Rampart—a scandal that cost the city tens of millions of dollars and led to the federal consent decree levied on the LAPD—got 'tons of attention' while 'cops working with gangsters got almost no attention.'"

The only breaking news in the *Daily News* story came from Don Vincent, who told the newspaper, "There are no ongoing settlement talks because 'so much money' is being demanded, and the city believes it will prevail." For the first time, Sanders and Frank felt certain that the city would not.

The two attorneys would admit their surprise that in interviews with jurors after the mistrial they were told they had been winning the case. The most significant event of the trial, as the members of the jury recalled it, had been Sanders's questioning of Bernard Parks. Now "Councilman Parks," and the most powerful black politician in the city, Parks couldn't be quite as opaque in front of a judge and jury as he had been during his deposition. Within his first few questions, Sanders got the former LAPD chief to endorse his theory about cop "tools." Yes, guns, badges, and radios were all police tools, Parks agreed, as were "camaraderie and special access to other officers." The moment that the jurors remembered best, though, had come during Sanders's follow-up questioning of Parks. "Is it fair to say that David Mack is an individual who's capable of being involved in very, very serious crime and taking the facts to his grave?" Sanders asked. Don Vincent's vociferous objection turned into the perfect setup for what Sanders would offer in defense of his question. With the court's permission, he asked Parks to read a passage from his deposition in which he had specifically agreed that David Mack was quite capable of "taking to his grave facts that the police would like."

"I was right next to the jury and I could see how riveted they were," Sanders recalled. "But I didn't understand what an impact it had on them until we talked to them after the mistrial."

Parks's statement about Mack, combined with testimony from Russell Poole's former partner Fred Miller that he had taken the case against Suge Knight for orchestrating Biggie's murder to the district attorney's office, had made a powerful impact on them, jurors said. Their conversations with the jury affirmed for Sanders and Frank something each had learned again and again over the years, which was that seemingly small victories can echo loudly in a courtroom. One of their big advantages in the abbreviated trial, the attorneys said, had been the fact that their paralegal Audrey Matheny "was the only person in the courtroom who knew how to manipulate the technology," as Frank put it. Because of Matheny, a single mother raising a young son, "we had our best exhibits sitting on-screen in the courtroom while the other side was questioning witnesses." The jurors had been amused and affected by the contrast between what they were seeing and what they were hearing.

They were headed into the second trial far better armed than they had been in the first, Sanders and Frank knew, with perhaps the most important ruling that could be made by the judge already in their favor. The two attorneys understood, though, that their return trip to the courtroom would be a long and arduous journey. The city's first submission of discovery evidence included eighty-one CDs of new Perez-related evidence that were provided initially to Judge Cooper, then to Sanders and Frank. The CDs contained hundreds of thousands of pages that would have to be pored over before the case could move toward trial. On top of that, many new witnesses, among them Rafael Perez, would have to be deposed.

Kenneth Boagni, of course, would be first and foremost among these new witnesses. Or so Sanders and Frank hoped. On the day the mistrial was declared, Sanders had sent Bradley Gage to Calipatria to conduct a deposition of Boagni. Nearly the first words out of the prisoner's mouth, though, were, "I'm not going to give you any testimony."

Sanders and Frank, in particular, had been furious during the court hearings that led to the mistrial when Assistant City Attorney Vincent repeatedly identified Boagni as the informant whose claims about Rafael Perez were at issue. Vincent had even paused to spell Boagni's name aloud during a hearing on June 27, knowing that *Los Angeles Times* reporters were present. The newspaper published Boagni's name the next day (along with Vincent's attacks on his credibility), and the man was naturally upset when officials at the Calipatria prison informed him his life was now at risk. Gage had been met by three attorneys for the city, plus two LAPD officers, when he arrived at Calipatria to depose Boagni. The inmate spoke with furious intensity when he informed Gage that he had been "told by a few people here in this institution about my—about the concern they had about my name being mentioned in the paper as an informant." When Boagni demanded to know who had disclosed his name to the press, Gage recalled, Vincent told him it had been Perry Sanders. He insisted to Boagni that this was not true, Gage said, but by then the man had made up his mind not to cooperate. "I have concerns about my family," he said. The deposition was canceled.

"It has become a clear pattern," Frank told me when I interviewed him for *Rolling Stone*. "The LAPD and the city try to hide the existence of witnesses who can help our case, then they try to block our access to those witnesses, and when that fails, they leak the witnesses' identities to Chuck Philips, knowing he will use that information in the pages of the *L.A. Times* to hurt our case in any way he can."

Three months passed before Boagni agreed to a one-on-one meeting with Sanders. "I kept reaching out and finally he said come see him," Sanders recalled. "I got on a plane to L.A. the next day and drove out there through the desert to Calipatria." Though he refused to disclose the details of his conversation with Boagni—"I promised him I wouldn't share that with anybody"—Sanders did say that he had been reassured by how composed and articulate the inmate was, and that he "might now be the best witness we have." Just days later, though, Sanders was alerted that LAPD officials were spreading word that Boagni had recanted. Sanders sent a message to Calipatria asking if that was true, and in reply received a letter in which Boagni wrote that he stood by his earlier testimony "100,000 percent." The letter also made it clear, however, that Boagni was beginning to recognize the powerful position in which recent events had placed him. He had just been visited in prison by an LAPD representative who "made it perfectly clear that if I was to testify, I would bury the city and the LAPD," Boagni wrote, adding that this same person "made it clear he hoped I wouldn't depose or testify."

This raised the obvious concern, Sanders acknowledged, that the city and the police department might be able to manipulate Boagni with the hope of a reduced prison sentence.

During the next six months, Sanders and Frank repeatedly told Judge Cooper that they believed the LAPD was still withholding evidence related not only to Perez and Boagni, but also to Mack and Muhammad. The attorneys pointed to new information they were finding in documents they were receiving years after those documents should have been handed over in discovery, including sightings of Muhammad at a 1993 meeting in the offices of Death Row Records and at the party that celebrated Snoop Dogg's acquittal on murder charges in 1996. They had also found a cryptic reference to an LAPD report that, shortly before his arrest in 1998, Perez had visited an inmate in the Los Angeles County Jail who was cooperating with authorities and warned the man, "Don't talk about Biggie." But what they hadn't gotten from the city, the attorneys said, was the single most important piece of evidence in the case, the "clue sheet" that listed the details of every tip or piece of evidence collected by detectives assigned to the investigation of the Biggie Smalls murder. The LAPD was maintaining that it couldn't find the sheet. In the clue sheet's absence, Sanders and Frank were planning to demand that the judge instruct the jury to make the most negative assessment available of the LAPD's failure to produce that document. What the judge did instead was warn the city's attorneys that if she discovered that either they or the LAPD were continuing to withhold documents, there would be "consequences."

Judge Cooper got the chance to decide what those consequences were in April 2006, when the city and its police department coughed up what Sanders and Frank recognized instantly as the most significant document they had put their hands on to date. It was a Los Angeles Police Department complaint form for Case No. 01-0190 revealing that, on the basis of allegations by Kenneth Boagni, the LAPD had been forced to open an investigation into whether Rafael Perez and David Mack had "conspired to kill Christopher Wallace." Because of what Boagni had told them about his conversations with Perez, the department also had been compelled to make a formal record of the allegations that Perez and Sammy Martin were Mack's accomplices in the Bank of America robbery, and that Perez and Mack together committed "multiple home invasion robberies."

The complaint form had been turned over to the plaintiffs' attorneys only at the insistence of the recently appointed head of the LAPD's newly formed Consent Decree Bureau, Gerald Chaleff. He was a former president of the Los Angeles County Bar Association who had for years been one of the city's top defense attorneys, most famous for representing Lyle and Erik Menendez, the Beverly Hills brothers convicted of their parents' 1989 murder. Now an LAPD employee with the rank of deputy chief, Chaleff said he was determined to make sure there was no repetition of the mistakes that led to the mistrial in *Wallace v. Los Angeles.* "I was at the city attorney's office, and I saw this box of stuff there that should have been exchanged in discovery a long time ago," Chaleff recalled. "The city attorney on the case, Don Vincent, was just sitting on it all. I was shocked and furious. I told him you need to deliver that to the other side right now. I didn't even know what was in the box. I just knew it must be something pretty important."

That it was. What the complaint form mainly exposed was that the LAPD had made zero effort to explore Boagni's allegations. Beneath the finding of "insufficient evidence to adjudicate" the LAPD had provided, as required by the city code, its "rationale": "This investigation did not provide sufficient information to adjudicate these allegations. The investigation did not address numerous issues. Interview[s] of all the witnesses identified in the complaint investigation were not completed, and follow-up homicide investigations were not included for review . . . Another issue that was not addressed in the investigation is the fact of whether Boagni was actually housed with Perez in the detention facility. Therefore, absent further investigation that would garner additional information that will substantiate or refute the allegations, the most appropriate classification for these allegations is Insufficient Evidence to Adjudicate."

In other words, Sanders observed, "they couldn't do anything because they didn't do anything." Even as the attorneys publicly expressed fury that the LAPD had hidden the complaint form and its attached documents from them for years, Sanders and Frank were privately reveling in the knowledge that they were now in possession of what they called blatant evidence of a police department cover-up, and along with it proof that numerous high-ranking police officials had been aware of Boagni's claims long before the lawsuit went to trial and had almost certainly conspired to hide them. "We wanted the judge to have a look at that stuff right away," Sanders said, "because we thought it would change the whole case."

"The smoking gun of all time," Brizzolara called the complaint form.

On page two of the document, it was explained that the investigation of Boagni's claims was considered "confidential" and that the Rampart Task Force "retained all related documents pertaining to this complaint." The investigators assigned to the Boagni complaint, that is, had never been permitted—if they had even attempted—to look at any of the evidence that might have supported the prisoner's allegations. "They're going to have to show it to us, though," Frank said, "and I bet they're more afraid of that than anything else in this case."

The only information in the complaint form that revealed anything new—beyond the degree of the LAPD's determination to suppress the Boagni materials—concerned Sammy Martin. The LAPD had managed to shuffle Martin off the department with an under-the-table negotiation that resulted in his dismissal from the force for having lied about the trip to Las Vegas he made with Mack and Perez in the aftermath of the Bank of America robbery. As Sergio Robleto observed, "Letting Sammy Martin slide on all the other stuff he was suspected of being involved in was the most convenient way to make sure that no evidence that might discredit Rafael Perez ever surfaced."

While much was known about the police careers of Mack and Perez, almost nothing had been previously revealed about Martin's. Part of the paperwork the detectives assigned to the Boagni complaint were required to submit, however, had been a "work/complaint history analysis" for each of the accused officers. Martin's stated that between 1990 and 1995 he had been "the subject of six sustained complaints" that included warnings, admonishments, and suspensions for neglect of duty, unbecoming conduct, and unauthorized tactics. Said Robleto, "Nobody gets six sustained complaints in a six-year period and stays on the department. Yet somehow Martin did. There are some questions to answer about that."

They would be asking those questions, Sanders and Frank assured Robleto; Sammy Martin was now part of a case that would be vastly broader than what they had imagined when they filed their original claim in federal court. The attorneys were already working on a motion to transform their lawsuit into a racketeering case by the time they came before Judge Cooper on April 26, 2006, to present her with the complaint form and to request permission to depose "any and all" LAPD officers and officials who knew of its existence.

"We think it's appropriate to get to the bottom of everyone who has laid a finger on that document," Sanders said. Therefore, he and his cocounsel were proposing that they be permitted to conduct a special two-week round of discovery depositions beginning on May 1.

"Stunning information," Judge Cooper called the complaint form after she had a chance to look through it. "Not to have turned this information over to the plaintiff, I'm just amazed," she told the city's lawyers. "I don't know how that can be justified."

The attorney speaking for the City of Los Angeles, John Wright, conceded, "The timing of the release of the document is unfortunate; it should have been handed over earlier." But he argued that it contained "nothing of any significant information more than what Mr. Sanders and his colleagues learned" during the week preceding the judge's declaration of a mistrial. The plaintiffs' request for new and greatly expanded discovery was based on an obstruction-of-justice theory that was not a cause of action in the lawsuit their attorneys had filed, and essentially permitted Sanders and his colleagues to interrogate police officials before deciding what to accuse them of, Wright added.

The court also heard from Gerald Chaleff, who assured Judge Cooper that he had "formed a specialized unit consisting of about eleven people whose only job was to scour the department in the attempt to find any material that anybody might think related to this investigation" and that he was "confident that, one, we are finding everything that there is, and, two, nobody is attempting to hide

anything." Chaleff made no mention of his having personally compelled the city attorney's office to turn over the box of materials that
included the complaint form

Sanders responded, "We intend to find out about who and at
what level and in what offices and in what departments were involved
in this cover-up, which goes directly to a racketeering complaint,
because there was an FBI investigation going on at the time. It was
public record and public knowledge that the FBI thought that Suge
Knight was involved in this homicide and Death Row Records was
involved in it. They were investigating it as a racketeering complaint.
We happen to know and believe that there's plenty of evidence already
on the record that people within the LAPD were involved with that
racketeering organization [Death Row]."

The city's posture toward the plaintiffs had been, "'Let's see what
they know now so we can figure out what else to hide,'" Sanders told
the judge. "We shouldn't be put in that position again."

Cooper agreed. She had heard from the city at least a dozen
times, and probably more, that "there was not one shred of evidence
that Detective Mack or anybody in the Los Angeles Police Department had anything to do with the murder of Biggie Smalls," the judge
reminded the city's attorneys. "There was such righteous indignation
on the part of the city and the police department that these allegations were being brought forward . . . and there have been years and
years of heels being dug in and absolute insistence that there was not
any evidence anywhere that the police had any connection with this
case. And now we see more and more and more is surfacing. And so
I am very concerned that this is, in fact, a different case from the one
we started out with, and that the plaintiffs are looking at a deliberate
concealment and cover-up, which is extremely disturbing to me."

Therefore, she granted Sanders and his colleagues not just the
two weeks for depositions that they had requested, but double that
time, four weeks.

For Sanders and Frank, the judge's ruling was nearly as big a
victory as her declaration of the mistrial and an award of sanctions

against the city. "We walked out of the courtroom that day bursting with confidence," Frank recalled.

He and Sanders, however, were about to learn what it meant to be up against Vincent Marella, who would be coming at them with a tactical move so calculated and targeted that it seemed, for a while at least, to have turned the case upside down one more time.

CHAPTER ELEVEN

The four weeks following the presentation of the complaint form before Judge Cooper were immensely productive, from the plaintiffs' point of view. Their depositions had generated enough new information to justify adding a number of new defendants to the case, most notably the commander of the LAPD's Risk Management Group, as well as his lead investigator on the *Wallace v. Los Angeles* lawsuit, plus Detective Steve Katz.

The next scheduled court hearing in the case was a routine status conference, in which the scope of the plaintiffs' new filing would be considered. Sanders and Frank had chosen to stay in Colorado Springs and join the proceeding by telephone, dispatching Bradley Gage to appear on their behalf before Judge Cooper. The two were so relaxed that they were sitting with their wives in a booth at the Famous Steak House, drinks on the table in front of them, when the judge's bailiff called the court to order.

The moment Marella began speaking, though, the two attorneys knew that they should have made the trip to Los Angeles.

"Your Honor, we requested this status conference for a very serious purpose," Marella told Judge Cooper, "and that is, we believe the court has been misled with very serious consequences in the case."

Sanders and Frank exchanged glances, each wondering if the other had any idea what this was about. Both shook their heads.

Marella quickly summarized the developments of the past ten months, how an anonymous caller—"we still don't know who he was"—had alerted Sanders to the Board of Rights hearing where Kenneth Boagni had testified "as to an alleged connection between David Mack and the Wallace murder."

"Over the next several days," Marella continued, "Mr. Sanders made critical representations to the court about the information that Mr. Boagni possessed and the fact that it went to the heart of the plaintiffs' case and, very significantly, that they had no knowledge of this, that the plaintiffs were completely unaware of the information and it was because that information had been withheld by the city . . . Your Honor, we now know that these representations were false, as we can demonstrate to the court—and we're prepared to do that today, not by anonymous phone calls or not by innuendo or inference—that the plaintiffs had in their possession as far back as November of 2002, in detail and directly from Kenneth Boagni, the very information they stood here during trial and represented to the court that they knew nothing about."

The proof of his claims that Marella was about to offer appeared damning on its face: a four-page witness interview report prepared by the private investigator who had been working for the plaintiffs prior to Sergio Robleto. Dated November 7, 2002, and bearing the heading "Privileged and Confidential Attorney Work Product," the report summarized an interview with Kenneth Boagni at Calipatria State Prison earlier that day. Boagni had described in detail what he was told by Rafael Perez about the Biggie Smalls murder and about the work Perez and David Mack had done for Suge Knight and Death Row Records, as well as the false claims Perez had made about the corruption in the Rampart Division.

What Boagni had told the investigator in that interview was even more detailed than his statements to the LAPD. Perez had made it clear that the hit on Biggie was a response to Tupac Shakur's slaying, Boagni said, claiming to have been at a meeting with Suge Knight and David Mack where Suge instructed the LAPD officers to obtain the weapon that would be used to kill Biggie. Perez told him they had done this, Boagni said, then described how he had been stationed outside the Petersen Automotive Museum on the night of Biggie's murder. When he spotted the Bad Boy Records entourage preparing to leave in a caravan of SUVs, Perez said, he had phoned Mack, who was inside the museum, to say that Biggie was "available." Mack phoned back five minutes later to tell him to "get out of the way," said Perez, who told Boagni he withdrew from the immediate vicinity of the museum to a spot where he could watch what went down. After witnessing the shooting, Perez said, he saw the killer drive off in a "black Monte Carlo SS" with someone in the passenger seat. Later, he had made his way to the county morgue, Perez said, where he viewed Biggie's corpse. Boagni also claimed that Perez had given him the name of the shooter, but refused to disclose it, because he wanted to "hold some things back."

Boagni described being interviewed at Calipatria by a team of LAPD detectives who turned off their tape recorder before asking what he knew about the Biggie murder. Steve Katz came to see him later and recorded that conversation, recalled Boagni, who said he had told Katz that Perez claimed there was an LAPD captain who knew about his and Mack's involvement in the murder.

So, it was clear that Sanders and Frank had the Boagni allegations in late 2002, Marella told the judge, yet "they never pursued the information during discovery, although they had the opportunity do so. They didn't produce the information in response to the city's discovery request, although they had the obligation to do so. Instead, what happened, Your Honor, was that the plaintiffs waited until trial was under way to stage what I think can only be called a drama of outrage about the very information that we now know they had."

He then asked Cooper to rule that there should be no further discovery in the case and that the plaintiffs should return the $1.1 million they had been awarded after the mistrial was declared.

Judge Cooper declared herself "speechless," then scolded Sanders over the phone in a voice that rose steadily as she spoke. "What I don't understand is how you could have received this report that is almost four pages of detail about Mack and Perez and their connection to Death Row Records and all the details about how this murder went down the night that B.I.G. was murdered, how you could have seen this, decided to ignore it, and then carried on in front of this court as if a bombshell had been dropped in your lap when you heard about it in the middle of trial. I'm absolutely astonished that you could have pulled that off, and I believe you have absolutely deceived this court into believing that you knew nothing about this until it was suddenly revealed by the defense . . . I'm so angry right now I can hardly speak to you."

Gage had saved the day, arguing that his colleague deserved a chance to see the document Marella had submitted to the court and to file a written response to the claims that had been made against him. Judge Cooper conceded that this was fair and gave Sanders seven days to submit his reply.

At the Famous, looking at Frank's stricken expression, Sanders reminded his partner that they were protected by one very significant fact: in the same remarks from the June 30, 2005, hearing that Marella had selectively quoted, Sanders advised the judge and the city's attorneys that he and his colleagues had been contacted by Kenneth Boagni "several years ago" and that he believed they had a witness statement from him.

Boagni had been that prison inmate who had reached out through BiggieHotline.com and wanted to send someone living in Lake Charles to meet with Sanders back in 2002. The proposed envoy turned out to be Boagni's wife, Darlene, but he hadn't known that at the time, said Sanders, admitting he was "scared off" by the suggested meeting. "We were already havin' people tell us to be careful," he explained, "sayin', 'These people are for sure gonna want to kill you.'"

He had not recognized the name Kenneth Boagni when he heard it spoken by Don Vincent in open court on June 27, 2005, Sanders said. It was only when Sergio Robleto told him that Boagni said he had spoken to their investigator three years earlier that he made the connection, Sanders explained.

Sanders knew that defeating Marella's claims against him was likely to be the single most important piece of work he did on this case. What he did not know was that the city's attorneys had made sure the courtroom was filled with reporters while Marella was accusing Sanders of defrauding the court, and that every local television news broadcast would lead that evening with a story about this "shocking revelation," as one broadcaster put it. By the time he heard about the news coverage in L.A., Sanders was already at work on his five-page declaration, and the pressure, he admitted, was "gigantic." "Pissed off as I was, I had to admit that Marella is one hell of a lawyer," Sanders recalled. "He can orchestrate a courtroom."

In his declaration to Judge Cooper, Sanders began with a recitation of the facts that the judge already knew, from the time Don Vincent had spoken the name Kenneth Boagni in open court to his own announcement three days later that Boagni had contacted Dennis Chang's office in 2002 and given Chang's investigator a witness statement. Sanders then explained that BiggieHotline.com had produced hundreds upon hundreds of tips, "most of which proved fruitless." Still, he had given the entire BiggieHotline.com file—every tip that had come in, including the one from Boagni—to FBI agent Phil Carson and the two LAPD Internal Affairs investigators, Roger Mora and Steve Sambar, when they visited him in Lake Charles in late 2002, Sanders wrote, "and redacted nothing whatsoever from the file." Included in what he had given Carson and the LAPD investigators, Sanders noted, was Chang's investigator's report of his interview with Boagni; that, in fact, was how the city attorney's office obtained the report—it had been given to the office by Mora.

The tips that had come in on BiggieHotline.com were all eventually separated into two groups, "Active Leads" and "Dead Leads,"

Sanders explained. Kenneth Boagni's claims had ended up in the Dead Leads file, he wrote, because in the discovery documents provided by the city and the LAPD there was no shred of evidence that the meetings with LAPD detectives that Boagni claimed had taken place ever had.

Some of the tips they had received through BiggieHotline .com, "such as the LAPD file contains clues on a D Mack being involved . . . actually were in the LAPD file as we were told they would be," Sanders noted. "There were dozens if not hundreds of things we had been told would be in the file, which when checked against the file were indeed in the LAPD Murder Books produced by the city." In other words, he and his colleagues had no reason to suspect that the LAPD was holding anything back, Sanders wrote. So when "plaintiffs found no corroborative information in the LAPD file that [Boagni] had spoken to Detective Katz and others regarding Rafael Perez," he and the plaintiffs' other attorneys had naturally put Boagni's claims with the other "unsubstantiated or uncorroborated" tips in the Dead Leads file, Sanders explained. The fact that Katz had specifically denied under oath in a deposition ever performing any investigation of Perez only confirmed this decision.

Judge Cooper found Sanders's answer to the accusations against him so persuasive that she not only issued a court order that discovery in the case could resume and that the plaintiffs were welcome to submit their amended complaint, but also wrote it in a way that read like a personal apology to the attorney.

"The *Times*, naturally, barely reported that," Sanders noted, "and the rest of the L.A. media pretty much ignored it, too. So I still sorta felt like the whole thing was hangin' over me whenever I came back to town, because a lot more people knew about the accusations that had been made against me, which were a big deal in the L.A. media when Marella made them, than knew that the judge had ruled they weren't true."

Gage would say he saw the effect of Marella's claims, and how they were reported in the media, when he accompanied Sanders to a settlement conference that Judge Cooper had ruled should be conducted by senior federal judge Dickran Tevrizian. "The judge refused to hear from Perry because of what Marella had accused him of," Gage recalled. "So I had to do all the talking."

It possibly hadn't boosted Tevrizian's opinion of Sanders when the attorney began by demanding a billion-dollar settlement. "I wanted these people to know I wasn't backing down, and I wasn't backing away," Sanders said. "I was still comin' after them, because I knew I had done nothing wrong. You can't show any flinch when you're up against people like this."

The most stunning revelation to emerge from the May 30, 2006, hearing was that four days earlier, on May 26, one of Sergio Robleto's operatives had finally caught up with Kendrick Knox and obtained a signed declaration from him that was everything Sanders and Frank had hoped for—and more.

After the mistrial, Robleto assigned a retired LAPD sergeant and homicide investigator named Bruce Stoughton to locate Knox and speak to him, in part because Stoughton "lived way out in the Valley, like Knox did." Even for Stoughton, though, Knox was a hard man to find. "The guy was never at home," he recalled.

Stoughton was already familiar with Knox and his investigation of Death Row Records because, he said, "basically Knox had picked up where I had left off." It all started with a vacant medical care center in Van Nuys on Oxnard Boulevard, Stoughton said. "I heard scuttlebutt that the abandoned building had been taken over by people from South-Central L.A. who were using it as a combination of recording studio and party pad," Stoughton explained, so he and other LAPD officers began to routinely check the building to see if it was being vandalized or broken into. "It clearly was," Stoughton recalled. "There were people milling around in the parking lot, which had resulted in a number of confrontations and threats against people who lived in the neighborhood." Eventually the abandoned building had become, effectively, the first Death Row Records recording studio. The LAPD brass seemed reluctant to do anything about it, Stoughton noted, fearing some sort of "racial incident," but eventually had pushed out the congregation of "gangbangers and rappers," forcing Death Row to relocate to Can-Am studios in Tarzana, where Ken Knox's investigation had begun.

One advantage Stoughton had in searching for Knox was his own status as a recipient of LAPD's highest honor, the Medal of Valor, awarded for risking his life to save the lives of three suburban teenagers who had made an idiotic decision to surf the storm-swollen waters of the concrete-encased Los Angeles River, as well as the two firemen who'd been pulled into the seething water while attempting to rescue them. The respect Stoughton commanded for having saved those five lives had helped him convince other retired cops to assist in locating Knox. "I bird-dogged him for some time," Stoughton recalled. "He did his best to avoid me, but I eventually ran him to ground and got him to give a statement. He said he was scared. He didn't want reprisal on his family. He said his wife was terrified of Suge Knight, and I think Knox himself was afraid of the LAPD. He told me that when the department began to close down his investigation, and the investigation into LAPD officers working for Death Row, he had decided to accept it and keep his mouth shut. He said he wanted to protect his family and didn't see any way the investigation could go forward, so why expose himself? He said it was hard to know how much of what had happened was the PD protecting itself, and how much was racial politics. Some of each, probably, he thought. Now, Knox had a nice home out in Sylmar and a comfortable retirement. He was reluctant to risk it, but he told me enough to know that he was going to be a great witness in court."

In his declaration, Knox briefly summarized his "investigation of Death Row Records and a studio being leased by Death Row Records in my service area in Tarzana, California." Then he unspooled a series of astounding revelations. The first was that while conducting surveillance in late 1996 and early 1997, Knox said, "I observed LAPD officer Rafael Perez on approximately three occasions at the recording studio dressed in baggy shirts, pants and tennis shoes. I further observed LAPD Officer David Mack in the company of Rafael Perez at least three times at the studio."

Through his chain of command, Knox stated, "I reported the presence of LAPD and other law enforcement officers I believed to be working as security guards at the studio for Death Row Records." In response? "I received complaints from and was confronted by some of these officers regarding these reports"—meaning that at least one of his superiors had leaked Knox's investigation to its targets.

He shared the findings of his investigation with the LAPD's Internal Affairs and Robbery-Homicide divisions, Knox said. He also had personally given Detective Russell Poole "a three-ring binder containing some of the surveillance reports, interviews of people at the studio, photographs of people at the studio and other documents." He was subsequently interviewed by an IA officer named Cindy Benes, Knox stated, and told her that he "believed that several if not more LAPD officers were working off-duty for Death Row Records as security guards and in other capacities."

Immediately afterward, Knox continued, "I was informed by a lieutenant from LAPD Robbery-Homicide Division that I was ordered to cease my investigation because of the sensitive nature of the investigation." That Knox refused to name this lieutenant was frustrating, Stoughton said, "but he knew the guy was following orders and didn't want to drag him into it." And besides, what Knox added in the next sentence of his declaration was what really mattered: "I was told by this same lieutenant that this order had come 'from the chief,' referring to Chief of Police Bernard Parks. I was further ordered not to discuss my investigation or findings with anyone inside or outside the Los Angeles Police Department."

By then, he had compiled an investigative file that filled a large blue binder with four inches of intelligence and surveillance reports, Knox went on, along with photographs, mug shots, interview records, field investigation reports, and "potential homicide investigative leads."

When a back injury unrelated to the investigation forced him to take a months-long leave of absence from active duty, Knox explained, he had given some of his records to two LAPD captains. "Upon my return to active duty, I was advised that these records had been 'lost.' My divisional copy of these records stored within my desk in the nonpublic area of my senior lead officer office was missing. I conducted a diligent but unsuccessful search for my documents and other materials. At that time, I also observed that the digital records and other data and material regarding the investigation which had previously been contained on my senior lead officer unit computer had been deleted and/or destroyed, and could not be duplicated or re-created from other sources. I also contacted LAPD Robbery-Homicide Division to request that they return the copy of the documents and other materials regarding my investigation that I had previously given Detective Russell Poole. I was advised by an individual in Robbery-Homicide Division that Detective Poole was no longer with the division, and that they did not know where the documents and other materials were located."

The former senior lead officer then finished by stating, "Because of my involvement with the investigation of Death Row Records and its employment of off-duty LAPD and other law enforcement agencies and security guards, I have been and am concerned for the physical safety and well-being of myself and my family."

As far as Sanders and Frank were concerned, the Knox declaration had put Bernard Parks in a box. Parks no doubt would claim executive privilege in an attempt to avoid answering questions about the Knox investigation, but Sanders doubted the judge would buy it. Most importantly, Knox had corroborated Poole's claims about the investigation of LAPD officers working for Death Row Records and possibly involved in the murder of Notorious B.I.G. having been shut down on orders from Parks. "The city and the LAPD have been bent on makin' some 'lone nut' attack on Russ Poole's integrity," Sanders said. "But he's not alone anymore. Knox is there with him."

Another explosive declaration was revealed at that same May 30 hearing before Judge Cooper. This one was signed by an active-duty

LAPD officer. She was Ya-May Christle, a former Internal Affairs Division supervisor who began her declaration with a paragraph reading: "I have spent almost 17½ years in the Los Angeles Police Department. I was a Sergeant II until I complained about the inappropriate conduct of Chief [Michael] Berkow, including my computer being taken after I input discovery information related to the lawsuit of Wallace v. City of Los Angeles. The information was input following the mistrial."

Christle's dispute with Berkow had just recently gone public, when she filed a lawsuit against the LAPD in which her main claim was that Berkow was promoting women for consenting to sexual relationships with him and that she had been demoted when she complained about him. According to Christle, the married Berkow had openly carried on a three-year affair with a female LAPD sergeant under his supervision. During that same period, Christle added, Berkow also had engaged in affairs with several other female subordinates out of "the apartment" (it was actually a curtained alcove off his office that contained only a bed and a nightstand) he kept in the Bradbury Building, where most LAPD Board of Rights hearings were held. (Berkow denied that latter allegation.) More relevant to the *Wallace v. Los Angeles* lawsuit, though, was Christle's claim that her demotion was in part due to her complaint that Berkow had conspired to cover up evidence that linked LAPD officers to the murder of Notorious B.I.G.

In August 2005, the month after the mistrial in the B.I.G. case had been declared, Christle explained, she received a department-wide notice from Gerald Chaleff directing LAPD officers to provide "all materials pertaining to the Christopher Wallace (AKA Biggie Smalls and Notorious B.I.G.) homicide investigation." Chaleff's memorandum had resulted in "more than one foot worth of discovery information" being delivered to the office where she and an LAPD lieutenant were to prepare a "discovery matrix" of the information on her work computer. The materials she and the lieutenant were collating included "information about the alleged involvement by LAPD officers" in the Biggie Smalls murder, Christle went on. Immediately after she prepared her summary of the evidence she had received, Christle stated, "my computer was taken from me. I complained to the Inspector General of misconduct. The subject matter of my complaint included suspicion that information regarding the Wallace murder was purged from my computer."

The city was so concerned about the sexual harassment claims against Berkow, recalled Bradley Gage, who was representing Christle in her civil suit, that "they basically conceded the retaliation aspect of the case." According to Gage, the LAPD "more or less agreed" that it had taken her computer to hide the evidence in the Biggie case.

A little more than one year after her declaration in the B.I.G. case, Christle was awarded $1.07 million by a Los Angeles jury that agreed her accusations against the LAPD (which included a claim that she was discriminated against as an Asian woman) were true. "She was gonna be a great witness for us and the city knew it," said Sanders, who believed that the revelations of the Knox and Christle declarations were "what started the LAPD and the city looking for a backdoor way to shut us down."*

---

* Berkow's defense of himself in the Christle case and the response to it by those on the other side are considered in Appendix A.

CHAPTER TWELVE

Adding Rafael Perez to the case, Sanders and Frank knew, meant they needed to play a fast game of catch-up with the so-called Rampart Scandal. Considering that it had mostly been ginned up based on lies told by a sociopathic criminal, the attorneys found, the Rampart Scandal had cut through an astonishingly large swath of Los Angeles. The leaked "confessions" of Rafael Perez had spawned more than 150 civil lawsuits filed by those who claimed to have been falsely charged or convicted in criminal court on the basis of perjured testimony by Perez and other officers from the Rampart Division. The settlement of those cases had already cost the city nearly $125 million. Of the seventy officers implicated by Perez, fifty-eight had been referred to Boards of Rights. More than two-thirds of those officers were found not guilty. Yet despite overwhelming evidence that Perez had made up most of what he told Rampart Task Force investigators, in 1999 Bernard Parks and his right-hand man Emmanuel Hernandez told the *Los Angeles Times* that "70 to 80 percent" of what Perez said was accurate. By 2006 it was obvious that the true figure was more like 7 or 8 percent.

The Rampart Scandal narrative had been challenged repeatedly—by two *Rolling Stone* articles as well as stories produced by the *New Yorker*, PBS's *Frontline*, and *Front Page* magazine. The *Los Angeles Times*, though, had yet to inform its readers of how Perez had failed five lie detector tests. And the rest of the city's media was even less probative. This meant, Sanders and Frank knew, that they were likely to be arguing their case before jurors who had swallowed the Rampart Scandal narrative whole. The two attorneys only had to look at the first criminal case spawned by Perez's claims to see what that might mean.

The charges brought in what was known as the "Alley Incident" case had resulted in the prosecution of four LAPD officers accused by Perez. The case was based on what had occurred, according to Perez, during two 1996 "gang sweeps" by Rampart CRASH officers. According to Perez, the accused officers had conspired to obstruct justice by framing 18th Street gang members with fabricated police reports, planted evidence, and perjured testimony.

The Alley Incident took place on June 19, 1996, when a CRASH team that included Perez confronted a group of 18th Street gang-bangers from the Temple Street set in the alley where they had gathered. Among them was a murder suspect named Anthony "Stymie" Adams.* According to the police, the gang members had tried to flee before they could be apprehended. One of the Temple Street set jumped behind the wheel of the car that the CRASH team sergeant had driven to the scene and tried to speed down the alley, striking one LAPD officer while a gang member in the passenger seat swung his door at a second officer. Both officers were knocked to the ground, according to the report they filed.

Only that wasn't what had happened, according to Perez. What actually took place, he said, was that the CRASH team had staged the scene to support their story, even going so far as to break the windshield of the car that they were falsely claiming had struck two of them.

---

* Stymie Adams pleaded no contest to manslaughter in the death of a Mexican Mafia member and was sentenced to twelve years in prison. That conviction was overturned by a Los Angeles Superior Court judge on the basis of evidence that Rafael Perez had falsified evidence in the case. After criminal charges were dropped, Adams won $800,000 in a civil rights lawsuit against the City of Los Angeles.

At trial, the officers had taken the stand to passionately deny the accusations against them. Their attorneys had hoped earlier for the opportunity to cross-examine Perez, but the Los Angeles County district attorney's office decided not to put him on the stand. Because of that, jurors never got the opportunity to learn that the LAPD sergeant who had been accused by Perez of ordering another officer to break his windshield on the night of June 19, 1996, had been ticketed two weeks before that date in the San Fernando Valley for driving that same car with a cracked windshield. Thus it could be proved beyond any doubt that the most damning of the claims Perez had made against his fellow officers was a lie. "So was just about everything else Perez said in that case," according to Cliff Armas.

Nevertheless, the jurors, who had read or heard Perez's leaked claims in the Los Angeles media for months on end, ultimately voted to convict three of the four accused officers of perjury, filing a false report, and obstructing justice. That conviction hadn't lasted long. The presiding judge, Jacqueline Connor, swiftly overturned the jury, declaring that the evidence presented at trial had not supported a guilty verdict. What Connor received for bravely doing the right thing was a heaping of abuse from the local media and in various online forums. Los Angeles County D.A. Steve Cooley promptly announced his office would appeal the judge's decision. The three officers remained under the gun for another four years, until finally, in 2004, the district attorney's office announced they would not be retried.

The three falsely accused officers filed a wrongful prosecution lawsuit that went to trial at the federal courthouse in Orange County. There, the jury awarded the three $15 million in damages—$5 million apiece. The Orange County jurors had needed just thirty minutes to return their verdict, and the judge who heard the case affirmed them by stating in open court that the "LAPD ruined the lives of three dedicated and highly skilled police officers." Nevertheless, L.A. mayor Antonio Villaraigosa directed the city to appeal the verdict. It would not be until 2008 that the Ninth Circuit Court of Appeals upheld the Orange County jury's verdict and ordered Los Angeles to pay the $15 million.

In the aftermath of the 2006 case, the attorney who had represented the three officers in the Orange County trial, Joseph Avrahamy, would write the first article published in Los Angeles that directly challenged the false narrative of the Rampart Scandal. Avrahamy was responding to what was known as the "Blue Ribbon Rampart Review Panel Report," a document that had just been delivered by a team assembled by Chief Bratton and headed by the best-known civil rights attorney in Los Angeles, Constance Rice. That report was astoundingly false, even if its lies were more those of omission than commission. What the "Blue Ribbon" panel had done, Avrahamy wrote in the *Los Angeles Daily News*, was merely "perpetuate the 7-year-old myth that Rafael Perez exposed wide-scale corruption in the Rampart CRASH unit."

Avrahamy asked that the citizens of Los Angeles consider the Rampart Scandal in light of its final tally: Of the ninety-three officers identified by Perez as having committed crimes while on duty, just eight were criminally charged, and only four were convicted. Of those four convictions, three were cases in which, to avoid going to trial on charges that could have put them in state prison, officers had pleaded guilty to excessive force, not to the corruption charges Perez had made against them. A "media frenzy" had created "the public's false belief of extensive corruption in the LAPD," Avrahamy wrote, and this had resulted not only in the overturning of felony convictions of "dangerous gang members who were properly arrested and convicted" but also in the creation of a game known as "Rampart Lotto," in which dozens of civil rights lawsuits had cost the taxpayers of Los Angeles $70 million.

Cliff Armas had been part of one Board of Rights hearing after another in which it was obvious that Rafael Perez had falsely accused his fellow officers. He was most haunted and angered, though, Armas said, by what he had learned about how far those assigned to the Rampart Task Force had gone to back Perez. He recalled a case in which Perez had accused Officer Humberto Tovar of having conspired to pin a gun charge on two gang members. According to the arrest report, Perez and Tovar had been part of a CRASH team that was following up on a tip about armed gang members at a Rampart apartment complex. "They stake out the apartment complex, and Perez sees a gang member with a gun walking around the block," Armas recalled. "He gives the gun to another guy, who also walks around the block. Perez and Tovar call for backup unit. Sergeant Ortiz arrives and they arrest the two guys they had seen with a gun, then go inside and search the apartment, where they find their original suspect but no gun. Perez, though, says this is a bad arrest. He said what really happened is: 'We take these guys into custody but there's no gun. So we go inside and search the apartment, where we find a gun inside a heater vent.' So then what to do? Perez says they huddle around Ortiz, who contrives the story about two gangsters outside with one gun."

He had visited the gang member who was substantiating Perez's account in prison, Armas remembered. "He backs Perez, says he had hidden the gun in a heater vent. So then I listen to the tape of him being interviewed by the task force guys. The first time they ask about the gun, the guy says, 'What gun?' Then they go off tape, and when they go back on, he tells the story about the gun in the heater vent. So I go see him again, and this time he admits they turned off the tape and told him the officers were dirty and planting evidence on people. He said the task force guys were tapping their fingers on the heater vent, 'so I think they want me to say the gun was hidden there.' And he did. I filed a complaint. All the two task force guys got was a verbal [i.e., unwritten] warning that if you go off tape, you have to announce why before you do."

One of those accused along with Tovar had been represented by attorney Darryl Mounger. After Perez testified at a Board of Rights hearing that a tip from an informant he had met on a street corner led him and the other CRASH officers to the building where they found the hidden gun, Mounger asked Perez to name the informant. When Perez did, the attorney was able to show that the man was in jail at the time Perez claimed to have met him on a street corner. "The problem with Perez is that he's told so many lies that he's confused," Mounger said after Tovar was acquitted. "He doesn't know what the truth is anymore."

Armas wondered if the members of the Rampart Task Force didn't, either. Armas had been assigned as departmental rep when the four officers accused in the Alley Incident case were brought before a trial board. He wanted to interview the gang member accused of driving the car that had struck two of those officers, Armas recalled, "but the guy had been deported to El Salvador. The task force sends two guys down there to interview him, and they come back saying he backs Perez's story. So I want to interview him, too. I find him in El Salvador and get him to agree to meet me at a hotel. I have my plane tickets and my hotel reservation, but then just as I'm getting ready to leave, Assistant Chief Berkow cancels the trip. Several months later I'm at the scene of an officer-involved shooting and I see Berkow. So I ask him why he canceled my trip to El Salvador. And he asks me, 'What good would it have done me to let you go?' Then Berkow tells me straight to my face that if I had gone down there and gotten the guy to recant, it would have ruined a case he and the task force had invested a lot of time and energy in, and that it wouldn't have been good for any of their careers. This guy and the people working for him all cared more about getting promoted than they did about wrecking the lives of LAPD officers."

The entire Rampart Scandal flowed from Rafael Perez, Sanders and Frank understood, so finding the most effective way to present the former detective to a jury, and to explain where he fit into their case, would be central going forward.

Sanders planned to describe Perez as a calculating fiend who had largely escaped the consequences of his depravity. Certainly, given the magnitude of his crimes, Perez had paid very little for them. Perez had served just three years of his five-year sentence for stealing eight pounds of cocaine from the LAPD evidence locker, and most of that in protective custody. After his release in July 2001, Perez pleaded guilty to the most terrible of the crimes that he had admitted: the shooting of Javier Ovando, which had put the gang member in a wheelchair for the rest of his life, followed by the planting of a gun on Ovando to get him sent to state prison. For this, Perez was sentenced to just five years' imprisonment and served only two. Not long after his release in 2004, he legally changed his name to Ray Lopez and found a home near the beach in the South Bay, where he was living comfortably.

His former partner Nino Durden also had been convicted in the Ovando case. Sentenced to five years in state prison, he was released in April 2005 after spending fifty-seven months in custody. As part of his deal with law enforcement, Durden had consented to interviews with federal prosecutors in which he told a story markedly different from the one Perez had sold to the LAPD. While he confirmed that he and Perez had indeed planted guns, fabricated evidence, and perjured themselves, Durden disputed the claims made about widespread misconduct in the Rampart CRASH unit. It had been just him and Rafael, really, Durden said, and mostly Rafael. Since Durden's arrest in 2000, the LAPD had possessed an alternative account of the Rampart Scandal from a far more credible witness who had not been caught in any false statements. Instead, the department had chosen to stand by a proven liar to prop up the false narrative of the Rampart Scandal and support the task force probe based on it.

Apart from the complex scheming of Bernard Parks, what motivated the LAPD's investigation of the Rampart Scandal was very simple, said Cliff Armas: "The guys with a bar wanted a star, and the guys with a star wanted two stars. Career advancement was what it all boiled down to."

Finding their way to the best method of deconstructing Perez in front of a jury was not the main problem Sanders and Frank faced in the summer of 2007, however. Simply finding him was. Under the name Ray Lopez, Perez had proved remarkably slippery. "Part of it was the LAPD still protecting him," said Robleto. "They had helped him keep his exact location and other details secret, and they'd gotten other law enforcement agencies to help, too."

Through Chris Brizzolara, Sanders and Frank had eventually turned the task of compelling Perez's deposition over to the most storied process server and street investigator in Southern California, Thurston Limar Sr. "With him, we figure out that Perez has got some misdemeanor traffic deal in the Torrance court," Sanders recalled. "Rafael has been ducking us for a long time, so we wanna make sure we get him this time."

Perez had been charged with possessing a California driver's license in a name that was not legally his. On the day of his arraignment, Limar, who suffered from emphysema and sometimes got about aboard a motorized scooter, had hooked up his oxygen tank and stationed himself outside the courtroom where Perez was to appear. When he saw Perez walking down the hallway toward the courtroom, Limar maneuvered his scooter through the double doors that separated the anteroom from the courtroom, just in front of Perez, then let the papers he was holding slide off his lap onto the floor.

Unable to get past the scooter, Perez stooped to pick up the papers and extended them to Limar, who smiled and said, "No, those are for you." According to Limar, Perez became furious when he saw that he was holding a subpoena. Before he could exit the courthouse, Limar (since deceased) said in a sworn statement, "I was confronted by an individual who represented that he was the attorney for Mr. Perez. This individual told me that I 'was less than a man,' and that I was 'a lowdown motherfucker' and 'a son of a bitch.' He went on to state that: 'I ain't going to have any pity for you because you are going to be hit by a fucking bus,' and that he 'would not have any pity on your ass then.'"

Perez finally testified under oath on August 28, 2007, at Brizzolara's offices in Santa Monica. It had been agreed that Brizzolara and Gage would ask all the questions for the plaintiffs' side, with Sanders permitted to speak only when he was instructing the other two attorneys. Perez, who had "come in unbelievably cocky," Sanders recalled, was accompanied by his own attorney, John Yslas.

Brizzolara asked Perez if, while serving in West Bureau Narcotics, he had become a close friend of David Mack's. Yslas immediately began to object. What followed was an almost cartoonish colloquy in which Yslas did more talking than did his client. Yslas was "a veritable fount of what I believed were unmeritorious objections," recalled Brizzolara, whose frustration was only increased by the fact that when Perez was finally allowed to answer, his most common reply was, "I don't recall."

The point of Yslas's interruptions, Brizzolara knew, was delay. Federal court trials limited depositions to seven hours maximum, and Perez's attorney seemed determined to run out the clock before anything substantive was said.

Perez had to answer at least *some* questions, though. Brizzolara had gotten Perez to acknowledge that the keys to various LAPD vehicles were found in his home when it was searched after his arrest. Perez said he'd simply forgotten to turn the keys back in after driving the cars, but Sanders and Frank intended to show that Perez had driven one of those vehicles while helping to coordinate the Notorious B.I.G. murder. Perez also admitted that he and Durden were on duty the night of Biggie's slaying and that they were equipped with LAPD-issued Astro radios. Sanders and Frank would argue that Perez had used his radio to help coordinate the hit on Biggie.

Most important to the attorneys, however, was getting Perez to deny that he had any connection to Death Row Records. "I have never been into any Death Row Records studio, never ever. Not standing out in front, not going inside; never," he said. His answer meant that Perez was still unaware of the Kendrick Knox deposition. A jury that knew Perez had lied about ever being at Death Row's studio would be inclined to believe he was lying about the rest of his denials of association with Suge Knight and the Bloods gang.

During the deposition, Perez also denied his close relationship with Kenneth Boagni while the two of them were locked up together in the Lynwood jail, something that had been attested to by at least two witnesses who were prisoners there during this same period. Those two had each described seeing Perez and Boagni make pruno wine in a toilet and get drunk on it together. "He was an 11th Street gang member, tatted up, guy I wouldn't trust as far as I could throw him," Perez said of Boagni. "I had no type of—other than we were housed in the same pod—I didn't have a relationship with him."

Perez also played down his friendship with Mack, yet his answers on that subject revealed something never publicly disclosed: Perez and Sammy Martin had visited Mack while he was locked up following his arrest for the Bank of America robbery. Amid serial objections by Yslas, Perez declined to say what the three of them had discussed.

For Sanders, the signature moment of the deposition had come when Perez was being questioned by Brizzolara about a photograph of him recovered by Russell Poole, in which Perez was shown wearing a red sweat suit and flashing the West Coast gang sign. After Perez said he was merely "joking around" when he made the sign, Brizzolara asked, "Did you think gangs were a joke? Do you think the Bloods gang is a joke?"

Remembered Sanders, "I'm telling you the guy became a different person in that fraction of a second. He went from being cool and cocky to deathly scared that fast. I mean, the guy was havin' a fear-of-God experience right in front of my eyes. You couldn't have driven a needle up his behind. Perez wasn't afraid of the LAPD, and he wasn't afraid much of us, either. But he was scared out of his mind of the Bloods." That was a lever that would move Perez, Sanders knew, if only he could figure out the best way to use it.

Even though he denied any relationship with Bernard Parks's daughter Michelle, Perez said a little too much when he was asked about the photograph of Michelle Parks standing between himself and David Mack. "I can't answer that question because I could have been at a fund-raiser and David Mack is there, and I don't know who Parks's daughter is, and she decides to take a picture with Mack and I'm standing there. And if I answered no, unbeknownst to me I actually did [have my picture taken with Parks's daughter]. So if you have the picture and you can produce it, I can answer the question."

Said Sanders, "I figure he probably knew that photograph had been destroyed, but he couldn't be sure there wasn't another copy out there somewhere, so he had to play it cagey. And juries don't like cagey."

Perez was cagey again, though, when Brizzolara got him to agree that he had traveled to Las Vegas with Mack and Martin, along with his girlfriend and drug-dealing accomplice Veronica Quesada, on November 8, 1997, two days after the Bank of America robbery. "Had you told Veronica Quesada previously that she should be ready to go to Las Vegas on a day's notice?" Brizzolara asked. Perez no doubt suspected that Quesada had told this to the authorities while trying to get the drug charges against her reduced—and in fact she had. He thought for a long time before answering, then said, "Not to my knowledge."

When Brizzolara turned finally to the night of the Biggie murder, his questions were all based on the activity log Perez and Durden had turned in on the morning of March 9, 1997, just hours after the 12:40 a.m. slaying. There were no entries for any activity later than 11 p.m. on March 8. But he did recall what he was doing at 12:40 a.m. on March 9, Perez said: "Talking to La Mirada gang members" near the corner of Virgil and Normal streets in Rampart, miles from the Petersen Automotive Museum. Which gang members? Brizzolara wanted to know.

A: Just La Mirada gang members.

Q: Who in particular?

A: We didn't put down—or I didn't put down which particular gang members.

Q: How many gang members were there?

A: I have no idea.

Q: Was there more than one?

A: I don't recall.

Q: Was there more than fifty?

A: Don't recall.

Q: What were they doing?

A: Don't recall.

"Perez thought he was smart, thought he was makin' us look stupid," Sanders recalled. "Gettin' him to show that cocky grin of his on the witness stand was gonna be easy, I thought. And the jury would only need to see it once."

They hadn't gotten a lot during that seven-hour deposition, Sanders would admit, but it was enough, he figured. "The key to Perez is playing to his overconfidence," Sanders said. "And we do that by playin' dumb ourselves. I'm good at that."

CHAPTER THIRTEEN

Less than a month before the Rafael Perez deposition, the Los Angeles Police Department had given its first indication of how it intended to shut down the *Wallace v. Los Angeles* lawsuit and permanently erase the implication of LAPD officers in the murder of Notorious B.I.G. Once again, the department had chosen Chuck Philips as its conduit. Sanders and Frank took one look at the headline on the July 31, 2006, *Los Angeles Times* article "LAPD Renews Search for Rapper's Killer," saw Philips's byline, and immediately recognized that the city's attorneys were telegraphing their intentions.

The two attorneys did not have to read far to discover what those were. After reporting that Chief Bratton had "launched a task force of senior homicide detectives to hunt down [Biggie's] killer," Philips added, "Whatever new evidence the police turn up could bolster the city's contention that LAPD officers played no role in the rapper's death."

"So we knew right then that this so-called investigation wasn't gonna be about solving the case," Sanders said. "It was gonna be about protecting the city from us."

The Wallace Discovery Task Force was the official title of this new unit of detectives dedicated to what Bratton had chosen to call Operation Transparency.

Philips wrote, "The leading theory being pursued by the LAPD task force involves the possibility that Wallace was killed by a member of Compton's vicious Southside Crips gang as part of a bicoastal rap feud linked to Shakur's death." It was a theory that had been discarded early on by the first team of RHD investigators assigned to the Wallace case, Russell Poole and Fred Miller.

Philips swept aside Poole's investigation, with a sentence that read, "Poole did not interview Mack or Muhammad and he did not produce any evidence to support his theory." No mention was made of the fact that Poole had been prevented from interviewing Mack and Muhammad by his LAPD superiors. And the statement that the detective had not produced any evidence to support his theory was simply false; Poole had in fact produced a raft of it, as Philips knew. The reporter did briefly mention, however, that Amir Muhammad, the man who Poole believed shot Biggie, had been arrested five days earlier by Department of Motor Vehicles investigators on charges "connected to his possession of four false identifications."

"Just your average mortgage broker," Sanders said, "one who needs four phony driver's licenses in different names."

Sergio Robleto read the *Times* article from the point of view of one who knew exactly where the story was coming from. "Bill Bratton is more politician than police officer," he observed. "He knows how to game the system as well as anybody."

Robleto, who had consulted with Bratton on what became the consent decree that placed the LAPD under the supervision of the U.S. Justice Department, said he'd realized how adept and opportunistic his former colleague was when Bratton applied for the position of LAPD chief just weeks later. "And of course he got it."

He laughed after learning Bratton had recast the LAPD's Internal Affairs Division into what was now called the Professional Standards Bureau, Robleto recalled. Bratton had long been a big believer in the notion that words changed not only perception but also reality.

Still, he had admired Bratton, Robleto said, until he read in the *Times* how the chief had responded to Judge Cooper's declaration of a mistrial in the *Wallace v. Los Angeles* case. "The failure to turn over some documents does not equal a deliberate cover-up by the LAPD," stated Bratton, who suggested that "better tracking procedures for case files" were all that was needed.

"Katz had been caught red-handed," Robleto said, "and Chief Bratton is saying it was at worst a careless mistake. I lost a lot of respect for him that day."

He might have read even more into Bratton's motives, Robleto said, if he'd known then that the two lead investigators on the Operation Transparency task force the chief had "launched" were detectives Daryn Dupree and Greg Kading. "If I had wanted to make sure a crime never got solved and that the investigation could be used as a cover-up," Robleto said, "giving the case to a couple of guys with the kind of baggage those two carry would have been exactly my strategy."

In 2000, FBI agents conducting a wiretap had overheard Dupree talking on the phone with his wife about a target of a federal drug-trafficking probe. He shouldn't be using the phone he was speaking to her on during that brief conversation, Dupree had said, because it was "chipped." What Dupree meant was that he was talking on a burner phone that had been cloned to use an illegally captured cellular account. The feds told the LAPD's Internal Affairs Division, which discovered that Dupree had improperly entered the department's computer system on eight occasions to obtain information about the girlfriend of the target in the FBI investigation.

Nevertheless, Dupree escaped prosecution, and Robleto found this "amazing." The district attorney assigned to the case acknowledged that Dupree had broken the law by using a chipped phone, but reasoned that the detective could argue he had broken into the computer system while investigating a crime. "In the interest of justice," the memo explained, "disciplinary action against Officer Dupree would be best handled administratively." At his Board of Rights hearing, Dupree was found guilty on both the chipped phone and the illicit computer access charges and suspended without pay for forty-four days.

"A troubling result," Robleto called it. "He should have been fired."

There was even less doubt that Greg Kading was a bad cop, Robleto said: "A bunch of federal judges called him one."

Robleto was referring to a Ninth Circuit Court of Appeals ruling that had condemned Kading's conduct on the morning of March 18, 1999. Kading was a uniformed officer assigned to the LAPD's Newton Division in South-Central Los Angeles back then. On the morning in question, he had been accompanied by two agents from the federal Bureau of Alcohol, Tobacco, and Firearms and a California state parole officer when they arrived at what they believed to be the residence of a Four-Trey Crips gang member named Janae Jamerson.

Jamerson was actually in state prison at the time, but Kading and the others had failed to check his status before arriving at the house.

The only people in the home were Jamerson's girlfriend, Darla Motley, and their five-week-old son. Motley, who had been sleeping with her baby, answered the banging on the front door in her pajamas. It was Kading who spoke, Motley said, identifying himself as an LAPD officer, stating that the man standing next to him was Jamerson's parole officer, then claiming that he and the other officers had a search warrant. In fact, they had no warrant, and the man with Kading was not Jamerson's parole officer.

Motley said that Jamerson did not live there and that anyway he was in the penitentiary. Kading responded by telling her that if she did not let them in, she would be arrested and her baby placed in foster care. This latter threat persuaded her to open the security door, Motley said. The moment she did, Kading shoved her aside, drawing his gun as he entered the house with one of the ATF agents. Motley told them her baby was in the back bedroom, and that was where Kading headed,. When she heard her baby screaming, she ran to the bedroom, Motley said, and saw Kading pointing his gun at her son, demanding to know where Jamerson was. Only when the ATF agent stepped through the door did Kading lower his weapon. During a search of the room that lasted twenty minutes, Kading taunted and mocked her the entire time, according to Motley, while she tried to comfort her baby. As he left the house, Kading shouted that she should let Jamerson's mother know "Newton Street's been here," recalled Motley. She moved a few weeks later, afraid to remain in the Newton Division area.

Motley filed a federal lawsuit against the LAPD accusing Kading of unlawful search and of using excessive force against her infant son. The case made it to the Ninth Circuit, where a panel of judges sided with Motley. The opinion, written by Judge Betty B. Fletcher, was damning in its assessment of Kading's conduct. Not only had Kading shown "no respect for Motley, her baby, her home, or her privacy," Fletcher wrote, but he had "lied to Motley" about her boyfriend's parole officer being present and his own possession of a search warrant. While police officers were to be broadly given qualified immunity for their actions during a search, Fletcher wrote, Kading had forfeited it by "pointing a deadly weapon at a tiny infant." The judge described his conduct as not simply harassing but "terrorizing."

Eventually Kading would win separation from the Motley case by arguing that "the LAPD never trained him to know that pointing a gun at a baby was an improper procedure," said Robleto, who had looked into the case. "Can you imagine? And this is the guy, along with Dupree, that is put on the task force to investigate the Biggie murder. To me, that tells you all you need to know about what the LAPD was really up to."

As much as Sanders hoped he might be, Chuck Philips wasn't going away—at least not yet. On September 26, 2007, a month after the Perez deposition, the *Los Angeles Times* ran a story on the front page of its Metro section under the headline "Inmate Recants Story About LAPD Link to Rapper's Slaying." The article focused on Waymond Anderson, a former R&B recording star who in April 1997 told Wilshire detectives that Suge Knight had previously offered him the contract on Biggie's life. Anderson, now serving a life sentence on an arson-murder conviction, later told Robbery-Homicide detectives that the hit on Biggie resulted from a conspiracy that included not only Knight but also Rafael Perez and David Mack.

But then Anderson began to change his story. Two *Los Angeles Times* articles by Chuck Philips published in January and April 2007 made a seemingly compelling case that the singer had been wrongly convicted. Not long afterward, Anderson claimed during a deposition in the Biggie case that his story of LAPD involvement in the rapper's murder was a fabrication invented as part of "a scam," one prompted in part by Perry Sanders's offer of money if he would implicate Perez and Mack in the crime. Sanders hired a Los Angeles lawyer to send the *Times* a series of letters threatening a libel suit if it published Anderson's claims against him. The *Times* ran the story anyway, replete with phrasing that portrayed Anderson as a credible witness whose "explosive testimony" had been an "unexpected twist" in the Notorious B.I.G. lawsuit.

Sanders had been quoted in the article as calling Anderson's allegations against him "100 percent demonstrably false." "This is wholesale, made-up-out-of-whole-cloth perjury," Sanders told the *Times*. Anderson "clearly would like to please Mr. Philips, because he's singing his song, first, second and third verse and certainly the chorus."

Philips retorted that Sanders's accusations against him were "idiotic," adding, "This guy clearly doesn't understand what an investigative reporter does for a living. I don't make stories up. I report them." *Times* editor in chief James O'Shea backed his reporter, calling Sanders's claims against Philips "utterly groundless."

Sanders would learn while sitting with his new bride Lorn Lee at a coffee shop in Santa Monica that the U.S. attorney for the Central District of California had launched an investigation based on the allegations of attempted bribery reported by the *Times*. "Rob was telling me I might lose my right to practice in California," he recalled. When Sanders prepared a press release and a court motion to counter Anderson's allegations, Philips wrote a letter to the inmate telling him, "It's all bullshit desperation on Perry Sanders' part. And it will make him look even worse when the truth comes out."

But on November 13, 2007, after reviewing the evidence presented by Sanders to refute the claims Anderson had made against him, Judge Cooper issued an order stating that Sanders and his colleagues "provide substantial evidence to prove that Mr. Anderson is a liar," and dismissing his claims. The *Times* did not report a word about this ruling.

Then, in July 2008, during a hearing on his habeas corpus petition in the arson-murder case, Anderson informed the court that his claims against Sanders had been made at the behest of Chuck Philips. Don Vincent was heavily implicated as well.

Vincent had said to him "that if I kept saying that David Mack and Rafael Perez was responsible for the murder of Biggie Smalls, I would never get out of jail," Anderson also told the judge. He was threatened by Suge Knight as well, Anderson told the judge, via "kites" (tightly folded letters) smuggled into prison by Chuck Philips. Philips had also brought him materials provided by Vincent. These were an assortment of documents from the Notorious B.I.G. lawsuit, Anderson said, passed on so that he could familiarize himself with the case as part of a scheme "to disqualify Perry Sanders from the Christopher Wallace case." He made the claim that Sanders attempted to bribe him, Anderson said, only "because Chuck Philips told me to."

The *Times* ran a brief story about what Anderson had said in the habeas hearing that ended with a quote from Philips: "That never happened. I'm flabbergasted by this whole thing. This is the ultimate betrayal."

By then, though, there wasn't much more damage that could be done to Philips's reputation. He had taken care of that himself with a front-page story for the *Times* that ran on March 19, 2008, under the headline "An Attack on Tupac Shakur Launched a Hip-Hop War." Based on "FBI records obtained by The Times," Philips wrote, the feds were sitting on informant statements that the shooting of Shakur at Quad Studios in 1994 had been arranged by talent manager James Rosemond (better known as "Jimmy Henchman") in collusion with

Jacques "Haitian Jack" Agnant and "promoter" James Sabatino in order to curry favor with Puffy Combs.

There was one considerable problem with the article: the "FBI records" that had been Philips's main source were fakes created by James Sabatino using a prison typewriter and a photocopier. The Smoking Gun website figured out within forty-eight hours of the publication of Philips's article that "the *Times* appears to have been hoaxed by an imprisoned con man."

Jimmy Henchman's lawyer Marc Lichtman issued a statement reading, "I would suggest to Mr. Philips and his editors that they immediately print an apology and take out their checkbooks." Puffy Combs's attorney Howard Weitzman sent the *Times* a letter that not only demanded a retraction but also warned that the Philips article met the legal standard for "actual malice" that would allow a public figure like Combs to sue for libel.

On March 27, 2008, nine days after Philips's article had run on its front page, the *Times* published a new page-one story under the headline "The Times Apologizes over Article on Rapper." A statement from Philips was quoted: "In relying on documents that I now believe were fake, I failed to do my job. I'm sorry." His editor, Marc Duvoisin, issued his own statement: "We should not have let ourselves be fooled. That we were is as much my fault as Chuck's. I deeply regret that we have let our readers down."

Philips paid the price for his mistake. In July 2008, he was among 150 editorial employees who were let go by the *Times* as part of a staff reduction meant to address the paper's increasingly dire financial condition. It was a steep fall for a reporter who had won a Pulitzer Prize nine years earlier.

Richard Valdemar, still aching over the demise of Mike Robinson, complained bitterly in *Police* magazine that Philips had not been "outright fired."

"The *Times* never admitted its faults or apologized to the victims of the suspects it protected and witnesses it exposed," Valdemar wrote. "The *Los Angeles Times* has the attitude that it has done nothing wrong, and it has nothing to apologize for."

Waymond Anderson, whose hopes for release from state prison had been raised by a Philips story that ran under the headline "New Evidence Could Set Singer Free," would learn on December 11, 2008, that his murder conviction had been affirmed by William C. Ryan, the judge who had heard his habeas corpus plea. Anderson would be spending the rest of his life behind bars.

CHAPTER FOURTEEN

Three months after the Rafael Perez deposition, the city got serious about asserting investigative privilege to shut down the *Wallace v. Los Angeles* lawsuit.

Just two days after Judge Cooper allowed the plaintiffs to add more LAPD officials to the lawsuit, Gerald Chaleff took the witness stand in the locked courtroom of Magistrate Judge Stephen J. Hillman. There, Chaleff made the argument that the LAPD's "ongoing investigation" in the Christopher Wallace murder would be jeopardized by the sharing of "open clues," and that therefore a raft of evidence in the case should be sealed and made off-limits to the plaintiffs' discovery motions.

"I get a call from Perry, who says, 'You need to get down to the court right now, because there's this in camera hearing going on with Chaleff on the stand,'" Brizzolara recalled. "So Brad and I rush down there, and sure enough, Chaleff is on the stand laying the foundation for their claim of investigative privilege."

But he and Gage couldn't get into the courtroom; the doors were locked. "I don't remember a single other case where the judge has locked the courtroom doors to have a hearing," Brizzolara said. "I've gone back into chambers, but never seen a locked courtroom."

Eventually the magistrate's bailiff admitted the two attorneys. Gage, who hadn't had time even to put on a suit, began to challenge Chaleff with a series of aggressive questions. "Chaleff didn't like what

I was asking him so much that he tried to stand up and walk off the witness stand," Gage recalled. Hillman made the witness sit back down, but just moments later agreed with a suggestion by the city's attorneys that he review the disputed evidence in chambers—with Chaleff there to interpret it, and the attorneys for the Wallace family excluded. What Chaleff testified to on the stand can't be reported, because every word of it was placed under a protective order by Hillman, who was handling the case's evidentiary hearings.

Hillman's order, affirmed by Cooper, still stands—nearly eleven years later.

"All I'm sure of is that whatever Chaleff said in there, which we will never know, made the difference," Sanders said.

On January 17, 2008, Hillman issued a ruling that stated, "Based on Gerald Chaleff's testimony at the November 28, 2007, hearing, the court finds that defendant City of Los Angeles has sufficiently met its threshold burden of assertion that the certain documents at issue are covered by an active investigation privilege invoked by the defendant."*

It was the beginning of the end for a lawsuit that had already gone on for six years. Even if they couldn't believe it, Sanders and his colleagues had seen it coming for a long time.

From the time the Internal Affairs Division complaint form for Case No. 01-0190 had been produced before Cooper, the city and the LAPD had played a maddening game of hide-and-seek with other documents. "The LAPD withheld forty thousand pages of evidence—all related to Perez—that we had to fight to see," Gage recalled. The police department insisted for months that it could not find Perez's

---

*I offered Chaleff repeated opportunities to explain his arguments to the magistrate and what he based them on. First, he told me he didn't recall any such appearance before Hillman, and demanded that I give him a date and evidence that such a hearing had taken place. After providing this, I called three additional times to repeat my questions. On each occasion, Chaleff told me he would get back to me later that day with a statement on his own behalf and a response from his friend William Bratton. "I promise," Chaleff said each time, and each time he failed to call back.

daily field activity report for March 9, 1997—the date of the Biggie murder—"then after being threatened by the judge suddenly said they found it, somewhere on the mezzanine level of Parker Center," Brizzolara remembered. "It was like somebody just happened to notice it lying in a corner."

After the production of the Internal Affairs complaint form on the LAPD "investigation" of Perez and Mack in the Biggie murder, Sanders and Frank had moved for summary judgment on the basis of the city's continued concealment of evidence. "Judge Cooper was strong," Brizzolara said. "I don't think she was swayed by political considerations—until we brought the motion for default judgment and an award of hundreds of millions of dollars. That was *too* much. She said, 'No, the jury will have to decide that.'"

Said Sanders, "When the city realized they were in no real danger of losin' the case by hidin' evidence, they were emboldened."

On July 31, 2006, the same day that the *Los Angeles Times* announced the launch of the LAPD's "Operation Transparency," the city's attorneys responded to a discovery demand by the plaintiffs with a "privilege log" listing 183 "items" that they were withholding on the grounds of attorney-client privilege, attorney work product, and active investigative privilege. On October 2, 2006, Sanders, Frank, and company sent the city a letter challenging the "privileged" claim for each of the 183 clues being withheld. After a meeting on October 10, the city withdrew its assertion of privilege for 71 clues and the plaintiffs withdrew their demand for 12 others, leaving exactly 100 items in dispute.

Chaleff had weighed in on November 14, 2006, with a declaration in which he claimed that, based on his "personal knowledge," he could state that the LAPD "is conducting an active homicide investigation pertaining to the murder of Christopher Wallace," and that he himself was "involved in the investigation."

"That was red flag right there," Brizzolara said. "Why was Chaleff being allowed to look at clues from an ongoing homicide case? He wasn't an investigator or an investigative supervisor."

The LAPD was classifying clues in the Wallace case as either "open" or "closed," Chaleff explained in his declaration. Closed clues could be turned over to the plaintiffs, but open clues could not be. "Disclosure of these open clues to any third party, regardless of any preferred protective order, would potentially jeopardize the ongoing investigation, and the LAPD therefore objects to the production of open clue files," Chaleff concluded.

The battle that might very well decide the war had begun, and all the attorneys on the case knew it. On the plaintiffs' side, the lawyers were increasingly confounded by Judge Cooper's discovery rulings. "I had no clue—still have no clue—why we weren't allowed to take Nino Durden's deposition when she let us take Perez's," Brizzolara said. "And I have no idea why the judge ruled that we couldn't take Sammy Martin's, either."

The most stunning and disappointing ruling Judge Cooper made was that the plaintiffs would not be permitted to take a deposition from Kendrick Knox. "It might not have mattered, because we had his declaration," Brizzolara said. "But if he died, his declaration wouldn't have been admissible, while his deposition would have been."

"So that ruling might have had the effect of putting Knox's life in danger," said Gage, "considering who the people on the other side were in this case."

Brizzolara and Gage, who had been handling LAPD-related cases for years, found themselves increasingly appalled by the department's maneuvering in *Wallace v. Los Angeles*. "I already knew that the main thing the LAPD uses Internal Affairs for is to cover up things they don't want the public to know," Brizzolara said. "But it went to a new level in this case. And look who headed up IA at the beginning and at the end of this case: Parks and Berkow, guys who have no scruples whatsoever."

"What has always troubled me about this case is that it's not just Parks," Gage said. "Bratton was just as responsible for the cover-up."

"Bratton is one of the villains of this story," Brizzolara agreed. "He could walk through raindrops, but he was not a good guy."

It looked increasingly as if Gerry Chaleff had replaced Berkow as Bratton's bulwark against the *Wallace v. Los Angeles* lawsuit. On October 11, 2007, Chaleff submitted to the court a declaration that the city had produced "each of the closed clues from the Wallace homicide investigation," then in the next paragraph conceded there was one clue being held back that "potentially relates to the plaintiff's theory of the case." He requested a one-on-one in camera meeting with the judge to discuss it. "That was the beginning of the city and the LAPD trying to have private conversations with the judge about why they needed to withhold certain evidence from us," Brizzolara recalled. "We should have fought it harder right then, but we were waiting to see what the judge ruled."

When Hillman and Cooper each ruled that the city could withhold that one clue, Sanders and company began to fight back. On November 20, 2007, they filed a complaint that the city was refusing to provide clues "relating to the five named 'Death Row' individuals [in their new lawsuit filing], regardless of whether or not they relate to the Wallace murder." The city answered that it couldn't explain why it could not turn over the clues except in an in camera hearing from which the plaintiffs' attorneys were excluded, because "the explanation itself would potentially compromise [the LAPD] investigation."

Said Sanders, "They started makin' these kinds of Catch-22 arguments, and the court bought them."

By January 2008, when Cooper agreed that the LAPD had reopened the Wallace murder investigation, the plaintiffs were trying to push back against a steamroller that was coming downhill at them. "The city said they couldn't turn some of these new clues over because they would interfere with the investigation, and we said, 'What? We have a protective order. We *can't* reveal these clues. We just want to see them,'" Brizzolara recalled. "But a lot of these evidentiary hearings were before magistrates who looked at us very skeptically."

When the plaintiffs asked to have at least the opportunity to review a transcript of the sealed proceeding at which Chaleff had testified before Hillman on November 28, 2007, first the magistrate refused, then Judge Cooper backed him. Six days later, on January 30, 2008, the city submitted a list of 978 clues it had classified as confidential for in camera inspection. "Again, they're all in the judge's chambers looking at this stuff, and we don't get to see any of it," Brizzolara recalled. "They were slowly tying our hands."

On February 6, Chaleff submitted a declaration that only seven of the clues on that list were "open clues in the Wallace murder investigation." One of the seven clues, though, was a hard drive that could have contained tens, hundreds, or thousands of individual clues, so far as the plaintiffs knew.

"When I say that the city pulled out all the stops to keep this case from coming back to court, that's an understatement," said Brizzolara, whose frustration doubled when Hillman ruled on March 11, 2008, that clues "00001 through 00978" would remain under seal and withheld from the plaintiffs. Citing the in camera testimony of Chaleff, Hillman agreed that "the disclosure of the documents would likely discourage people from cooperating with the police." He was rejecting the plaintiffs' offer to look at the clues under a protective order, Hillman added, because that would not "adequately protect the anonymity of witnesses or the integrity of the ongoing murder investigation."

At a June 9, 2008, hearing before Judge Cooper, Brizzolara challenged Hillman's ruling, detailing how the city and the LAPD had used Operation Transparency as a screen to prevent the plaintiffs from seeing the evidence in the case. Many of the clues the city had tried to hold back weren't "new" at all, Brizzolara pointed out: the daily field activity reports for the night of the Biggie murder, for instance, "as well as numerous documents prepared by and/or transmitted to Det. Steve Katz." The court should bear in mind that "Det. Katz is the disgraced former lead detective on the case who was found to have willfully secreted documents regarding the involvement of LAPD offices in the homicide," noted Brizzolara. The city, he went on, "has employed the ongoing investigative privilege since the time that [the

LAPD] was caught withholding documents directly relevant to the plaintiffs' case."

When the judge agreed with the city that even the various documents prepared by Katz were protected work product that should be placed under seal, the attorneys on the plaintiffs' side knew they were being put in an untenable position.

"We were facing the prospect of trial by ambush," Brizzolara explained. "They could have admitted one of these clues as evidence and we wouldn't even know what it was, wouldn't know whether it was one of the protected clues or not. We'd have no way to prepare and no way to respond."

Added Gage, "They could walk us down a road where we didn't know what we were facing. They could have decided a clue was invalid or no longer relevant and we wouldn't know that. Or it could mean something, but we wouldn't know what. In our wildest dreams we might not have been able to guess what was coming at us."

After consulting with his colleagues and his clients, Sanders decided that the only course open to them was to negotiate some sort of suspension of the lawsuit until the LAPD's alleged investigation had run its course. That became imperative after Judge Cooper's death in January 2010. The new judge assigned to the case, Jacqueline Nguyen, made it clear from the first that she had no intention of lifting any of the protective orders that had been placed on the evidence in the Wallace murder investigation.

On April 2, 2010, the two sides of the *Wallace v. Los Angeles* lawsuit signed a joint stipulation to dismiss without prejudice. Part of the deal was a "tolling" agreement that allowed the case to be refiled at any time and that suspended the statute of limitations. "The point is to give the LAPD another year to close the case, which they keep claiming they are close to doing," Sanders said. Whatever Chaleff and others were saying in their closeted sessions with the judges must have provided a strong indication that Operation Transparency was on the brink of arrests and criminal charges, Sanders and his colleagues reasoned. "What my clients want, first and foremost, is to see the killers of Christopher Wallace brought to justice," Sanders said. "This isn't about money for them."

However, the prospect of an enormous payday *was* a motivation for most of the attorneys on the case. The disconnect from the objectives of their clients—one client in particular, Voletta Wallace—was creating strains within the legal team. Brizzolara and Gage both felt they had enough to take the case to trial, even under the difficult circumstances created by the protective orders that had been put on much of the evidence. "No doubt in my mind, at all," said Gage. "I've won millions of dollars in cases where I didn't have a tenth of what we had in this case."

Brizzolara was concerned by how the dismissal was being spun in the local media. "When we moved to dismiss our own case without prejudice, it had absolutely nothing to do with the merits and the *L.A. Times* knew that, but of course they didn't report it that way."

The *New York Times* article about the dismissal did include a long quote from Sanders, who "insisted the case was being withdrawn only to avoid interfering with what he called a 'reinvigorated' police investigation," as the newspaper put it. Sanders had also "emphasized that since the suit was dismissed without prejudice, it could be refiled," the *New York Times* reported: "'The criminal investigation has been opened back up full-force,' Mr. Sanders said. 'The bottom line is that we did this because the family only wanted justice to be done.'"

What Sanders didn't say was that eight years of litigation had worn on Voletta Wallace. She had endured cancer treatment during much of that time and was increasingly concerned not only about the toll on her own health, but also about the way the constant drama of the case was affecting her grandchildren, now teenagers, who had "basically grown up with this thing going on around them," as Sanders put it. Also, "Voletta felt that the mistrial and the evidence that came out afterward proved police involvement in the murder and that the case had basically been won," Sanders said. "Now she wanted to believe that the LAPD was finally committed to solving her son's murder, and she wanted to see what they did with that commitment."

The dismissal was a "wait-and-see strategy," Sanders said.

In the meantime, the evidence that had been the subject of court disputes consuming most of the past three years in the case was locked up in a safe-deposit box at the First Street Federal Courthouse in Los Angeles. Clues 00001 through 00978 were all inside that box, along with transcripts of the hearings that had taken place behind closed doors.

"None of that stuff is going anyplace," Sanders said.

CHAPTER FIFTEEN

Sanders and his colleagues would not obtain even a fleeting glimpse into what had gone on inside the LAPD's purported investigation of the Christopher Wallace murder—its Operation Transparency—until late 2011, more than a year after the dismissal of the lawsuit. Even then, what they learned came to them indirectly, through former LAPD detective Greg Kading's self-published book titled *Murder Rap*.

Sanders knew that Kading had left the LAPD under a cloud more than a year earlier. For a few days in early autumn 2009, the Los Angeles media had been filled with stories about how U.S. District Court judge Steven V. Wilson had thrown out more than fifty federal convictions because of what the judge described as Kading's "reckless disregard for the truth."

Before joining the Wallace Discovery Task Force, Kading had been a member of Operation Corrido, a federally run team of agencies from across Southern California that made an immense racketeering case against a Los Angeles supermarket chain owner named George Torres. He was accused of using his business as a front for the drug-trafficking empire he allegedly maintained by, among other things, ordering the murders of those who threatened it. In April 2009, Torres was convicted in federal court on more than fifty counts. Five months later, Judge Wilson voided every one of those guilty verdicts and placed most of the blame for his decision on Kading.

In a scathing 147-page ruling, Wilson stated that Kading had unlawfully obtained the cooperation of witnesses by, among other things, making "promises of immunity, money, and benefits, while in prison, to drug dealers who faced decades of prison time." The judge was also infuriated by his discovery that Kading had misquoted conversations caught on a wiretap of Torres's phone in a search warrant affidavit.

Wilson had been swayed by the testimony of former LAPD detective Steve Strong, the investigator for Torres's attorneys. He had known Kading when they were both in the department, Strong recalled, adding, "and I thought he was a good guy." Strong's wife had been Kading's LAPD training officer. "She thought he was okay, too," Strong said. "But then I started listening to the tapes of his witness interviews and I was shocked. I couldn't believe how overboard the guy went."

On those tapes, Kading could be heard offering the sole government witness in an alleged murder "big money" if would testify that Torres had ordered the execution of one Jose Maldonado. Judge Wilson would say it was obvious from listening to the tape of the interview that Kading had then supplied the witness with the answers he wanted to hear. "It all had to do with a guy [Maldonado] who worked for Mr. Torres and disappeared," Strong recalled. "Nobody knew where he was. There was no evidence of any kind. Some people said he'd gone back to Mexico. But Kading got this one guy to say he'd been killed on orders from Torres." On another tape, Kading had persuaded a second key witness to testify against Torres by promising to have domestic violence charges against his brother dropped. "When they put me on the stand, I told the judge Kading was totally out of control and had no idea what he was doing," Strong recalled.

The government would argue that Kading had not violated any LAPD protocols in those interviews. "Kading was telling them there's no informant manual," Strong recalled. "So they put me on the stand and I said yes, there is, and that it offers very clear instructions that Kading blatantly violated. The judge tells the U.S.

attorney on the case, 'I want that manual.' Kading again says there is no manual, and the U.S. attorney tells that to the court. But a senior LAPD officer took the stand and said, 'Yes, there is a manual.' The judge came unglued and said he wanted the manual in his courtroom in two hours."

After the manual was delivered and Judge Wilson had had an opportunity to read it, "he told Kading to get out of the courthouse and never come back," Strong remembered.

Sanders was keenly interested in what *Murder Rap* might reveal about the LAPD's "reinvigorated" investigation of the Biggie murder. Mostly, what the book told him, Sanders said, was that Operation Transparency had been an utter sham dedicated to a single purpose: steering public attention away from the implication of police officers in the assassination of Notorious B.I.G. Virtually everything Kading had written about Russell Poole's work on the case was riddled with misrepresentations, distortions, and lies of both omission and commission. In short, Sanders said, "What I learned from reading his book was that the investigation was a fraud, and so was Kading."

The falsest claim Kading made in his book was that what he called the "exculpatory truth" of Poole's theory that David Mack and Amir Muhammad were involved in Biggie's murder had been "painstakingly uncovered" by the LAPD investigation. In fact, the truth had been sloppily slathered over.

Kading's relentless misrepresentation of Poole's investigation, and of the evidence that implicated Mack and Muhammad in the Biggie murder, was what most damned him in Sanders's mind. The former Operation Transparency detective had portrayed Muhammad as the innocent victim of a witch hunt that Poole had created out of gossamer-thin evidence. Muhammad had "a reasonable alibi" for the visit to Mack in jail after his bank robbery arrest that Poole had made so much of, Kading wrote: He was simply checking on an old friend who had gotten into trouble with the law. That Kading knew, but made no mention of, the fact that Muhammad had used a name that wasn't legally his, a false address, a false Social Security number, and an out-of-service phone number to arrange that visit was just one among many glaring distortions of the truth.

An equally if not even more telling omission by Kading was Muhammad's 1998 "gun brandishing" arrest in Chino and the subsequent shooting deaths of the couple he had menaced—again, facts that it could be proved Kading knew about. Muhammad's arrest by Department of Motor Vehicles investigators for possession of four falsely obtained driver's licenses also went unmentioned in *Murder Rap*.

Kading was even more misleading in his "analysis" of the evidence that Poole believed pointed to Mack as part of the conspiracy to kill Biggie. He began creating his portrait of Poole as a monomaniac who'd lost sight of the forest for the trees by suggesting it was the discovery that David Mack owned a black Impala that most persuaded the detective of Mack's involvement in the Biggie murder. The truth was that, while hearing about the Impala found in Mack's garage when he was arrested for the Bank of America robbery was what first interested Poole in that particular dirty cop, the vehicle was not even among the top five pieces of evidence Poole had cited in his outline of the Mack-Muhammad theory of the Notorious B.I.G. assassination. Kading dealt with those more significant clues by distorting them, omitting them, or simply misrepresenting them.

There was no mention in *Murder Rap*, for instance, of the fact that the same brand of bullets that had killed Biggie—the GECO ammunition that the LAPD's own investigative reports described as "very rare"—had been found in David Mack's home after he was arrested. Kading did acknowledge that Mack had taken sick days just prior to the Biggie murder, but ignored what made that significant in Poole's eyes—the fact that Mack had taken one other set of sick days during 1997 and 1998, coinciding with the Bank of America robbery. To Poole, this was evidence that Mack "took time off when he wanted to plan and commit major crimes."

The fact that key witnesses, including Biggie's close friend Damion Butler, had stated that they saw Mack at the Petersen

Automotive Museum on the night of the murder was also left out of
Kading's critique of the Mack-Muhammad theory.

What Kading additionally failed to mention was the implication
of Rafael Perez as Mack's partner in setting up the Biggie murder.
There was no consideration of the sworn testimony of Kenneth Boagni
or Felipe Sanchez, or of the adjudicators who heard that testimony
and believed it; no reference whatsoever to the sworn testimony of
Mario Ha'mmonds; and not a word anywhere in *Murder Rap* about
the multiple additional clues that pointed to the involvement of Perez
in the Biggie slaying.

At times Kading made statements that were simply false. The
most brazen was his claim that only one LAPD officer, Richard
McCauley, had ever worked for Death Row. But Kading knew (not
least from reading *LAbyrinth*) that in 1998, under pressure from an
LAPD Internal Affairs investigator, Death Row's director of security,
Reggie Wright Jr., had named three other officers working for the
label. Kading also failed to mention that Kendrick Knox had identified Mack and Perez as among the several LAPD officers he saw
coming and going at Death Row's studio while he was conducting
surveillance of it.

The strangest and most insidious line of attack Kading made
against Poole involved his contention that the detective should have
recognized that the investigation of David Mack was an Internal
Affairs matter better left to IA detectives. "What Poole saw as a
concerted cover-up was instead a well-established precedent, making clear distinctions among all the various investigations in which
he had become involved," Kading wrote. To Sergio Robleto, "That
was maybe the most ridiculous thing I've ever heard about how
the LAPD operates." Apart from the fact that the LAPD Internal
Affairs Division never investigated Mack in any meaningful way,
and in fact contributed considerably to the cover-up Poole had
been complaining about back in 1998, Robleto noted, "IA does not
investigate homicides. That was Russ's assignment: to investigate
the murder of Notorious B.I.G. And a murder investigation always

takes priority over any other kind of investigation. Nothing is or ever should be held back from the detectives on a homicide case. What Kading wrote about that was to me the clearest evidence that he's nothing but a shill for the LAPD."

Kading's criticism of Poole's "reliance on jailhouse informants to support his case" was especially hypocritical. In the Torres case, Kading not only had relied almost entirely on jailhouse informants to make *his* case, but had persuaded them to say what he wanted them to say by offering inducements he had neither the authority nor the ability to deliver. The only "jailhouse informant" Poole had relied on in any significant way was Michael Robinson, known to be one of the most reliable CIs in Los Angeles County history. The contrast between the two detectives couldn't have been clearer.

"When I read the book, I thought, this has got to be a gag," Sanders recalled. "Because anybody who knew the case would have easily seen what a liar Kading was." What the former detective seemed to be counting on, though, was that most of his readers had no more than a passing knowledge of the Biggie murder investigation, and that those few who were better informed—LAPD officials and assistant city attorneys, mostly—would not be inclined to challenge a narrative that debunked the theory of cop involvement in the slaying.

It was in his description of how he had "solved" the murder of Notorious B.I.G., though—and along the way Tupac Shakur's slaying as well—that Kading wove a truly tangled web. Kading's claim was that he and his partner Dupree had determined that Biggie's killer was Wardell "Poochie" Fouse, Suge Knight's thug who had been shot to death in 2003. The only evidence they had to support this was what they had been told, according to Kading, by "a forty-two-year-old single mother of two by the name of Theresa Swann." Swann, as Kading described her, was Suge Knight's former girlfriend who had come to Los Angeles from Ohio and lived under an assortment of aliases that included Theresa Reed and Theresa Cross. The story Theresa told, according to Kading, was that Suge had hired Poochie to assassinate Biggie, and that she had actually delivered the money

($9,000) to Fouse while he was locked up by posing as David Kenner's legal secretary.

Kading's account omitted one extremely salient fact: there *was* no Theresa Swann. No Theresa Reed or Theresa Cross, either. No such person or persons.

There was, however, a Tammie Hawkins.

Hawkins was a Suge Knight baby mama who had been one of Suge's two main accomplices, along with Reggie Wright Jr., in concealing and conveying assets in the aftermath of the Death Row Records bankruptcy filing made in April 2006. Through a pair of companies Knight had set up in her name, Digital Revolution Holdings and Dimples Merchandising, Hawkins had been the pipeline for the hundreds of thousands of dollars Suge was funneling out of Death Row, as well as for the far more valuable master recordings of unreleased songs, including those by Tupac Shakur and Snoop Dogg.

Kading had written about his discovery of the masters in a Detroit storage facility as if it were the product of crack work by Dupree and himself. In fact, the two detectives had done little more than follow in the footsteps of the bankruptcy attorney who had been appointed trustee of the Death Row debt, R. Todd Neilson. It was Neilson who had found the $658,848 in cash that had been wired to Hawkins by Knight, and who had traced the missing master recordings to the companies in her name.

Hawkins was a criminal who had followed her criminal brother to Los Angeles from Detroit. Jerry Hawkins was a member of the Lueders Park Piru Bloods, and it was through him that she had met Suge Knight. Even as Tammie Hawkins was becoming Kading's sole source of the claim that Poochie Fouse had killed Biggie Smalls, the woman had been the target of a task force assembled by the Los Angeles County Sheriff Department's Commercial Crimes Unit. According to those investigators, Hawkins was one of the leaders of a ring that had been using fraudulent loan applications to buy new automobiles that it then quickly resold. When Hawkins's house was raided, sheriff's deputies recovered a pistol that had been reported stolen in Seattle. That house, on Thoroughbred Street in Rancho Cucamonga, a San Bernardino County community in the foothills of the San Gabriel Mountains, had once been the home of Suge Knight and his wife Sharitha, but in 2001 was purchased by Hawkins at the bargain price of $10,000.

Kading did not write a word in *Murder Rap* about how Hawkins had become his witness. In fact, the former detective had not offered solid evidence to support *any* of his claims, neither LAPD documents nor witness statements. "His whole attitude was, 'Take my word for it,'" Robleto said. "Sorry, there's no way I'm taking Kading's word for anything. I would need proof." Sanders was told by a source he would not name that "Suge's attorney" had provided Hawkins to Kading. But that made little sense, given that his ex-girlfriend had told the LAPD, according to Kading, that Suge was behind the hit on Biggie. "Why would Suge give Kading a witness who would say he was responsible for the Biggie murder?" Robleto asked.

Sanders proposed a possible explanation: "Getting the LAPD to arrest him based on bullshit might have been the best way Suge could have protected himself. If the case was filed and he beat it, that would mean he could never be charged again, under double jeopardy statutes."

A far simpler and more obvious explanation for how Hawkins had come to Kading was threaded through the pages of *Murder Rap*: she was fed to him by Reggie Wright Jr. It was clear even without Kading's acknowledging it that Wright had provided the detective's main path into the world of Death Row Records. "A valuable resource to law enforcement" is how Kading describes Wright in *Murder Rap*, writing that the former Death Row director of security had been unfairly placed under a "cloud of suspicion" in the Biggie murder, "despite those allegations being conclusively proven false." *How* those allegations had been "proven false," Kading didn't say, but that's his modus operandi throughout the book: to simply claim that this or that had been shown to be true or untrue without offering a shred of proof to support those assertions. What everyone who had investigated Death Row before Kading knew was that Wright had been a dirty cop who became an even dirtier ex-cop, involved in virtually every criminal enterprise associated with the record label. Multiple informants described how Suge and Reggie had financed their operations before Death Row began producing hit records: by ripping off drug dealers, then selling their product on the streets in Compton and surrounding communities.

In *Murder Rap*, Kading fails to mention that Wright was an even more significant coconspirator than Tammie Hawkins in helping Knight conceal assets during Death Row's bankruptcy. The single biggest scam Suge and Reggie had cooked up together in that regard involved the sixteen-floor office building at 6200 Wilshire Boulevard in Los Angeles, where the Death Row Records offices had been housed. Valued at approximately $8 million, the building (half a block from the Petersen Automotive Museum) had been transferred from Knight to Wright in early 2006, shortly before the Death Row bankruptcy filing. Neilson, the bankruptcy trustee, had unraveled the scheme and filed suit against Knight and Wright for fraudulent conveyance, eventually claiming all the proceeds from the sale of the 6200 building. That process took several years, however, and in the interim Wright was collecting every penny of the rents on the property. He had also used his ownership of the 6200 building to acquire $1 million loan on a house in Corona, out in Riverside County, at a time when houses in that community sold, on average, for about a quarter of that amount. How Wright, who claimed to live on a disability pension from the Compton Police Department and reported about $45,000 a year in income on his tax returns, could afford to live in a mansion was one more question that didn't interest Kading.

Wright and Hawkins had been involved with each other—at least financially—since the late 1990s or before. In 2001, the two had been jointly evicted from a house in Malibu. Wright might possibly have rented the property with Hawkins as a beard for Knight, but that wasn't evident from the public record.

According to law enforcement sources, Reggie and Tammie each had turned on Suge in the years after 2006, when they became allies in working against Knight. It was Wright who had pointed Kading toward the idea that Biggie Smalls was killed by Poochie Fouse on orders from Suge Knight, telling the detective that Suge had bought Poochie an Impala—a green Impala—at George Chevrolet in Bellflower.

Hawkins's animus toward Suge had spiked in 2010, when her court filing to collect child support for their four-year-old son, Taz Maree Knight, had resulted in a ruling that she should receive just $312 a month. Knight had claimed he was earning only $1,217 a month, an amount that was about a tenth of what he spent on attorneys. Just a few months later, Kading came out with the book in which he claimed that "Theresa Swann" had implicated Suge and Poochie Fouse in the Biggie murder. In short, Kading's entire case in the Biggie murder consisted of what he claimed he had been told by Reggie Wright Jr. and Tammie Hawkins. Kading barely mentioned that he had arranged for Wright and Hawkins to receive blanket immunity before they became his witnesses. In Hawkins's case, that immunity extended to her role in the auto theft ring.

Kading contended in *Murder Rap* that he had made a winnable case against Suge that was never filed, because of the problems that had spilled over from the George Torres prosecution. There was a delicious irony in Kading's explanation for why Suge was never charged with Biggie's murder. Just as Russell Poole had charged a decade earlier, Kading now accused the LAPD of "undercutting the ability of it its own investigators to solve the case." The difference was that, unlike Poole, Kading wasn't suggesting that the police department was protecting corrupt cops in order to hide its own culpability. Instead, he accused the LAPD of "a studied disregard for justice": "It was expedient for them to cripple the case in the interests of avoiding a potentially difficult prosecution," he explained.

Another, and more forthright, way of saying the same thing was that Kading and Dupree hadn't succeeded in making a case sufficient for the D.A.'s office to file on, especially when the detective who would have to explain the investigation on the witness stand—Kading—was certain to be impugned for his conduct in the Torres case.

Kading lamented that Eugene Deal had never been shown a mug shot of Poochie Fouse, seemingly oblivious to the fact that Deal had already made a positive identification of Amir Muhammad as the killer. But there was so much else he hadn't accounted for. For instance, why hadn't Kading shown Poochie's picture to Lil' Cease or any of the other witnesses who had seen the killer's face as he was firing the bullets that took Biggie's life? Sanders wondered. Why would Poochie Fouse be dressed and groomed like a Nation of Islam member when he went to kill Biggie? And how had he known where the police were that night in the area surrounding the Petersen Automotive Museum and been so successful in avoiding them? Plus, how would Poochie, a low-level thug, come into possession of "very rare" ammunition typically seen only on the East Coast? Poochie was "conveniently dead," as Robleto put it, so he could never be asked those or other questions.

Sanders had compiled a long list of the inaccuracies in *Murder Rap* by the time he contacted Kading in November 2011 to arrange a meeting at the Hilton Garden Inn in Calabasas. The attorney brought along a new associate, a young lawyer from the Bay Area named Sandra Ribera.

Sanders did most of the talking when their November 3 meeting with Kading began. "My main point, obviously, was to see what it was he'd done to supposedly eliminate cops [as suspects in the Biggie murder]," Sanders recalled. "I went through it point by point, and he hadn't run down even one of the things I asked about. Not one! So, when he says the first thing he did was absolutely eliminate cops as suspects by running down every piece of supposed evidence, that's a lie. It's a blatant lie."

What was most interesting to him about the entire meeting, Sanders said, was watching the way Kading changed while he was being questioned: "He started out with this sort of Boy Scout persona—'I'm just here to help'—but as I began to ask more and more pointed questions, he literally became a different person right in front of my eyes. I've never seen a bigger Jekyll-and-Hyde transformation in my life! He started out innocent and charming, but, believe me, that went away fast when he was put under pressure. You could see the fury in his eyes. His face was getting redder and redder, and the atmosphere was getting more and more tense. Kading looked like he was about to pop at any second, so I took my foot off the gas and let Sandy ask some questions."

Ribera, a self-described "huge fan" of Tupac Shakur, had become obsessed with the case after reading the 2005 *Rolling Stone* article while on a plane to Hawaii, shortly after her graduation from law school. "I basically stalked Perry for a year until he brought me on the case," she recalled. Sanders said, "I thought maybe her familiarity with the world of hip-hop would be a help, plus she was willing to work really hard for very little guaranteed money." It probably didn't hurt that Ribera's father had been the chief of police in San Francisco at the same time Bernard Parks was running the LAPD and that the two men had been in frequent communication. Ribera, though, said she never would have asked her father to involve himself in the case. "I was actually surprised that my dad never seemed upset when I got into it," she said, "even though he was friends with Parks."

Ribera had come into the Calabasas meeting with a far more sympathetic attitude toward Kading than Sanders had, as she recalled it, "at least at the beginning."

"It was obvious that there was a lot he didn't know," Ribera said. "The LAPD had kept a lot from him, including all of the informant interviews. He did know about Mike Robinson, and he admitted to us that Mike was credible, even though he had written exactly the opposite of that in his book. He hadn't gotten a copy of the Knox declaration, and he wasn't given access to any of the stuff connected to Boagni. So I was thinking, 'This poor guy doesn't realize how the LAPD pulled the wool over his eyes.' Gradually, though, it became

obvious that Kading hadn't really minded having the wool pulled
over his eyes. He didn't get upset or pissed off at the LAPD when
Perry told him all the stuff he didn't know, but he did get pissed at
Perry for pointing it all out and telling him how little he actually
knew about the case.

   "I figured, 'Okay, now this guy has a choice. Now that he knows
how much of what he's saying is bullshit, he can go back and try to
make it right. But Kading didn't do anything like that. He just stuck
with the bullshit. Whether it was laziness or he doesn't give a shit, I
couldn't tell you. What I really think, his book was out and he didn't
want to deal with any new information. But saying he ruled out cops
in the Biggie murder was disingenuous at best. He knew the LAPD
was happy to have him out there saying it had been 'proven' no cops
were involved. They weren't going to make an arrest or do anything
that would force them to produce evidence and answer questions.
They were just going to wait for it to all go away."

   During the interview Kading did reveal at least once significant fact that stunned Sanders: the LAPD had shut down Operation
Transparency one month after the dismissal of the lawsuit.

   "The strange thing was," Sanders said, "Kading seemed to know
that his so-called investigation had just been used by the LAPD to
protect itself from our claim of cop involvement in Biggie's murder."

   Ribera remembered, "Kading said that Internal Affairs had
refused to share any of their stuff with him and that the Risk Management guys had told him he couldn't have anything connected to our
lawsuit. So it seemed like this totally circular situation where Kading
ruled out cops being involved because the evidence indicating cops
had been involved was kept from him. At one point he more or less
admitted that his job had been to come up with some theory of the
case that didn't implicate police officers. And he was fine with that.
When I saw that, I knew there was no hope with this guy. He could
have cared less what the truth was."

   For Sanders, the bottom line was that Kading had rested his
"case closed" argument about Biggie's murder on the claims of a

single dubious witness, Tammie Hawkins. "We had way, way, way more to implicate Mack and Muhammad and Perez in the Biggie murder than he had to implicate the guy he was pointing at. When I actually got in a room with Kading, I couldn't believe how thin his whole deal was. The guy was almost entirely bluff and bluster. All he had in the Biggie case was a demonstrably false theory that a four-year-old could have beaten in court."

CHAPTER SIXTEEN

In the review of *Murder Rap* he posted on Amazon.com, Russell Poole began by stating, "Greg Kading has no credibility on this subject matter. He became a task force member on the Biggie case 10 years after the fact." Poole's review ended with his observation that "Kading never attempted to interview me regarding the Biggie investigation. He makes a lot of false statements about me & my part in the investigation."

Poole's failure to thrive after he left the force had been gradual up to that point. The attention he received following the publication of *LAbyrinth* in 2002 and his appearance in Nick Broomfield's movie *Biggie & Tupac* just a few months later had made Poole into something of a cultural icon, a symbol of the solitary figure pitted against the institutional corruption of a sprawling metropolis. But that image slowly faded over the next few years, leaving him more and more bereft. After several years out of law enforcement, Poole found a new job with the U.S. Marshals Service, working as a bailiff at the federal court in downtown Los Angeles. He savored the sense of connection to the city's dramatic churn, but the job was a far cry from working as an LAPD homicide detective. There was a sense about him of someone forever attempting to keep hope alive, the hope that what he knew still mattered and that history would not be permitted to rest on a foundation of lies.

"It will all come out, eventually," he would repeat again and again during those years. "In the end, the cover always comes off a cover-up." Not enough people in Los Angeles cared what was true, however, and those who helmed the city's institutions found it increasingly easy to marginalize Poole and to dismiss the threat he posed. He looked more and more like someone following the attenuated thread of a narrative that was fraying into oblivion.

As the *Wallace v. Los Angeles* lawsuit began to stall and fade away, Poole sought a return to relevance through a partnership with Richard "R.J." Bond, a data retrieval expert who moonlighted as a documentary filmmaker, one who was obsessed by the murder of Tupac Shakur.

Bond emerged in 2007 with the release of *Tupac Assassination: Conspiracy or Revenge*, a documentary he produced in association with Frank Alexander, the bodyguard who was supposed to be protecting Shakur on the night he was killed. The crux of the film was a theory that the man who had orchestrated the Tupac murder was Reggie Wright Jr. Wright had prevented Shakur's favorite bodyguard, Kevin Hackie, from being in Las Vegas and had refused to allow the bodyguard who was supposed to protect him, Alexander, to carry his weapon, according to those interviewed on-screen. Those facts conformed with Russell Poole's initial suspicion about Shakur's death. The difference was that Bond and Alexander believed both Suge and Tupac had been targets of a hit arranged by Wright, attorney David Kenner, and Knight's estranged wife Sharitha as part of a Death Row Records takeover.

It wasn't a theory that went over well with a number of others who had investigated the Tupac and Biggie murders. Sergio Robleto pointed out how obviously it failed to accord with the physics of what had taken place in Las Vegas: five-foot-eight-inch, 160-pound Tupac Shakur had been hit by four of the thirteen bullets fired at the BMW, while six-foot-two-inch, 300-pound-plus Suge Knight—a much larger target—hadn't caught a single slug. "Anybody who thinks Suge was the target has to be smoking crack," Robleto said.

Bond, though, along with Alexander, believed Knight had simply gotten lucky that night. "So they went to plan B," Bond said. "They reinforced the Crips-killed-Tupac-for-revenge story, then arranged the Biggie murder so they could lay it off on Suge and send him away to prison forever."

By 2012, Bond was beginning to forge a relationship with Russell Poole, who had been trained by Bond's father as a cadet at the Los Angeles Police Academy. The two men connected through their belief that the police departments in Las Vegas and Los Angeles had no intention of trying to solve the Tupac and Biggie murders. Bond sent Poole copies of *Tupac Assassination* and its sequel, *Tupac Assassination 2*. Poole replied by asking Bond to distill the information in the films into a "case sheet" for him to take to Phil Carson at the FBI. Bond did that, then sent Poole a partial manuscript of the book about the Tupac murder he was trying to write. Gradually, Poole was drawn into both Bond's investigation and his theory of the case.

In December 2013, Poole and Bond announced that they had obtained a "confession letter" written by a Blood who said Reggie Wright had paid him and two others to kill Tupac. There were compelling reasons to doubt the letter, not the least of which was that it had actually been handwritten by the sister of the informant who had turned it over. Those who had been Poole's closest allies up this point were appalled by his immersion in what Sanders called "a junk theory." Sergio Robleto said, "I'm worried about Russ. He's really getting off track here."

Both men, and others, suggested that Bond had taken advantage of Poole's deteriorating condition and need to remain part of the investigation of the Biggie and Tupac murders. Bond, though, was a dogged and resourceful investigator who was turning up facts no one else had found, and Poole admired him for that.

Not long after teaming up with Bond, Poole lost his job at the U.S. Marshals Service. He had suffered a major hearing loss, Poole said, that made it impossible for him to work at the federal courthouse. Few thought it was quite that simple. Poole had been morose since the dismissal of the *Wallace v. Los Angeles* lawsuit; when a year passed and the case was not refiled, he grew despondent. He was gaining weight and drinking too much. Bloated and red-faced, "Russ didn't look well," is how Robleto put it, and Poole's obsessive focus on the Biggie and Tupac investigations increasingly separated him from both family and friends. Like Robleto, Sanders was sympathetic. "A guy can only take so much," he said. "Russ has been shredded by what the LAPD and the city have put him through. He keeps trying to believe, but nobody's given him much reason to. Nobody can stand up forever under the pounding he's taken."

Bond was more loyal to and supportive of Poole during this period than any other person. He let the former detective and his wife, Megan, move rent-free into the house in Corona where Bond and his wife, Athena, were living with their children. While Bond worked full-time to support his family and his book and movie projects, Poole scuffled from one temporary gig to another and was burning through savings at a rate that unnerved his wife.

Immersing himself in Bond's investigation of the Tupac murder became both Poole's therapy and his avocation. The two men worked as a team to set up a June 2014 meeting with LAPD deputy chief Kirk Albanese at which they planned to brief him on their theory of the case. "Russ and I were so happy," Bond recalled. "I remember Russ got a haircut that day, and really groomed himself up. We were goin' to town. We go all the way to the top floor of New Parker Center; get seated in this conference room, still excited; and then Daryn Dupree walks in. I should have stopped the meeting right then and said I needed a minute to talk to Russ. But Russ still believed in the LAPD deep down and so did I, sort of, because of my dad and my grandfather."

Albanese had been respectful during the meeting, and he and Poole were hopeful something might come of it, Bond said.

Not long after Poole and his wife, Megan, moved out of Bond's home, she left him, unable to bear the cost of her husband's unending obsession with the Biggie and Tupac cases. Bond said the couple had separated because Megan was trying to protect her pension, fearing that Russ would spend that money in furtherance of his investigations. It may have been more complicated than that, but by the beginning of 2015 Poole was living out of a suitcase. For a time, he had a room in a San Bernardino hotel where he was doing security work, but he eventually began to move back and forth between the spare rooms at his parents' home and his adult son's. At age fifty-nine, he was drinking himself to sleep at night, and his weight was a good fifty pounds more than it had been when he retired from the LAPD. A blood pressure condition brought warnings from doctors that Poole needed to monitor himself on a daily basis. Too proud to apply for Medicaid and too poor to afford his prescribed medications, "Russ was making his own medicines from materials he bought online," Bond said.

Sergio Robleto found it difficult to connect with Poole by this point. "I wanted to remember Russ the way he was," Robleto explained, "and I couldn't pretend enthusiasm for his theory of the Tupac case." He was left trying to reconcile feelings of sorrow and rage whenever the two of them spoke on the phone, Robleto said. "When it's threatened, the LAPD is like an elephant stomping through mice, just rolling downhill on anything or anyone that gets in its way," he reflected. "Russ experienced what it was to try to stand up alone against that. He had no chance. And it caught up with him."

In August 2015, though, Poole's spirits were lifted by word that Los Angeles County sheriff Jim McDonnell had agreed to set up a meeting with his homicide investigators to hear what Poole had to say about the Biggie and Tupac murders. The meeting had been orchestrated by Poole's new collaborator, Michael Carlin, publisher and editor of the *Century City News*, a weekly shopper that served one of the wealthiest zip codes in Los Angeles. Together, Poole and Carlin had approached a senior deputy in the Los Angeles County district attorney's office named Dave Demerjian with the evidence that supported their theories of the Tupac and Biggie murders.

"Demerjian was about to retire," Carlin recalled, "and wanted one last big case. He told us he was interested in what we had but would need a homicide investigator to work with him." Carlin saw an opportunity to secure such an investigator while attending a meeting of Leadership L.A., a training program sponsored by the Los Angeles Chamber of Commerce. Carlin was a graduate of the program and so was Jim McDonnell.

McDonnell had been with the LAPD for twenty-eight years and was mentored for a good many of those years by William Bratton. Both men had grown up back east in the Boston area and their connection went back decades. "I remember when Bratton was with Kroll while it was preparing its draft of the consent decree," Robleto recalled. "Bratton would meet with Jimmy every time he came to L.A. When Bratton decided he wanted to be LAPD chief, Jimmy was his inside guy. They're both operators."

McDonnell rose to the number two position in the department while Bratton was serving as LAPD chief, and it was widely assumed he would succeed his mentor. Instead the City Council had chosen Charlie Beck, a shameless political opportunist who had exploited Rafael Perez's Rampart Scandal narrative to gain a reputation as the division commander who "rehabilitated" Rampart. Furious, McDonnell had accepted the position of chief of police in Long Beach, then run for county sheriff, winning election to the position in 2014.

In early summer 2015, Carlin was in the audience at a Leadership L.A. event where Sheriff McDonnell gave the keynote speech. Afterward he had "cornered" McDonnell, "who didn't seem too happy about it," as Carlin recalled, but agreed to set up a meeting for him and Poole with his senior homicide investigators.

"McDonnell knew Russ from the LAPD and sincerely respected him, I think," Carlin recalled. "For a period of time, the two of us were texting back and forth with the sheriff and getting on conference calls with him. Russ and Jim were reminiscing and seemed really friendly. Then all of a sudden McDonnell stopped replying." Through his assistant, though, McDonnell helped arrange the meeting Carlin and Poole had been asking for. The two were told that Captain Rod

Kusch of the Sheriff's Homicide Bureau and his top investigator, Richard Biddle, would be there. "Russ was really excited," Carlin recalled, "and so was I."

Three or four days before the meeting was scheduled to take place, Carlin recalled, he and Poole learned that the August 24, 2014, shooting of Suge Knight at the 1 Oak nightclub in Las Vegas had been facilitated by an off-duty Los Angeles County sheriff's deputy. (Knight had been shot seven times while attending a party at 1 Oak thrown by singer Chris Brown on the evening of the Video Music Awards ceremony; he later sued Brown for failing to provide adequate security.) Poole made contact with Knight's attorneys to share what he had learned and to suggest a deal: Suge would cooperate in nailing Reggie Wright Jr. for the Tupac and Biggie murders, and in exchange Poole would persuade the Sheriff's Department to drop a murder case that had been filed against Knight in Compton. That, Poole and Carlin decided, would be what they pitched at their meeting with Kusch, Biddle, and whoever else was present.

Two days before the meeting was to take place, Poole phoned to tell me how excited he was about it. "I've been promised by Jim McDonnell that the Sheriff's Department will really listen," he said. "I think this is the best chance left to get a real investigation going."

The next day, "Russ gets a call from somebody at the Sheriff's Department to ask what exactly the meeting is about," Carlin recalled. "Russ starts by telling what we've learned about the sheriff's deputy who walked the shooters into 1 Oak right before the attempt on Suge's life. The sheriff's person says, 'How did you find out?' Russ told them a little of how we knew, but not everything. So the sheriff's person says, 'Look, this is a cop thing, and we'd rather not have Carlin there.'"

This had all been explained to him, Carlin said, when Poole called to say he would be going to the meeting alone. "Russ believed he and McDonnell had a great rapport and he told me, 'I don't want to disappoint Jim,'" Carlin recalled.

An hour before the 10 a.m. meeting at the Sheriff's Department's Monterey Park station, Carlin recalled, Poole phoned to say he was in Diamond Bar, stuck in freeway traffic, but thought he could make the meeting on time. A little more than two hours later, Carlin got a call informing him that Poole had died of a massive heart attack during his meeting with Sheriff's Department officials and investigators. "I believe Russ was murdered during that meeting," Carlin said.

CHAPTER SEVENTEEN

Mostly, what gave traction to Michael Carlin's unsubstantiated claims about Russell Poole's death was how little the Los Angeles County Sheriff's Department was willing to reveal about its circumstances. Poole's family had received a copy of the medical examiner's report that listed the cause of death as "cardiac arrest," but no calls from McDonnell or anyone else in a senior position at the Sheriff's Department to explain what had happened. Only when she read the medical examiner's report, Megan Poole said, did she realize that Russ had collapsed as the Monterey Park meeting was coming to an end and that the efforts of those present to revive him had failed. There was nothing in that report, though, about who those present were or what Russ had discussed with them.*

Michael Carlin claimed that McDonnell had phoned him after Poole's death, with Rod Kusch on the line. "Jim said Rod was in the meeting along with two investigators, but would not name them,"

---

* My own call to the Sheriff's Department to ask for that information, and for an interview with Jim McDonnell, resulted in a conference call joined by four of the sheriff's subordinates. McDonnell's strategic communications director Carol Lin did most of the talking. Lin told me absolutely nothing other than that a meeting had taken place and that it had been arranged as "a courtesy" to Russell Poole. Sheriff McDonnell hadn't been present, she added. I asked for the names of those who had attended the meeting and a chance to talk to them about what had taken place in it. Without revealing a single name, Lin said she would check on the "availability" of those who were present when Poole died and get back to me. She never did.

Carlin said. "He said there were a total of six people in the room [but] withheld the names of four people." McDonnell told him that "at the conclusion of the meeting they were all in the room when Russ had a heart attack and died before he hit the floor," Carlin said. "He wouldn't give me any information at all about what was discussed in the meeting."

This conversation hadn't prevented Carlin from making online postings in which he claimed to have an inside source who alleged that those in the meeting had used a defibrillator, not to stimulate Poole's heart but to stop it. When I spoke to Carlin, he told me, "I do not believe Jim McDonnell had anything to do with Russ's death. This was Death Row behind it." His "sources" had told him that Reggie Wright Jr. and Daryn Dupree were in the room when Poole died, Carlin said.

Richard Bond called Carlin's claims "tinfoil hat stuff" and offered a theory of what had happened at the Sheriff's Department meeting that was considerably more plausible: "Russ was desperate to have somebody hear him, and he felt McDonnell owed him, so he went to that meeting alone. Russ had barely enough money to pay for the gas to get there, but this was a mission of the heart for him. Whatever was said at the meeting, I think Russ heard it and knew this was the end of the road, the end of the journey, the end of any hope for vindication. I think the realization hit him like a lightning bolt. And it killed him."

Nevertheless, Bond admitted being impressed by at least one solid piece of evidence that supported Carlin's claims about who was present at the meeting. This was that within two hours of Poole's death, well before it was being reported in the media, an interview with Reggie Wright Jr. had been posted on YouTube by the Bomb1st.com website. In it, Wright said he knew Poole was dead, then added, "It's a good day for me because I believe in karma, and you know, all these people that keep coming out with the bullcrap ... first was [former Tupac Shakur bodyguard] Michael Moore, then Frank Alexander, and now Russell Poole ... All these people is dropping dead there, so I keep telling people, 'God don't like ugly, so people learn a lesson from this one . . . the next person probably is to be an R.J. Bond, but, uh, I don't know."

The only possible explanation for the fact that Wright had learned of Poole's death "at almost the same time Russ's family was being told," Bond said, was that he had heard it from someone at the meeting or high up in the Sheriff's Department. For Bond, this suggested Carlin's claim that Daryn Dupree was in the meeting was true: "If Dupree told Kading, Kading would have told Reggie."

Of course he had been alarmed by Wright's suggestion that he would probably be "the next person" to die, Bond said: "I put it in the same category as Kading's remark about how I would be a dead man if Poochie Fouse was still alive. I've seen Reggie Wright issue 'orders by insinuation' before. He makes a suggestion, and someone else acts."

The Wright video was taken down from YouTube within twenty-four hours of being posted, and Wright himself was considerably more circumspect when asked in subsequent interviews about Poole. Greg Kading, though, was remorseless. "I apologize for sounding insensitive," Kading told one interviewer, "but Poole was not promoting 'truth' in the Biggie murder. He was promoting unsubstantiated and disprovable theories, which only lead to public confusion about the murders. In [my] documentary you see how easily his original theory was dismantled and his 'new' theory is even more implausible. My condolences to the family and friends of Mr. Poole and it is not my intent to disparage him, but my loyalty is to the truth in these murders and to the public who has been eagerly awaiting answers for nearly twenty years."

"Sickening," Perry Sanders called Kading's remarks. "A guy who has absolutely no interest in the truth, and who didn't even put a dent in Russ's original theory of the Biggie shooting, out there talking about how he 'dismantled' it."

Sanders was particularly incensed by the claim Kading was regularly making in interviews that Biggie's mom, Voletta Wallace, now "supported" his theory of the case. This assertion was based mostly on sections of a March 22, 2012, article written for the *L.A. Weekly* by Chris Vogel, who was now serving, effectively, as Kading's publicist. With "the ground shifting in one of the most baffling cold cases in Los Angeles history," Voletta Wallace, "while she has not ruled out dirty cops, [now] leans toward Kading's new evidence."*

"I believe everything in [Kading's] book," Vogel quoted Voletta Wallace as saying. "So if Greg Kading found out all this truth, why isn't Suge Knight behind bars? What are the police waiting for? They murdered my son. LAPD, make a goddamn arrest."

Vogel had "completely distorted" both Voletta Wallace's remarks and his own, Sanders said: "Voletta and I both just in essence said, 'If the case is solved, as your detective says it is solved, prosecute someone.' Nothing more, nothing less. No embracing Kading. That article was one more part of a disinformation campaign that has gone on for fifteen years."

As proof that the article was "invalid," Sanders pointed to Vogel's claim that he believed the confession of Theresa Swann was "solid, unimpeachable evidence." That was "total B.S.," Sanders said. "I never vouched for Swann in any way, shape, or form."

Voletta Wallace said that when Kading had come to see her in Brooklyn, she had refused his offer to meet with his prize witness. "I told him I would only meet with her if she was locked up," Wallace said. "I told him I would believe his case was true only if the people he said were responsible had been arrested. I was never with Greg Kading, or on Greg Kading's side. Never! I have always believed and still believe that the one person who truly tried to solve my son's murder was Russell Poole. If I'm with anyone, it's Poole, not Kading."

Despite the obvious flaws in both his investigation and his book, Kading's incessant self-promotion, combined with sloppy media coverage,

---

* A consideration of the accusations against Greg Kading by his two most public challengers is found in Appendix B.

had gradually established his account of the Biggie and Tupac investigations as the prevailing one. That Kading had superseded Poole was made more or less official when the USA Network began airing *Unsolved* in February 2018, claiming the series was based on *Murder Rap*. At least half of the show, however, was based on *LAbyrinth*, which writer Kyle Long and producer Anthony Hemingway had used without my permission. Knowing that I had sold the rights to the companies using it as the basis for the film *City of Lies*, starring Johnny Depp and Forest Whitaker, and that I therefore *couldn't* sue them, Long and Hemingway had taken a calculated risk that Global Road, the company that now owned the book's rights, *wouldn't* sue them.

In Long and Hemingway and the executives at USA, Kading had found suitable collaborators. The result was a narrative that stuck close to *LAbyrinth*'s except when it served the Kading chronicle that was the other half of the story line. The big lie of *Unsolved*, apart from its pretense that Kading's had been a credible investigation, involved an invented scene that utterly misrepresented both Poole and Kading. It was set up by a false claim that Poole's storage locker had been abandoned after he stopped paying his bill. Then Kading showed up, as the series had it, and inherited Poole's files. Not only had nothing of the sort taken place, but Kading had never gained—or for that matter tried to gain—*any* access to the elements of Poole's investigation, and had thoroughly misrepresented even what he knew of them in *Murder Rap*.

The most telling thing about *Unsolved*, though, was how carefully it steered away from the actual facts of Kading's relationship with Reggie Wright Jr., just as Kading himself had in *Murder Rap*. Only in the various public statements they made after the release of Kading's book had he and Wright acknowledged—and then only implicitly—what a hand-in-glove pair they were. Kading was the more ambiguous of the two, acknowledging only "working with" Wright on the Biggie and Tupac murder investigations. Yes, he was "protective of Reggie," Kading acknowledged in one interview. In another he suggested that "people"—meaning Bond and Poole, mainly—should apologize to Wright because he had been interviewed by various law enforcement agencies and had passed several lie detector tests. There was no evidence of this on offer; it was yet another "take my word for it" claim by Kading.

Wright, though, wanted to revel in how central he was to Kading's claims of having solved the Tupac and Biggie murders. He and his people were continuing on from the point where his friend Kading had left off, Wright told one interviewer: "We're going to explore some things that they found out during the Greg Kading investigation. I helped a lot with that investigation." Whenever an interviewer challenged Wright, or pointed to evidence that implicated him in either the Biggie or the Tupac murder, his response was the same: "Read the Greg Kading book, *Murder Rap*. It answers that question."

Kading, though, had gone silent on the subject of Reggie Wright Jr. in May 2017. That was because Wright and his father Reggie Wright Sr. had just been indicted by a federal grand jury in Memphis, Tennessee, for operating a large-scale drug ring in coordination with a subset of the Watts-based Grape Street Crips.

Even a cursory reading of the indictment made it clear the feds had the Wrights cold. The FBI and the DEA had been monitoring the Memphis ring since 2013, focusing on a circle of known drug dealers who operated out of an inner-city apartment complex. What they had discovered was an astoundingly naked operation in which the Wrights were sending heroin, OxyContin, methamphetamine, and marijuana via the U.S. Postal Service directly to their Memphis dealers. Once they got the drugs, the Memphis Crips made deposits of between $5,000 and $10,000 in accounts in the Wrights' names at either Wells Fargo or Bank of America. No layer of distance between the dealers and the Wrights had been created at all. "Reggie became complacent after Kading came out with his book," Bond said, "because he knew Kading had his back."

The feds had not only the bank records but also video of each and every deposit. It was an unbeatable case and the Wrights knew it. Anyone familiar with Reggie Jr. knew his next move was going to be a snitch deal.

Suge Knight certainly knew it. At the first court hearing in his murder case after the Wrights' arrests, Knight had created a darkly comedic scene when he began to demand of the presiding magistrate, "Why can't I talk to my attorneys?" He *could* talk to his attorneys, the magistrate replied, but to only one of them directly; whatever he wanted to say to the other lawyers assisting him had to be communicated through his primary attorney. "That's how it works," the magistrate explained. Suge continued to protest, then looked around the courtroom until he spotted David Kenner seated among the spectators. "For instance, David Kenner," Suge said. "He's here and he wants to talk to me, but you guys won't let me talk to him." The law enforcement officials in the courtroom had to cover their smiles; every one of them knew that Suge was desperate to talk to Kenner because only Kenner could help him figure out how to deal with Wright Jr. before Reggie started talking to the feds. That Wright was capable of turning on Suge there could be no doubt after the Kading book was published; it was Reggie who had helped concoct the "Theresa Swann" account that put Biggie's murder off on Poochie Fouse, working for Suge.

Knight was just one among many who imagined that the indictments against the Wrights might result, finally, in the closure of the Biggie and Tupac murder cases. Whatever the degree of his involvement, there was little question that Reggie knew enough to make the case against all those who had conspired to kill the two most famous rappers in the history of hip-hop. Would the feds use their leverage to compel Wright's testimony against Suge Knight in the Biggie murder?

It quickly began to appear that this was not going to happen. Petty jurisdictional agendas were prevailing over larger questions of justice. "The DEA and ATF in Tennessee made this case," explained one embittered federal agent, "and neither agency gives a damn about a murder case in California they have nothing to do with. What they want are convictions that build their numbers. And they made sure the U.S. attorney in Tennessee understood that."

That Reggie Jr. was negotiating a plea deal as a government informant became apparent when he was separated from all the other defendants in the case—including his father—and scheduled for hearings independent of theirs. Reggie was telling people he had negotiated a deal under which he would serve no more than two or three years, with an additional promise that the prosecution against his father would be dropped. He had used Reggie Sr.'s name without his knowledge to set up some of the bank accounts where the drug money was deposited, Reggie Jr. was now claiming.

"If it's true, then one more time the opportunity to solve the Biggie and Tupac cases is squandered," Bond lamented. "That was probably the last best chance to break those cases open, and it looks like the feds threw it away. The only question is how much encouragement to do that they got from L.A."

Whatever deal he had made with the feds, Wright was clearly feeling fairly relaxed about his circumstances, something he signaled in March 2018 by agreeing to an interview with Internet radio host Jesse Surratt. The ostensible reason for the interview was to let Wright rebut reports that he was near death from some sort of ailment. He had developed a blocked esophagus, Wright explained, that led to his becoming dehydrated and losing weight. "All it meant was surgery," he told Surratt, "not being on my deathbed."

The Surratt interview was also about protecting and repairing his public image, as Wright made clear in his remarks about Russell Poole. A lot of people thought he was a bad guy because of the remarks he'd posted on YouTube after Poole's death, Wright acknowledged, but "I didn't speak negative on Russell until he came after me with this other stuff"—meaning the accusations Poole and Bond had made of Reggie Jr.'s involvement in the Tupac and Biggie murders. "A straight-up cop," Wright called Poole, the kind of detective "who wouldn't plant evidence when he searched my home or where I work." But he did disapprove of Poole's obsession with the Tupac and Biggie cases, Wright added: "You don't retire and leave the police department behind a case. You don't take it personal. You just move on to the next case."

The weirdest and most amusing moments of the interview came when Surratt brought up Tammie Hawkins. "I don't know who that is," Reggie lied. "You're talkin' about Theresa Swann, right?"

The interview turned into bilious farce when Wright denied that he and Hawkins/Swann had been a couple when Hawkins gave Kading the Poochie story. Not true, Reggie said: "Just 'cause I rented a house where she was livin' don't mean we was livin' together." Did he know Suge had herpes? Wright asked Surratt suddenly: "You think I'm gonna mess around with somebody that be with somebody who has herpes?"

Wright didn't do any of the bragging about how integral he was to Kading's investigation that he had done in other interviews. To Surratt, he claimed that he hadn't known Suge had paid Poochie to kill Biggie Smalls "until I read *Murder Rap*."

"What that told me was that Kading had warned Reggie to back off from telling everyone how involved he was in the so-called investigation," Bond said. "I was pretty sure I knew how Kading had done that, by telling Reggie that if Suge believed he had fed him the Poochie story, Suge was going to find a way to get to him."

If that was true, Wright might have been the last person on earth to see Suge Knight as a credible threat.

CHAPTER EIGHTEEN

S uge Knight had been in the news often during the past decade, mostly because of wounds inflicted on his body or his reputation. Knight for the first time became the public butt of jokes in summer 2005, around the time of the mistrial in *Wallace v. Los Angeles*, when he was shot in the right thigh while attending a party hosted by Kanye West at the Shore Club West in Miami. While it was never clear that the shooting had been an attempt on Suge's life—more likely, it seemed, he'd been caught in crossfire—this event revealed his vulnerability on at least two levels: he was no longer shielded by an entourage of thugs, and the lawsuit he filed against West for failure to provide adequate security at the event indicated how desperate Knight had become for money. That Suge now was being mocked by comedians and late-night television hosts was an unmistakable sign that people simply were not so afraid of him as they'd once been.

This humiliation was followed by a series of incidents that seemed to confirm the oft-repeated claims that Knight was a soft-bellied bully who liked to beat up smaller foes but couldn't stand his ground against a man the same size. In May 2008, at the Shag Nightclub in Hollywood, Knight had confronted a man he claimed owed him money, then let his bodyguards give the guy a beatdown. The man had popped up a few moments later, though, to throw a punch that put Suge on his back, apparently unconscious, for several minutes, before he was helped to his feet and half-carried from the club to a waiting vehicle. The incident was openly celebrated on a number of hip-hop websites.

Just four months later, Suge was arrested in a parking lot off the Las Vegas Strip by police officers who said they had come upon him "punching a naked woman with one hand and holding a knife in the other." The woman was Knight's then-girlfriend Melissa Issac, who'd grabbed the steering wheel of Suge's pickup truck after he punched her in the face during an argument. As he had done so often before in Las Vegas, Knight would hire well-connected attorneys who got the criminal charges dismissed. The lawyers, though, couldn't do a thing about the damage to his public image. Suge liked to whupass not only on smaller men, it was said, but also on even smaller women.

Only five months after that, Suge was attending a party at the W Hotel in Scottsdale, Arizona, when he got into an altercation with a man who claimed to be the business manager of the rapper Akon. Again, it was Knight who took the beating, one that left him with a broken nose and shattered facial bones.

Suge seemed to have become more prey than predator, lacking the resources to protect himself. His descent had been accelerating ever since March 2005, when a Los Angeles judge awarded Lydia Harris a $107 million judgment against Knight and Death Row Records. Harris was the wife of legendary L.A. gangster Michael "Harry-O" Harris, who had been proclaiming for nearly a decade that Death Row was launched in 1991 with $1.5 million in seed money he provided in exchange for a partnership in the label. That Harry-O's money had been the product of his vast cocaine empire, and that the man himself was serving a twenty-eight-year sentence in state prison for conspiracy to commit murder, had complicated his legal position. So had his refusal to accept a reduction of his sentence in exchange for testifying against Knight in court. Harris's wife, Lydia, however, found a clearer path: making a convincing case that she was a God-fearing woman who played no part in her husband's criminal activities and had been almost entirely unaware of them.

Suge filed his bankruptcy claim barely a year after Lydia Harris's court victory. In collusion with Reggie Wright Jr. and Tammie Hawkins, he had done his best to conceal the assets he had amassed during the fifteen-year run in which Death Row Records had earned more than $325 million from the recordings of Tupac Shakur, Snoop Dogg, Dr. Dre, and dozens of other hip-hop artists. The trustee in Knight's bankruptcy case had tracked down and seized most of that hidden wealth. The Internal Revenue Service, which stood first in line among Suge's creditors, would collect every penny of the $11.3 million it was owed. Lydia Harris's attorney stood right behind the government's. Lydia and Michael Harris would ultimately divide their piece of the pie in a divorce agreement they negotiated at the Monterey County courthouse in Northern California, where Harry-O had been transported from his current residence in San Quentin State Prison.

Suge had managed to hang on to at least some of his Death Row earnings, but his enormous legal bills were rapidly chewing through that money. By 2010, he was living not in a beachfront Malibu mansion, but in a Las Vegas tract house, from which he ran an assortment of nickel-and-dime enterprises. He rarely showed up in Los Angeles, and found trouble waiting whenever he did. His appearance at an MTV Video Music Awards party in West Hollywood hosted by singer Chris Brown resulted in an attempt on Knight's life in which he was shot seven times and needed emergency surgery.

Knight was writhing in fury and humiliation as those he had once terrorized celebrated his fall. It seemed a long time ago that Suge had decorated the foyer of the Death Row Records offices in Los Angeles with an oil painting of Dr. Dre being sodomized by a blond bodybuilder while Puffy Combs, skinny legs sticking out of a pink tutu, stood alongside a porcine Notorious B.I.G. watching with lascivious delight. B.I.G. may have been dead for years, but Puffy's business empire and celebrity status each continued to grow, while Dre was a mega-celebrity pocketing a big piece of the $3 billion sale of his Beats headphones enterprise to Apple. Suge had demanded

10 percent of the Beats deal but received nothing at all. Strapped, he attempted to impose a $30,000 "tax" on any out-of-town rapper who wanted to work in either Los Angeles or Las Vegas, according to the Los Angeles County district attorney's office, but he lacked the muscle to enforce it. Increasingly, Suge's badass posturing made him look pathetic rather than fearsome. In 2014, he had attempted to enforce his tax by calling out rapper Rick Ross in a video interview: "You know you owe me that bread, titty man," he said. "I'm gonna beat the dog shit out of you." Ross never paid him a penny.

A year later, there were people who actually professed to feel sorry for Suge. To him, being pitied was far worse than being hated. All his bills seemed to be coming due when, in early 2015, Suge was arrested for murder.

The circumstances of this crime derived entirely from the combustion of his egotism, his envy, and his desperation. The film *Straight Outta Compton*, based on N.W.A.'s seminal gangsta rap album, was shooting that winter in southwest Los Angeles County. Suge was infuriated to learn that he was the movie's villain. It wasn't so much being portrayed as a psychopathic thug that bothered him, though, as that he wasn't being paid by the producers of a film in which he was a major character. Determined to do something about it, Suge drove his Red Ford Raptor pickup onto the film's set on the afternoon of January 29, 2015, blowing past security guards until he was face-to-face with Dr. Dre's bodyguards. Dre and Ice Cube were among *Straight Outta Compton*'s producers. The bodyguards tried to chase him off the set, but Suge refused to budge. The panicked producers sent Cle "Bone" Sloan, a Bloods gang member who was working on the film as a technical adviser, to see what he could do. "Why don't you leave so we can move forward?" Sloan said he told Suge. "You got the white folks scared." Knight did leave eventually, but less than an hour later got a call from Terry Carter, a well-known entrepreneur in South-Central L.A. whose businesses included the rap label he had founded with Ice Cube, Heavyweight Records. A self-described "peacemaker," Carter was said to be friendly with Suge—the two had talked about starting a business together. He asked Knight if they could meet at Tam's, a burger joint in Compton near the *Straight Outta Compton* film's base camp, to talk things over. Suge arrived at Tam's just minutes later and found Carter waiting with a friend. According to the account Bone Sloan gave to the police, Knight was bad-mouthing him to Carter just as Sloan drove into the parking lot: "He was talking shit and I just popped out like a jack-in-the-box." Witnesses saw Sloan charge the Raptor's driver's side shouting, "Let's do it!" as he began throwing punches through the open window. Suge threw his pickup into reverse, knocking Sloan down, then put the truck into drive and lurched forward over the fallen man, crushing his ankles. The Raptor kept going until it plowed into the fleeing Carter and rolled over the fifty-five-year-old man's torso, killing him on the spot. The entire event had been captured on Tam's surveillance video.

Suge fled the scene, but turned himself in to the police twelve hours later, at around 3 a.m. The first of Knight's several attorneys in the case said his client was "heartbroken" over Carter's death, but soon after this a new lawyer began to argue that Suge had acted in self-defense. Eventually, a claim that Carter had "lured" Knight into an ambush became Suge's legal strategy. There were people who believed he could make it stick. One of them was the biggest name among the six attorneys Knight went through in the first two years after his arrest, Tom Mesereau. Famous mainly for winning the acquittal of Michael Jackson at his sex abuse trial in Santa Barbara County, Mesereau publicly claimed to be confident that he could prevail in Knight's case. "I am convinced of Knight's innocence," he told *Rolling Stone*, "and . . . I look forward to defending him. [Knight] was defending himself at all times, and should not be facing any charge of murder, attempted murder or hit-and-run. If I had been driving the truck, I would not even have been charged with a misdemeanor."

Even if Knight did manage to beat the murder charges against him, though, the district attorney's office seemed confident that a second case would send him to prison for a very long time. Suge had been arrested on robbery charges months before the death of

Terry Carter. The alleged crime had taken place in Beverly Hills on September 5, 2014. As Knight stepped through the back door of Film One Studios accompanied by one of his seven children, he found himself face-to-face with a female photographer named Leslie Redden. According to Redden, Suge charged her, warning that he had "a bitch to come beat your motherfucking ass." When Knight lifted his shirt to show her his waistband, Redden said, she turned to flee but took only a few steps before being confronted by Suge's friend, comedian Katt Williams, and his female companion. When the woman knocked Redden to the ground, she said, Williams stood over her, screaming that she had better delete the photos of Suge she had taken, before ripping her camera out of her hands. A little more than a month later, Knight and Williams were arrested and charged with one count of robbery.

Mesereau called that charge "utterly ridiculous," but *Rolling Stone* reported that the robbery case "may prove harder to beat" than the charges against Knight related to Terry Carter's death.

Yet another criminal case had stacked up behind that one during February 2017, when a grand jury indicted Knight for threatening the life of *Straight Outta Compton* director F. Gary Gray. Still raging about both his portrayal in the film and, especially, not being paid for the use of his character, Suge had sent a barrage of text messages and voice mails Gray's way, along the lines of, "I will see u in person . . . u have kids just like me so let's play hardball." In other text, Suge reminded the director he was "from Bomton," meaning he was a Blood, then promising to make sure Gray got some "hugs" from fellow gang members; what Suge meant by "hugs," Gray knew, was a serious beating. According to the prosecutors, Gray was so frightened by the messages Suge sent him that he spent two days dodging their questions. When they finally put him on the stand in front of a grand jury, the director claimed not to remember any messages from Suge or what they might have meant. The deputy D.A. prosecuting the case, Cynthia Barnes, told the grand jurors that Gray's performance as a witness only emphasized how terrified Knight had made him:

"He's perjuring himself because he's that afraid." The grand jurors had agreed with her.

It was the charges brought in the death of Terry Carter, though, that were keeping Suge locked up in solitary confinement at the Los Angeles County Men's Jail. On March 20, 2015, amid the sort of sideshow that had been playing off and on at the Criminal Courts building a few blocks away since the O.J. Simpson trial, Judge Ronald S. Coen had set Knight's bail at $25 million. Mesereau had left the case months earlier. Two explanations for his departure circulated: One was that Suge had failed to make fee payments as promised. The other was that Knight had attempted to use the attorney to commit crimes—including the elimination of witnesses—from behind bars.

Two other Knight attorneys had already cycled through the case by the time Suge's latest lawyer, Matthew Fletcher, began pleading with Judge Coen to reconsider the $25 million bail, complaining about the poor treatment Knight was receiving for ailments that included diabetes, blood clots, and vision loss. As if on cue, Suge, wearing an orange jumpsuit and heavy black-framed glasses, collapsed in the courtroom. Coen was not impressed by what he viewed as an encore performance; Knight had taken to passing out regularly in court and the judge seemed to be among the many observers who thought Suge was faking it. Outside the courthouse, Knight's supporters staged a protest featuring a woman with a blonde Afro who wore a red dress and shouted, "This is a public lynching! Black lives matter!" Coen, though, refused to budge.

Knight was still in jail sixteen months later when his attorneys filed papers informing the court they had a witness—professional informant Daniel Timms—who would testify that two sheriff's deputies had compelled him to testify falsely against Suge in the Carter murder. Knight's latest attorney, Thaddeus Culpepper, detailed Timms's story in letters to California attorney general Kamala Harris and U.S. attorney general Loretta Lynch, writing that the informant had been told his wife's nephew would receive a significantly reduced sentence in a murder case he was facing. Superior court judge William

C. Ryan ruled that Culpepper's claims about Timms were "patently and demonstrably false." Nevertheless, it was a near certainty that Timms would be called as a witness at trial.

Fletcher and Culpepper were both back in the news in March 2018, just weeks before Knight's murder trial was to begin. The two attorneys had been indicted by a grand jury for allegedly urging Suge to pay witnesses to testify in his favor. A month earlier, Suge's fiancée Toi-Lin Kelly had received a three-year prison sentence for violating a court order by arranging for the sale of the security footage that showed Knight's truck ramming Sloan and driving over Carter. "I can't wait to get this footage to you," Kelly had written to TMZ, seeking a $55,000 payment for the right to show it. Prosecutors were also looking for a way to charge Suge in that case.

Judge Coen had pledged that Suge's April 9, 2018, trial date would not be postponed, but it was once again when Suge's fifteenth attorney was replaced by his sixteenth, Albert DeBlanc Jr. Suge was making trips to the emergency room at Los Angeles County–USC Medical Center almost as often as he was changing attorneys. On April 5, 2018, he was once again rushed to the hospital by ambulance. Yet another "firm" trial date had been set for September 24, 2018. Most savvy observers were willing to take odds that it would be postponed also.

By late spring 2018, Suge had been in jail for more than three years awaiting a trial that seemed as if it would never happen. He was unlikely ever to live outside a jail or prison cell again. Whether or not that was justice, he couldn't say, Perry Sanders admitted. On the one hand, there were a lot of crimes that Suge Knight would never pay for, including the murder of Notorious B.I.G., and yet on the other hand he had only one life to spend behind bars, regardless of what he was being punished for.

"Fair is not the same as right," Sanders observed, "but sometimes it has to do."

EPILOGUE

Among those who had tried to make the case in *Wallace v. Los Angeles*, it was the belief that Knight's accomplices were still walking around free that rankled. At least Reggie Wright Jr. was headed for prison, but his would be only a short stay in a minimum-security federal prison. For a man many—including Sanders—suspected of crimes that should have put him away for life, it was essentially a skate. The only consolation was that Reggie Jr. would be marked forever as a snitch, and that a whole lot of Crips knew it was members of their gang that he had testified against.

Infinitely more galling was that Rafael Perez continued to live comfortably near the beach as Ray Lopez, not only unpursued by law enforcement in Southern California, but actually protected by it. The Rampart Scandal narrative Perez had mostly made up out of whole cloth had been embraced across the entire spectrum of power and influence in Los Angeles; these days, it was actually taught in history classes.

David Mack finished his fourteen-year prison sentence in May 2010 and was apparently proving that the money from the Bank of America robbery really *was* well invested. After taking alternative-energy courses at Los Angeles Trade-Technical College, he established a firm that installed solar panels under minority set-aside contracts. He did well enough to purchase a bungalow in L.A.'s pricey Laurel Canyon. Mack was a vocal Bernie Sanders supporter who had actually organized rallies to back the candidate in black communities. The photographs on Mack's Facebook page depicted a genial grand-dad posing with his four granddaughters and his wife, Carla, who had remained married to him during all those years he spent in prison.

Six months before Mack bought the Laurel Canyon house, Harry Billups, a.k.a. Amir Muhammad, a.k.a. Harry Muhammad, purchased a home in Dallas, Georgia, an Atlanta suburb. He was still claiming to be a simple mortgage broker.

That there was no easily observed justice in this world was driven home for Sanders when Sergio Robleto died suddenly of pneumonia in March 2018 at age sixty-nine. The previous year, Robleto had worked as a technical adviser on the film made from my book *LAby-rinth*. He had donated all his earnings from that job to the family of Russell Poole. "Two of the only three people who ever really tried to investigate the Biggie murder are now gone," Sanders lamented. "In this case, the good guys keep dropping and the bad guys keep walking away. It's not right, but it's the way it is."

Nearly as unbearable to Sanders was that Greg Kading's bogus investigation had been legitimized by a national television network and his claims about who was responsible for Biggie's murder went largely unchallenged in the media. "It's absolutely sickening to me," Sanders said. "Is there anybody in L.A. who cares even a little about what's right and true?" In May 2018 Sanders was alerted at his Colo-rado Springs home to a radio interview Kading was doing on Denver's KOA station. "It was one lie after another," said Sanders, who was most upset by Kading's claim that Mike Robinson had recanted his claims about Amir Muhammad, something that had never happened. Sanders remembered when Kading had told interviewers virtually the same story about Eugene Deal's identification of Muhammad as the likely killer. "Kading has never parsed evidence like a true detective does," Sanders said. "Instead he takes eyewitness evidence that has never been refuted and just bald-faced lies, saying it was all recanted."

Sanders's associate Sandy Ribera said she was most "horrified" to learn that Detective Steve Katz—"the biggest cover-up artist I've ever seen"—was not only still an LAPD detective but also an adjunct professor in the Los Angeles Southwest College Administration of Justice program.

The truly big-time bad guys in the history of the case had done even better. Almost immediately after retiring as LAPD chief, Bernard Parks won a seat in 2003 on the Los Angeles City Council, one he would occupy for a dozen years as the most powerful black official in the city's government. He finished fourth in the Democratic primary when he ran for Los Angeles mayor in 2005, and in 2008 was edged out in a runoff election for a seat on the Los Angeles County Board of Supervisors. Term limits had forced Parks to surrender his City Council seat in 2015 at the age of seventy-two, but he was managing his retirement on a pair of city pensions that paid him nearly a million dollars a year.

Michael Berkow also escaped major consequences for his behavior as a member of the LAPD command staff and prospered financially in the years that followed. Berkow left the LAPD in 2006 to take the position of chief of police in Savannah, Georgia. His disgrace was hidden from the citizens there for only a month before the *Savannah Morning News* uncovered the depositions from the Christle case, in particular the one in which Berkow admitted to sleeping with two of his female subordinates while serving as LAPD deputy chief. When asked about the Christle allegations, Berkow replied, "I categorically deny her assertions and look forward to my day in court. My attention, my energies, my talent is completely dedicated to making Savannah safer. I deeply regret that a bad personal decision in Los Angeles is distracting me from this task."

Berkow would leave the Savannah job, but again did more than simply land on his feet afterward. His old pal William Bratton had helped arrange for Berkow to receive a highly paid position as president and chief operating officer of the new Kroll Associates division Altegrity. (Bratton had also arranged to return to working at Kroll himself when he retired from his position as LAPD chief a few months later.) Berkow ran Altegrity for two and a half years, then in 2012 was hired by the Boston Police Department (where a younger William

Bratton had served in the department's second-highest post, executive superintendent) to "streamline" the BPD's internal affairs complaint process. A *Boston Globe* article on Berkow's background was not published until after he had also been hired, with a little help from his friends, as director of the U.S. Coast Guard's Investigative Services, a position placing him in charge of this armed service's detectives worldwide. It's a job he holds to this day.

"Unbelievable," said Phil Carson, who had retired from the FBI and was now working in private security jobs in Los Angeles. "Berkow still working in law enforcement is maybe the part of this whole thing that bothers me most."*

In 2012, Berkow's former collaborator Chuck Philips defended his reporting on the murders of Biggie and Tupac in an article published by the *Village Voice*. He argued that in his *Los Angeles Times* article about the shooting of Tupac Shakur that relied on fraudulent documents, "at worst what I had done was make a mistake." His editors were ultimately responsible, Philips said, but let him take the fall for it. The most painful part of his firing, Philips said, was learning that the *Times* had settled the legal claim against it by paying "Jimmy Henchman" Rosemond $200,000 in cash on the same day Philips lost his job.

Since then, he had applied for hundreds of jobs in journalism, Philips wrote, and had been turned down every time.

---

* Asked to explain how it could reconcile Michael Berkow's current position as head of its Investigative Services division with the various accusations made against him, including the findings of the jury in the Christle case, the U.S. Coast Guard replied with this written statement:

> *Mr. Berkow is a valued member of the Senior Executive Service. While the Coast Guard will not discuss the hiring process in a particular case, it's important to point out that a suitability screening is conducted to ensure a candidate meets federal standards of character and conduct. Also, the Coast Guard validates whether a candidate has an existing security clearance which meets the senior executive position requirements. If a candidate does not have an existing security clearance (as was the case with Mr. Berkow), the appropriate background investigation and suitability determination are conducted pursuant to the hiring process for a member of the Senior Executive Service. Mr. Berkow currently holds an active security clearance.*

By focusing his wrath on Rosemond and pointing a finger at his former *Times* editors, Philips had persuaded the *L.A. Weekly* to run an article under the headline "Chuck Philips Demands L.A. Times Apology on Tupac Shakur." After years of correspondence with various prison inmates, Philips had found his way to one named Dexter Isaac, a convicted murderer who claimed to have participated in the Quad Studios shooting and said it was orchestrated by Rosemond. Isaac had validated the essence of the article that got him fired, Philips insisted, and now the *Times* should run another front-page correction, this one aimed at rehabilitating his career.

The man owned no end of gall. "I never had a major error in a story before," he told the *Weekly*. "I had a couple of small corrections. No serious drama."

His own editors at the *Times* first "fucked up my story," Philips added, then "threw me under the bus." Since he named no names, it couldn't be said for certain that Philips was talking about his former hands-on boss Marc Duvoisin, who by then had been promoted to *Los Angeles Times* managing editor. Duvoisin would lose that job in March 2016 after he was caught up in a controversy over claims the *Times* had delayed a story about how the former dean of the USC Keck School of Medicine partied on campus with a prostitute and drug dealers. In June 2018, Duvoisin was hired as editor and vice president of the *San Antonio Express-News*.

Thirteen years after the mistrial was declared in *Wallace v. Los Angeles*, eleven years after the city and the LAPD had succeeded in secreting much of the evidence in the case in a locked box, it was still there, in the bowels of the District Court.

That it would remain there forever, however, was no longer as certain as the city side imagined or hoped.

In late spring 2018, on the basis of information gathered for this book that I shared with Sanders, the attorney approached Voletta

Wallace to suggest that she consider supporting him in an attempt to refile the civil lawsuit.

The conversation was fraught. It had been Mrs. Wallace who decided, in consultation with Biggie's widow, Faith Evans, not to refile before the rapper's youngest child turned eighteen and the statute of limitations expired. Sanders had told her that the success of the city in withholding whatever new evidence the LAPD had uncovered made moving ahead with the lawsuit a high-risk proposition, one in which they could be blindsided from a hundred different directions. It increased the chances of losing in court tenfold at least, said Sanders, who wanted to proceed anyway.

She was exhausted by a case that had dragged on for a decade already, Voletta told the attorney. Her grandchildren had grown up with their father's murder at the center of their lives, and she wanted them to be free of it, finally. It wasn't as if she or they or Faith needed the money. Biggie's fame had only grown in the years since his death, and his work still continued to produce millions of dollars of income annually, more than enough to take care of them all.

"Voletta told me that she felt the mistrial had been the victory she needed, that she felt we had proved that LAPD officers were involved in her son's murder," Sanders recalled. She had decided, apparently, to be content with that.

When Sanders arranged for Voletta Wallace to speak with me, however, she began to change course. Hearing about the blocked investigation of FBI agent Phil Carson had been key. The decision by the U.S. attorney not to prosecute the case Carson had made, combined with the refusal of the federal government's lawyer to offer any explanation for that decision, infuriated Biggie's mother. So did what she heard about the collusion between LAPD deputy chief Mike Berkow and *Los Angeles Times* reporter Chuck Philips to derail the lawsuit she had filed against the City of Los Angeles. The pivotal moment, though, came when Biggie's mother heard what the city had argued in its efforts to end the FBI investigation and, in particular, to keep Phil Carson off the witness stand: did the FBI really want to throw away a working relationship with the LAPD that involved dozens of agents and tens of millions of dollars in order "to solve the murder of a four-hundred-pound black crack dealer turned rapper"?

"Oh, my God! They said that?" she asked. According to Phil Carson and another FBI agent who was present, yes, they had, I told her.

She went quiet for several moments, then declared, "I want justice for my son." Sanders should begin working on a filing to reopen the case, she said.

The expired statute of limitations would make that difficult, Sanders said. After consulting with Rob Frank, though, Sanders believed the two of them had found a legitimate basis for reviving the lawsuit. California had laws that permitted it in cases where discovery had been denied, in which evidence or information had been withheld or concealed. There was strong evidence that's exactly what had happened in *Wallace v. Los Angeles*, Sanders said. And if Phil Carson was ever allowed to take the witness stand, this lawsuit not only could but almost certainly would be won.

"This case had been covered over with lies," Sanders said, but when what was under those lies is revealed, justice might finally be done.

"They've been tellin' themselves they got away with it for years. Maybe now we get to tell them they haven't."

APPENDIX A

While researching and writing this book, I attempted to contact Michael Berkow directly (bypassing the U.S. Coast Guard) through his LinkedIn account, but there was no reply to my messages. When this book was about to go into production, I went directly to the Coast Guard, asking for both a reply from Berkow and one from the military service itself about how he had obtained his present position. The Coast Guard replied first, stating that Berkow had passed a background check, and I was able to put that into the body of the book as a footnote. Berkow himself replied a short time later. At that point, the best available means of incorporating his claims and denials was in this Appendix.

Berkow seemed to be most concerned about the Ya-May Christle case, and in particular her accusations concerning his sexual activities, and his promotion of the women subordinates who consented to sex with him. It's a subject that's of minor significance in the context of this book, but Berkow's lengthy statements have compelled me to clarification. The Christle lawsuit accused Berkow of having sex with as many as five different women under his command and stated, "All the paramours benefitted because of this sex." According to plaintiff filings in the case, "This rampant orgy of lust that Berkow enjoyed at work was known to [Christle] and was [so] severe and pervasive that it altered the conditions of her employment, creating an abusive working environment." Only one of the five "paramours" named in the lawsuit admitted to having sex with Berkow while under his command; both she and Berkow claimed that she enjoyed no professional benefits as a result of their relationship.

The judge hearing the Christle lawsuit, William Fahey, ruled that the evidence offered by Christle and her attorney to substantiate her accusations about Berkow's abuse of authority for sexual purposes was largely inadmissible. Berkow was dropped as a defendant in the case after Fahey dismissed the plaintiff's claims of sexual harassment and a hostile work environment. Judge Fahey, however, did *not* dismiss the claim that the LAPD, acting through Berkow and others, had retaliated against Christle both for reporting Berkow's suspected sexual activities and for her assertion that he had ordered her work computer taken from her and expunged of information relating to the Notorious B.I.G. murder case. The lawsuit went to trial on the basis of those claims and the jury not only ruled in Christle's favor but awarded her more than $1 million in damages. That ruling was appealed, but Christle prevailed at every level and eventually received nearly $5 million when the case was settled.

Berkow insists that he has no knowledge of what happened with the case after he was removed as a defendant. I find that difficult to believe, given that much if not most of the evidence offered by the plaintiffs centered on him and his behavior. Be that as it may, I do not see how Berkow can claim to have been vindicated by the litigation of the Christle lawsuit. As Christle's attorney Bradley Gage put it to me: "The entire lawsuit was based on Berkow's conduct. Our case involved the actions of Berkow."

Far more germane to this book, obviously, are the accusations against Berkow that involve the Notorious B.I.G. murder investigation, and in particular the claims that he exposed Michael Robinson as an FBI informant, communicated improperly with Amir Muhammad, and collaborated with Chuck Philips to destroy the reputation of Phil Carson, all in an effort to subvert the *Wallace v. Los Angeles* lawsuit. I believe that Berkow did all of those things, either directly or through subordinates. I acknowledge that this belief is based substantially upon what I've been told by others involved in the case, and that Phil Carson is the only one fully on the record. But Carson's recollections haven't been disputed by any of the others—current and former FBI agents, former LAPD officers and Los Angeles County sheriff's deputies, attorneys and investigators who worked on the case—that I've spoken to.

Berkow, though, denies everything. "I have no idea who many of the individuals you named are and while I do know who S/A Carson is, it is in connection with a completely different criminal matter that he was investigating with members of the LAPD Professional Standards Bureau. Nothing to do with Christopher Wallace's murder," he wrote to me. "That denial was underlined by his attorney, who said Berkow 'never asked the FBI to stop any investigation, much less the Wallace investigation.'"

In his emails to me, however, Berkow not only contradicted Phil Carson (along with several other FBI agents); he also contradicted himself. "I am unaware of any confidential informant or FBI investigation into this case or of any of the other allegations you are making," he wrote to me. This is the same man who, as LAPD deputy chief, was the single departmental source quoted by name in the *Los Angeles Times* March 20, 2004, article by Chuck Philips that revealed both the FBI investigation of the Biggie murder and the agency's use of Michael Robinson as the confidential informant who was sent to Amir Muhammad's home in an attempt to obtain incriminating evidence against him. Robinson's work as an informant in the Biggie murder investigation had been part of "a joint FBI-LAPD investigation," Berkow told the *Times*, one in which the LAPD was "cooperating with the feds 100%."

Perhaps reading that quote will jog his memory.

APPENDIX B

I acknowledge being every bit as offended as Perry Sanders by former LAPD detective Greg Kading's blatantly false characterization of Russell Poole's investigation of the Notorious B.I.G. murder. Most of Kading's misrepresentations have been described in the body of this book.

This appendix is intended in part to acknowledge two others who have investigated and denounced Kading: R.J. Bond and Jesse Surratt.

Of those two, Bond is the one who has contested with Kading longer and more frequently, filing complaints with the LAPD's Internal Affairs Division focusing on how and from whom Kading has obtained what should be confidential information. Bond was on good terms with Kading prior to the publication of *Murder Rap*. On the first day of 2008, Kading sent Bond an email that read, "Happy New Year friend, be safe and take care." By 2011 Kading was sending Jesse Surratt an email under the heading "Your Boy Bond," with an attached document titled "RJ Bond's an Idiot."

What first caused him to begin looking at Kading in a negative light, Bond said, was the way in which the former detective had tried to whitewash his conduct in the George Torres case. In *Murder Rap*, Bond observed, "Kading made it sound like all the trouble he had gotten into on the Torres case was about nothing more than some technical error he'd made in applying for a search warrant. There wasn't a word about the fact that he'd manipulated witnesses with false promises or lied to the judge, all stuff I knew a lot about. I had found some other things a lot of people seemed not to know about. For instance, there was this witness to whom Kading had made the promise that a relative of his would either get out of prison or receive a shorter sentence if the witness said what Kading wanted him to say. When the guy was called by the defense in the Torres case to testify about what Kading had said to him, Kading went ballistic. He told the guy, 'You fucked us. Just for that, your brother's not gonna get out of jail.' And the court has the transcript because the conversation was being recorded. The defense was able to use it in court to bury Kading. See, all of Kading's testimony in that case was sealed, so he thought it would never come out. He's quite calculating."

Eventually Bond, the son and grandson of LAPD officers, accused Kading of violating California Penal Code Section 404 (b) by "misappropriating" government property—specifically interview tapes and case files from the ongoing investigation into the murder of Christopher Wallace. "Russ Poole had preserved his notes and documents because he was suing the LAPD," Bond explained, "but Kading had no such motive. His pure reason for absconding with those materials was to promote himself in his book. The fact that the LAPD was looking the other way made me start thinking about why, and the only explanation, I realized, was that they wanted Kading out there putting down the Russell Poole theory of the case." Bond filed a complaint with the LAPD that was examined by Internal Affairs investigator Efrain Flores, whose work, from Bond's perspective, would produce exactly one significant piece of information: an admission that "Theresa Swann" was really Tammie Hawkins. When he read Flores's report, Bond was struck by an early statement that the investigator had found no evidence Daryn Dupree provided documents to Kading himself, or to the two *L.A. Weekly* reporters who had produced a fawning story about Kading's book (a story that made no reference whatsoever to the numerous false or skewed claims in *Murder Rap*). "But I never mentioned Dupree by name in my complaint," Bond observed. "So why was Flores bothering to try to exonerate him?"

More interestingly still, Flores wrote that he had contacted Dupree to discuss the claims made by Bond, and that immediately afterward he had received a call from Kading seeking to confirm that he was under investigation. "Obviously Dupree alerted Kading, which is a departmental violation right there, but Flores did nothing about it," Bond said. "Then he comes up with this report that states there's no rule against a retired LAPD officer 'discussing' an ongoing investigation. But that wasn't what my complaint was about. My complaint was about Kading illegally taking home LAPD documents containing information that could jeopardize the safety of witnesses, and Flores didn't even mention that in his report. So, to me, that was just more evidence that the LAPD was covering up for Kading because Kading was covering up for them."

He had decided to drop the matter, Bond said, until he met Jesse Surratt, who was at that time the moderator of an Internet chat forum called "Tupac Nation." Following the publication of *Murder Rap*, Surratt had developed every bit as much contempt for Kading as had Bond. "After I read his book, I did an interview with Kading," Surratt recalled. "When I asked about the inaccuracies in his book, he became very, very defensive. I read the judge's remarks during the Torres trial, which cited multiple examples of Kading's disregard for the truth, none of it mentioned in his book. I did some more research and realized that all of the cops put on that task force Kading was on were damaged cops, just like him. I came to believe that the LAPD banded together a certain task force of cops they knew would whitewash the Biggie murder investigation. They didn't look at a single bit of the evidence that implicated Mack and Perez."

Eventually, Surratt recalled, "I went to R.J. Bond to talk about my concerns, and when Kading found out about that, he sent me all of Bond's information, with a note that read, 'Be careful who you make friends with.'" Kading had attached a number of documents, which he asked Surratt to post on his website. Surratt was astonished to discover that the documents were the entire record of the LAPD's Internal Affairs investigation of Kading, which included R.J. Bond's home address. "When I asked Kading how he got the IA report," Surratt recalled, "he refused to answer."

Bond was "panicked" when Surratt forwarded Kading's email to him. He persuaded Surratt not to post the documents Kading had sent him, Bond recalled, but three other websites contacted by the former detective *did* put the documents up, unredacted. Kading followed up with a statement: "Bond has no hesitation in making false accusations against people based on unsubstantiated rumors. He's lucky Suge doesn't have guys like Poochie around anymore."

Bond responded by filing a second complaint with the LAPD, calling what Kading had written "a direct threat." The department seemed to take this complaint seriously, sending Threat Assessment Unit officers three times to interview Bond at his home in Corona, fifty miles from LAPD headquarters in downtown L.A. He consulted with his father, "who told me, 'If Kading wasn't a problem for them, they would never have done that.' I had my dad come and sit with me each time I was interviewed." It was no surprise to Bond that this complaint, too, was ultimately dismissed.

Bond tangled with Kading again after the meeting with Deputy Chief Kirk Albanese at LAPD headquarters that he and Russell Poole had attended in June 2014. Somehow, immediately after the meeting, Kading obtained a copy of the PowerPoint presentation Bond and Poole had made for Albanese and began posting portions of it, along with his commentaries, on a website registered to "Anton Batey."

"There was only one way Kading could have gotten that Power-Point, and that was from Dupree," Bond said. "Sharing evidence in a murder case with someone who is no longer a police officer is a crime, so I filed another complaint, against Dupree."

This time the LAPD really did seem to take Bond's concerns seriously. When Bond sent an email under the heading "I am in trouble—the letter is out now," an Internal Affairs investigator named Dollie Swanson responded with an email of her own conceding that the PowerPoint presentation seemed to have been leaked. "I have been pursuing several leads with the help of our information technology personnel, trying to track down how and who accessed your prior complaint," Swanson wrote.

Swanson sent Bond a detailed list of questions and scheduled a meeting with Russell Poole, who had filed his own complaint with Internal Affairs. After speaking with Poole, Swanson phoned Bond to say she was applying for search warrants on the computers of Daryn Dupree and Greg Kading. "And that was when the LAPD shut her down," Bond recalled. "She told me the LAPD brass wouldn't let her get the search warrants, wouldn't even let her finish the investigation. After that, she didn't want to talk to me anymore. When I got her on the phone, she sounded scared. She told me that LAPD was taking the position that the [PowerPoint] had been leaked by someone outside the department."

One more time, Bond said, "The LAPD showed me how committed it was to protecting Greg Kading, a cop who had left the department under a cloud if not in disgrace." There was little doubt that the LAPD was backing Kading when the former detective began leaking an Internal Affairs report that effectively vindicated him in the Torres case. IA had managed this by reducing the entire case to the question of whether Kading had intentionally lied in his search warrant affidavits. Being reckless with the truth and being untruthful were two different things, the IA report noted, before concluding that "there is absolutely no evidence in this investigation to show that Kading intentionally or maliciously misrepresented material facts." The LAPD had managed to reach such a conclusion by omitting completely any questions about what Kading had promised witnesses to get them to testify as he demanded and whether he had lied on the stand, the two most significant reasons Judge Wilson had excoriated him. The *L.A. Weekly* reporter Chris Vogel wrote an article that embraced the IA report without the slightest whiff of critical inquiry, and soon Kading was distributing that article across the Internet as well. Even Bond would concede that Kading seemed to possess a boundless energy for self-promotion. He was a constant presence on Tupac and Biggie Internet fan boards, posting something new almost every day. "Kading's MO is to simply call people names and dismiss them," Bond says. "He won't fight with you directly about the evidence; he just calls you a nut job. And he makes it work by just repeating it again and again and again."

By then, though, Bond had been joined by Surratt as a vocal critic of Kading. Surratt was relying on Kading's own words and works to expose him. After his initial interview of Kading, Surratt began posting long pieces that challenged the *Murder Rap* narrative. In the first, appearing under the title "Greg Kading's Bias Towards Mack and Muhammad," Surratt cataloged many of the intentional omissions and deliberate distortions of fact in *Murder Rap*. He took particular issue with how Kading not only ignored the fact that GECO ammunition had been found in Mack's garage after his arrest, but also played down how rare the ammunition used in the Biggie murder actually was. Kading had seen the FBI statement that GECO bullets were so uncommon in the United States that the agency couldn't find them in its database of crimes—except in the Christopher Wallace case, as Surratt knew. Kading was an LAPD "shill," Surratt wrote, who was refusing to admit the existence of important evidence in the Notorious B.I.G. case "because he doesn't want people to question if the evidence he has linking Wardell 'Poochie' Fouse to Biggie's murder might be false."

A week later, Surratt posted another article that focused on the shiftiest move Kading had made: his attempt to turn the black Impala driven by the Biggie shooter into an aqua-green Impala like the one Poochie drove. For the "incorrect" claim that the shooter's Impala had been black, Kading was blaming Russell Poole. "There was a misreport of a black Impala that was outside the Petersen that the suspect had apparently driven," Kading told one interviewer. "And then Russell Poole draws a conclusion: 'Look, David Mack has a black Impala.' But what Russell Poole doesn't do is tell people about how every single witness that was in those cars denied it being a black Impala. They said it was a green Impala."

His claims about the green Impala were possibly the single most glaring example of Kading's dishonesty, in Surratt's view. Gregory Young and James Lloyd actually *had* described the Impala as dark green (not aqua-green), but, as Kading well knew, Poole was just one of four detectives who had concluded that the vapor lights illuminating the shooting scene had given the shiny black sedan a greenish cast. Kenneth Story, the driver of the SUV Puffy Combs was riding in that night, told the police that three separate witnesses to the shooting had described the killer's car as "a clean, black Chevrolet Impala." The Metropolitan Transit Authority driver whose bus had been westbound on Wilshire when the shooting occurred, and who saw the vehicle after it had passed out from under the vapor lights, confirmed to the police on the night of the shooting that the killer's sedan was black. And Reggie Blaylock, the off-duty Inglewood police officer who had been in the passenger seat of the SUV right behind Biggie's at the time of the shooting, had described the killer's car as "a '94 or '95 Chevrolet Impala SS, black, with large wide tires." None of that, of course, was mentioned by Kading, whose claim that "every single witness that was in those cars denied it being a black Impala" was just one more of his many inaccuracies.

What most proved Kading's duplicity in Surratt's mind, though, was a second reading of the ex-detective's book. In at least three references to the Biggie shooter's vehicle in *Murder Rap*, Kading had described the car as a "black Impala." Not once in his 2011 book had Kading written that the car was green. His subsequent claim that he had known since 2009 that the Impala was green was, Surratt wrote, "a transparent attempt to draw attention away from David Mack, Amir Muhammad, Rafael Perez, and Reggie Wright."

Perhaps that was Kading's intention. I don't know. What I do know is that Kading has absolutely no credibility.

DEAD WRONG ROSTER

Christopher Wallace a.k.a. Notorious B.I.G. a.k.a. Biggie Smalls, seminal rapper whose March 9, 1997, murder remains unsolved

Voletta Wallace, mother of Christopher Wallace and main plaintiff in *Wallace v. Los Angeles*

Faith Evans, widow of Christopher Wallace and co-plaintiff in *Wallace v. Los Angeles*

Tupac Shakur, seminal rapper whose 1996 murder in Las Vegas, still unsolved, has been linked to the slaying of Notorious B.I.G. seven months later

WALLACE V. LOS ANGELES

Perry Sanders, lead attorney for the estate of Christopher Wallace a.k.a. Notorious B.I.G. a.k.a. Biggie Smalls

Rob Frank, Sanders's cocounsel on the *Wallace v. Los Angeles* lawsuit

Sergio Robleto, former LAPD South Bureau Homicide chief, lead investigator for the plaintiffs in *Wallace v. Los Angeles*

Chris Brizzolara, associate counsel for the plaintiffs in *Wallace v. Los Angeles*

Bradley Gage, associate counsel for the plaintiffs in *Wallace v. Los Angeles*

Sandra Ribera, junior cocounsel for the plaintiffs in *Wallace v. Los Angeles*

Audrey Matheny, paralegal for Sanders and Frank

Bruce Stoughton, former LAPD officer working for Robleto

Terri Baker, New York entertainment attorney pivotal in the decision to hire Perry Sanders as lead attorney in *Wallace v. Los Angeles*

Paul Paquette, Los Angeles assistant city attorney, original lead defense lawyer in *Wallace v. Los Angeles*

Don Vincent, Los Angeles assistant city attorney, second chair for the defense in *Wallace v. Los Angeles*

Vincent Marella, attorney hired by the Los Angeles City Council to take over as lead defense lawyer in *Wallace v. Los Angeles*

Florence Cooper, district court judge who presided over most of *Wallace v. Los Angeles* case

Xavier Hermosillo, political activist, talk show host, and civilian member of LAPD Board of Rights tribunals whose revelations led to the 2005 mistrial in *Wallace v. Los Angeles*

Kenneth Boagni, prison inmate whose testimony at an LAPD Board of Rights hearing led to the mistrial in *Wallace v. Los Angeles*

Felipe Sanchez, former prison inmate whose testimony about Rafael Perez agreed with Boagni's

Thurston Limar Sr., legendary private investigator who located and served subpoena on Rafael Perez in *Wallace v. Los Angeles*

John Yslas, attorney who represented Perez in *Wallace v. Los Angeles*

Steven J. Hillman, U.S. magistrate who ruled in multiple evidentiary hearings in *Wallace v. Los Angeles*

Gerald Chaleff, longtime Los Angeles criminal defense attorney appointed to head LAPD Consent Decree Bureau, key witness in suppressing release of clues in Notorious B.I.G. murder investigation

Jacqueline Nguyen, district court judge who replaced Cooper on *Wallace v. Los Angeles* case

FEDERAL BUREAU OF INVESTIGATION AND U.S. ATTORNEY

Phil Carson, former FBI agent whose investigation of the Notorious B.I.G. murder was stymied by the political intervention of the Los Angeles Police Department and its allies

Tim Flaherty, FBI agent who served as handler to informant Michael "Psycho Mike" Robinson

Cathy Viray, head of media relations in the FBI's Los Angeles office

Steve Kramer, associate counsel in the FBI's Los Angeles office

Louis Caprino, head of criminal investigations in the FBI's Los Angeles office

Richard T. Garcia, FBI assistant director, head of the bureau's Los Angeles office

Robert Mueller, FBI director during Carson's investigation of the Biggie murder

Steve Gomez, FBI agent who worked with Carson on the case

David Vaughn, former assistant U.S. attorney who first refused to prosecute the case Carson made in the Notorious B.I.G. murder, then refused to provide the standard letter of declination that would explain why that prosecution was declined; now in private practice in Los Angeles

LOS ANGELES POLICE DEPARTMENT/
LOS ANGELES COUNTY SHERIFF'S DEPARTMENT

Rafael Perez, former LAPD officer convicted of stealing large amounts of cocaine from the department's evidence locker; suspected in the murder of Notorious B.I.G.; best known as the progenitor of the Rampart Scandal

David Mack, former LAPD officer convicted of bank robbery and suspected in the murder of Notorious B.I.G.

Sammy Martin, former LAPD officer suspected of serving as an accomplice in the Mack bank robbery and in other crimes

Nino Durden, former LAPD partner of Rafael Perez who contradicted many of Perez's claims in the Rampart Scandal

Russell Poole, former LAPD detective who was the lead investigator on the original probe of the Notorious B.I.G. murder

Fred Miller, Poole's partner in the Notorious B.I.G. murder investigation

Bernard Parks, former Los Angeles chief of police accused of extensive malfeasance by Poole and multiple others

Michelle Parks, daughter of Chief Parks, LAPD clerk-typist, suspected of narcotics trafficking, possibly in association with Rafael Perez, David Mack, and other members of the Bloods gang

Kendrick Knox, former LAPD senior lead officer whose investigation of police officers working for Death Row Records was shut down by Bernard Parks

Steve Katz, LAPD detective who took over the investigation of the Notorious B.I.G. murder in 2000, caught concealing evidence that implicated police officers in the murder, leading to the 2005 mistrial in *Wallace v. Los Angeles*

Roger Mora and Steve Sambar, LAPD Internal Affairs investigators originally assigned to work with Phil Carson in his investigation of the Notorious B.I.G. murder, until their removal by then–Deputy Chief Michael Berkow

Michael Berkow, former LAPD deputy chief who left under a cloud after accusations that included the orchestration of a cover-up in the Notorious B.I.G. murder; now head of U.S. Coast Guard's Investigative Services

Ya-May Christle, LAPD sergeant who accused Berkow of seizing the computer on which she was "collating" evidence that implicated police officers in the murder of Notorious B.I.G.; awarded millions in a lawsuit against the LAPD

William Bratton, former LAPD chief and executive at Kroll Associates who appointed Berkow as deputy chief

Jim McDonnell, former LAPD deputy chief and current sheriff of Los Angeles County

Richard Valdemar, former Los Angeles County sheriff's deputy who worked as handler to Michael Robinson and as private detective for Sergio Robleto

Greg Kading, former LAPD detective assigned to "Operation Transparency" investigation of Notorious B.I.G. in 2006; author of self-published book *Murder Rap* in 2011

Daryn Dupree, LAPD detective, partner to Kading in Biggie murder investigation

Paul Byrnes, former LAPD Rampart Division sergeant accused by Rafael Perez, acquitted in four consecutive Board of Rights hearings

Cliff Armas, LAPD officer representative for Byrnes and other officers accused by Perez

Fabian Lizarraga and Gary Farmer, LAPD lieutenant and sergeant (respectively) who prosecuted the case against Byrnes and attempted to block the testimony of Kenneth Boagni and Felipe Sanchez about involvement of Rafael Perez in Notorious B.I.G. murder

Kenneth Hale and Earl Paysinger, LAPD captains who served with Xavier Hermosillo as adjudicators in the Byrnes Board of Rights hearing

Shelby Braverman, former LAPD narcotics detective who was incarcerated after learning that Michelle Parks was suspected of transporting narcotics between Los Angeles and Las Vegas

John Cook, former LAPD Internal Affairs investigator who was removed from Michelle Parks investigation after questioning her aggressively

Richard Ginelli, former LAPD senior detective and close associate of Bernard Parks who supervised Braverman and was eventually arrested for stealing heroin held as evidence by LAPD

Cliff Ruff, head of the LAPD officers' union, the Police Protective League, at time of Braverman's incarceration

Thomas Wich, Vincent Vicari, Michael Gannon, and Bill Brockway, members of the Rampart Task Force accused of attempting to suppress the testimony of Kenneth Boagni and Felipe Sanchez

Rod Kusch, head of homicide investigation for Los Angeles County Sheriff's Department who was in the room when Russell Poole died

DEATH ROW RECORDS/SUSPECTS IN MURDER OF NOTORIOUS B.I.G.

Suge Knight, former CEO of Death Row Records, suspected of ordering the execution of Notorious B.I.G.

Reggie Wright Jr., former director of security for Death Row Records, suspected of involvement in the murder of Notorious B.I.G.

David Kenner, longtime, on-and-off attorney for Suge Knight

Amir Muhammad a.k.a. Harry Billups a.k.a. Harry Muhammad (as spelled throughout the book; the variant Muhammed appears in some sources), Mack's friend suspected of being the triggerman in the murder of Notorious B.I.G.

Angelique Mitchell, ex-girlfriend of Amir Muhammad who accused him of multiple
    assaults and of menacing her with a firearm; killed by a gunshot to the head
    in what was ruled a murder-suicide
Tammie Hawkins a.k.a. "Theresa Swann," informant Greg Kading relied upon to
    make claim that Biggie was murdered by Wardell "Poochie" Fouse

BLOODS GANG

Aaron "Heron" Palmer, Suge Knight thug shot dead June 1, 1997
William "Chin" Walker, Knight thug shot dead April 4, 2000
Vence "V" Buchanan, turncoat Blood who reportedly arranged the shooting death
    of Walker, reportedly killed by Knight thugs Alton McDonald and David
    Dudley three weeks later
David "Brim" Dudley, Knight thug shot dead March 25, 2001
Alton "Buntry" McDonald, Knight thug shot dead April 3, 2002
Eric "Scar" Daniel, Fruit Town Piru, suspected in murder of Buntry, shot dead
    himself June 7, 2002
Henry "Hen Dog" Smith, Knight thug shot dead October 16, 2002
Wardell "Poochie" Fouse, Knight thug shot dead July 24, 2003

LOS ANGELES TIMES

Chuck Philips, disgraced former *Los Angeles Times* reporter accused of working
    with the LAPD and the City of Los Angeles to cover up the involvement of
    LAPD officers in the murder of Notorious B.I.G.
Marc Duvoisin, Philips's editor at the *Times*

BAD BOY RECORDS/WITNESSES IN BIGGIE MURDER

Sean "Puffy" Combs, a.k.a. Diddy, CEO of Bad Boy Records who was with Biggie
    in Los Angeles on the night of the murder
James "Lil' Cease" Lloyd, rapper who was riding with Notorious B.I.G. at the time
    of his murder
Eugene Deal, longtime Puffy Combs bodyguard who identified Amir Muhammad
    as the likely killer of Notorious B.I.G.

INFORMANTS/WITNESSES

Michael "Psycho Mike" Robinson, informant used by FBI, Los Angeles County Sheriff's Department, and multiple other law enforcement agencies; first to name Amir Muhammad as killer of Notorious B.I.G.

Mario Ha'mmonds, informant used by FBI and LAPD, among other agencies; prison neighbor of Suge Knight who reported Knight's alleged claims about the murder of Notorious B.I.G. and LAPD involvement

Kevin Hackie, former Compton school police officer, FBI informant, and Tupac Shakur bodyguard who made and recanted statements about involvement of Suge Knight, Reggie Wright, and David Mack in murder of Notorious B.I.G.

Reggie Blaylock, Inglewood police officer working as security for the Bad Boy Records entourage on night of Biggie murder

Benny Keys, police officer incarcerated with David Mack who was the first to report to law enforcement Mack's claims about membership in the Bloods gang and involvement in the Notorious B.I.G. murder

Waymond Anderson, former R&B recording star convicted of arson/murder who implicated Amir Mumammad and David Mack in Notorious B.I.G. murder, recanted that testimony, then reaffirmed it, accusing Chuck Philips, Don Vincent, and Suge Knight of inducing his perjury

Veronica Quesada, former girlfriend of Rafael Perez and accomplice in sale of drugs stolen from LAPD Property Division who cooperated with authorities

OTHERS

Nick Broomfield, documentary filmmaker to whom Eugene Deal first identified Amir Muhammad as the likely shooter in the Notorious B.I.G. murder

Reginald Gaithwright, suspected major drug dealer who was in the passenger seat while Michelle Parks was driving in Las Vegas with narcotics in the vehicle when they were stopped by police

Joseph Avrahamy, attorney who represented the LAPD officers accused by Rafael Perez in "Alley Incident" and wrote the first open challenge of the Rampart Scandal in Los Angeles after winning $15 million judgment for his clients

James "Jimmy Henchman" Rosemond, New York entertainment executive and promoter accused by Chuck Philips of orchestrating shooting of Tupac Shakur at Quad Studios

James Sabatino, prison inmate who fabricated the FBI files that Philips relied upon to accuse Rosemond on Quad shooting

Richard "R.J." Bond, documentary filmmaker, Russell Poole's partner, and critic of Greg Kading

Jesse Surratt, Internet radio host and critic of Greg Kading

DOCUMENTS

WALLACE V. LOS ANGELES

Los Angeles Police Department Complaint Form, CP No. 01-0190, David Mack, Rafael Perez, and Samuel Martin Jr., January 4, 2001

Privileged and Confidential Attorney Work Product, KSG Forensic and Investigative Services, Inc., Witness Interview, Kenneth Boagni, November 7, 2002

Cover Letter from Law Offices of Dennis W. Chang to Perry R. Sanders Jr. and Robert J. Frank, Esq., November 12, 2002

Letter from Office of Londell McMillan to Perry Sanders and Rob Frank, August 26, 2003

Federal Bureau of Investigation, Request for Information. From: Special Agent Phil Carson. To: Rob Frank/Perry Sanders, FBI Case 194C-LA-232722, November 14, 2003

Deposition of Bernard Parks, November 14, 2003

Deposition of Steven Katz, Case No. CV 02-02929 FMC, March 12, 2004

Deposition of David Mack, Case No. CV 02-02929 FMC, May 18, 2004

Memo. To: Perry R. Sanders Jr.; Robert J. Frank. From: Audrey C. Matheny, Deposition of David Mack (February 18, 2004), Summary

Defendant Harry Billups a.k.a. Amir Muhammad Answer to Plaintiff's First Amended Complaint, Case No. CV 02-02929 FMC, June 6, 2004

Deposition of Michael Robinson, Case No. CV 02-02929 FMC, February 3, 2005

Deposition of Jimmy L. Trahin, Deposition of Michael Robinson, Case No. CV 02-02929 FMC, February 4, 2005

Deposition of John Lodge, Case No. CV 02-02929 FMC, February 4, 2005

Deposition of Eugene Deal, Case No. CV 02-02929 FMC, February 14, 2005

Deposition of LAPD Detective Wayne Caffey, Case No. CV 02-02929 FMC, February 22, 2005

Deposition of Damion Butler, Case No. CV 02-02929 FMC, March 17, 2005

Comparison of Testimony of David Mack and Harry Billups, prepared by Audrey Matheny for Perry Sanders and Rob Frank, March 2005

Deposition of Mario Ha'mmonds, Case No. CV 02-02929 FMC, May 17, 2005

Exhibit A, Documents Produced by Defendants on June 27, 2005, Case No. CV 02-02929 FMC

Exhibit B, Documents Produced by Defendants on June 28, 2005, Case No. CV 02-02929 FMC

Exhibit C, Document Produced by Defendants on July 1, 2005; Defendant City of Los Angeles' Response to Request for Production of Documents, Case No. CV 02-02929 FMC

Exhibit D, Documents Produced by Defendants on July 21, 2005; Defendant City of Los Angeles' Supplemental Response to Request for Production of Documents, Case No. CV 02-02929 FMC

Deposition of Steven J. Katz, Case No. CV 02-02929 FMC, June 28, 2005

Deposition of Cliff Armas, Case No. CV 02-02929 FMC, June 28, 2005

Deposition of Fabian Lizarraga, Case No. CV 02-02929 FMC, June 28, 2005

Deposition of Earl C. Paysinger, Case No. CV 02-02929 FMC, June 28, 2005

Reporter's Daily Transcript, Case No. CV 02-02929 FMC, July 1, 2005

Reporter's Daily Transcript, Case No. CV 02-02929 FMC, July 5, 2005

Deposition (aborted) of Kenneth Boagni, July 5, 2005

Plaintiffs' Time Line (for collection of sanctions against City of Los Angeles), August, 2005

City of Los Angeles, Mayor Antonio Villaraigosa, Re: Request by the Office of the City Attorney for the Appropriation for Outside Counsel, October 17, 2005

Reporter's Daily Transcript, Case No. CV 02-02929 FMC, April 26, 2006

Reporter's Daily Transcript, Case No. CV 02-02929 FMC, May 23, 2006

Declaration of Kendrick Knox, Case No. CV 02-02929 FMC, May 26, 2006

Declaration of Ya-May Christle, Case No. CV 02-02929 FMC, May 27, 2006

Declaration of Perry R. Sanders Jr., Case No. CV 02-02929 FMC, May 30, 2006

Plaintiff's Response to Allegations of Defendants Made at the Status Conference on May 23, 2006, Case No. CV 02-02929 FMC, May 30, 2006

Order on Defense Request to Terminate Discovery, Case No. CV 02-02929 FMC, June 9, 2006

Declaration of Vincent Marella, Reporter's Daily Transcript, Case No. CV 02-02929 FMC, July 24, 2006

Plaintiff's Reply to Defendant's Response to Plaintiff's Motion for Leave to File Second Amended Complaint, July 31, 2006

Deposition of Michael Moore, Case No. CV 02-02929 FMC, October 3, 2006

Deposition of John Dunkin, Case No. CV 02-02929 FMC, October 12, 2006

Deposition of Emmanuel Hernandez, Case No. CV 02-02929 FMC, October 17, 2006

Deposition of Salvatore Piscopo, Case No. CV 02-02929 FMC, October 18, 2006

Deposition of John Cook, Case No. CV 02-02929 FMC, October 23, 2006

Deposition of Trevion Stokes Case No. CV 02-02929 FMC, October 24, 2006

Deposition of Mark Thompson, Case No. CV 02-02929 FMC, October 26, 2006

Deposition of Stuart A. Maislin, Case No. CV 02-02929 FMC, November 3, 2006

Deposition of Stanley Nalywaiko, Case No. CV 02-02929 FMC, November 8, 2006

Deposition of Daniel Randolph, Case No. CV 02-02929 FMC, November 13, 2006

Deposition of Nehanda Sankofa-Ra, Case No. CV 02-02929 FMC, November 15, 2006

Order Granting in Part and Denying in Part Plaintiff's Motion for Leave to File Third Amended Complaint, Case No. CV 02-02929 FMC, January 26, 2007

Complaint for Money Damages and Demand for Jury Trial, *Estate of Christopher G.L. Wallace v. City of Los Angeles, Rafael Perez, and Does 1 Through 100*, Case No. 88369597, filed in Superior Court April 16, 2007

Answer of Defendant Rafael Perez to Complaint for Money Damages; Demand for Jury Trial, Case No. CV 02-02929 FMC, April 16, 2007

Declaration of LAPD Sergeant William Kelly, *Wallace v. Los Angeles*, Case No. CV 02-02929 FMC, July 13, 2007

Supplemental Submission by Defendant City of Los Angeles Re: Privilege Log Items; Declaration of Sergeant William Kelly, Case No. CV 02-02929 FMC August 11, 2007

Plaintiff's Opposition to Defendant's Supplemental Submission Re: Privilege Lot Items and Declaration of Sergeant William Kelly, Case No. CV 02-02929 FMC, August 26, 2007

Deposition of Ray Lopez a.k.a. Rafael Perez, Case No. CV 02-02929 FMC, August 28, 2007

Defense Submission Before November 20, 2007, Conference, *Wallace v. Los Angeles*, Case No. CV 02-02929 FMC, November 20, 2007

Joint Submission Regarding Active Clues, Case No. CV 02-02929 FMC, November 20, 2007

Stipulation and Order Re: Case Status, Case No. CV 02-02929 FMC, December 13, 2007

Plaintiff's Response to Magistrate Hillman's Second Request for Plaintiff's Position Regarding Proposed Method of In Camera Inspection of Open Clues to Be Produced by Defendant, Case No. CV 02-02929 FMC, December 17, 2007

Order Granting Plaintiff's Request for Transcript of Sealed Proceeding Held Before Magistrate Judge Stephen J. Hillman on November 28, 2007, Case No. CV 02-02929 FMC, January 24, 2008

Defendant Nino Durden's Answer to Plaintiff's Complaint and Demand for Jury Trial, Case No. CV 02-02929 FMC February 6, 2008

Plaintiff's Objections to Proposed Method of In Camera Inspection of and Arguments Regarding the Allegedly Open Clues to Be Produced by the Defendant, *Wallace v Los Angeles*, Case No. CV 02-02929 FMC, May 5, 2008

Plaintiff's Objections to Proposed Method of In Camera Inspection of and Arguments Regarding the Allegedly Open Clues to Be Produced by the Defendant, *Wallace v Los Angeles*, Case No. CV 02-02929 FMC, May 5, 2008

Notice of Motion and Motion for Review of Magistrate Stephen J. Hillman's Order Dated March 11, 2008, Case No. CV 02-02929 FMC, May 5, 2008

Defendant's Joint Opposition to Plaintiff's Motion to Alter or Amend Judgment; Declaration of Thomas V. Reichart, Case No. CV 02-02929 FMC, May 12, 2008

Opposition to Plaintiff's Motion for Review of Magistrate Judge Rulings; Declaration of Thomas V. Reichart, Case No. CV 02-02929 FMC, May 19, 2008

Reply in Support of Motion for Review of Magistrate Judge Stephen J. Hillman's Order Dated March 11, 2008, Case No. CV 02-02929 FMC, May 23, 2008

Plaintiff's Request for Transcript of Sealed Proceeding Held Before Magistrate Judge Stephen J. Hillman on November 28, 2007, Case No. CV 02-02929 FMC, January 24, 2008

Notice of Submission of Open Clue Documents for In Camera Review, Case No. CV 02-02929 FMC, January 30, 2008

Defendant Steven Katz's Answer to Plaintiff's Third Amended Complaint and Demand for Jury Trial, Case No. CV 02-02929 FMC, December 15, 2009

Answer by Defendants Stuart Maislin and Stanley Nalywaiko to Plaintiff's Third Amended Complaint, Case No. CV 02-02929 FMC, December 15, 2009

Civil Minutes, In Camera Hearing Regarding Motion to Compel (Testimony of Gerald Chaleff), Case No. CV 02-02929 FMC, November 28, 2007

Joint Stipulation to Dismiss Without Prejudice, Case No. CV 02-02929 FMC, April 2, 2010

MUHAMMAD AMIR/HARRY BILLUPS

Correctional Systems Inc. Visiting Application and Approval List Form, Visitor Amir Muhammad, Inmate David Mack, December 21, 1997

Chino Police Department Suspect Report, Case No. 98-7205, Harry Muhammad, October 21, 1998

Chino Police Department Arrest-Booking Form, Case No. 98-7205, Harry Muhammad, October 21, 1998

Chino Police Department Control Report/Receipt, Case No. 98-7205, Harry Muhammad, October 21, 1998

City of Chino, California, Notice to Appear, Case No. 98-7205, Harry Muhammad, October 21, 1998

Criminal History Inquiry Report, California Department of Justice, Harry Billups a.k.a. Amir Muhammad a.k.a. Harry Muhammad

CHUCK PHILIPS/WAYMOND ANDERSON

Deposition of Waymond Anderson (by Rob Frank)

Proposed Stipulation, *People v. Waymond Anderson*, March 26 1997

Letter from Attorney Douglas E. McCann to Mrs. Allison Scott Anderson regarding Legal Fund-Raiser for Waymond Anderson, Overview of Case, December 14, 1998

Email from Waymond Anderson's attorney David Bernstein to Chuck Philips, October 7, 2006

Letter from Attorney David Bernstein to Congresswoman Maxine Waters, February 18, 2007

Handwritten note from *Los Angeles Times* reporter Chuck Philips to inmate Waymond Anderson, dated July 4, 2007

Six additional handwritten notes from Chuck Philips to inmate Waymond Anderson, undated, 2007

Los Angeles District Attorney, Bureau of Investigation, Investigator's Report on Waymond Anderson, August 23, 2007

Letter from Attorney David Bernstein and Waymond Anderson, Inmate K-882707, California State Prison at Lancaster, September 30, 2010

SUGE KNIGHT/TAMMIE HAWKINS/DEATH ROW BANKRUPTCY

Declaration of Steven J. Kahn in Support of Official Committee of Unsecured Creditors' Motion for Order Directing Bankruptcy Rule 2004 Examination of B Squared Inc., DBA, All California Funding and for Production of Documents, U.S. Bankruptcy Court, Central Division of California, Los Angeles Division, Case No. LA:06bk-11205-VZ, In re: Death Row Records, Debtor, February 26, 2006

Complaint for (1) Turnover of Property of the Estate; (2) Avoidance of Unauthorized Post-Petition Transfer; (3) Conversion; (4) Unjust Enrichment; (5) Accounting; and (6) Temporary and Permanent Injunction, U.S. Bankruptcy Court, Central Division of California, Los Angeles Division, Case No. LA:06bk-11205-VZ, In re: Death Row Records, Debtor, August 31, 2006

Preliminary Statement, Creditors' Trustee R. Todd Neilson, U.S. Bankruptcy Court, Central Division of California, Los Angeles Division, Case No. LA:06bk-11205-VZ, In re: Death Row Records, Debtor, June 5, 2007

REGGIE WRIGHT JR.

Deposition of Reginald Wright Jr. in *Watt v. California*, March 12, 2002

Grand Jury Indictment (30 pages) of Reginald Wright Jr., Reggie Wright Sr., and eighteen other defendants, filed (under seal) in United States District Court for Western District of Tennessee in Criminal Case No. 17-20151-JTF, May 25, 2017

Arrest Warrant for Reginald Wright Jr., issued by United States District Court for the Western District of Tennessee, May 25, 2017

Report Commencing Criminal Action, *U.S. v Reginald Wright Jr.*, CR 17-20151-JTF, June 28, 2017

Calendar/Proceedings Sheet, *U.S. v Reginald Wright Jr.*, CR 17-20151-JTF, June 28, 2017

Designation and Appearance of Counsel, Reginald Wright Jr., CR 17-20151-JTF, June 28, 2017

Acknowledgment of Defendant (release on bond) Reginald Wright Jr., CR 17-20151-JTF, June 28, 2017

Notice of *Lis Pendens* filed by U.S. Attorney's Office for the Western District of Tennessee, seeking forfeiture of Reginald Wright Jr. in County of San Bernardino, State of California, June 30, 2017

Notice of *Lis Pendens* filed by U.S. Attorney's Office for the Western District of Tennessee, seeking forfeiture of Reginald Wright Jr. in County of Riverside, State of California, June 30, 2017

Memorandum submitted on behalf of Reginald Wright Jr. in CR 17-20151-JTF seeking to modify the conditions of bail, November 29, 2017

RUSSELL POOLE, RICHARD BOND, JESSE SURRATT

Email Exchange Between Richard Bond and Dollie Swanson, LAPD Internal Affairs, August 18, 2014

Email Exchange Between Russell Poole and Dollie Swanson, LAPD Internal Affairs, August 18, 2014

Email Exchange Between LAPD Chief of Detectives Kirk Albanese and Richard Bond, August 18, 2014

Email Exchange Between Russell Poole and Richard Bond, November 9, 2013 to June 17, 2014

Email Exchange Between Russell Poole and Daisy Sanchez, assistant to Kirk Albanese, June 3, 2014

Email Exchange Between Jesse Surratt and Richard Bond, June 3, 2014

Greg Kading posting on Makaveli Board, July 7, 2014

Email from Greg Kading to Chris Blatchford, August 1, 2014

GREG KADING

United States District Court, Central District of California, Order Re Pretrial Motions in *Limine, Motley, et al. v. Parks et al.* (including Greg Kading), Case No. CV 00-01472 MMM (SHx), June 19, 2006

U.S. Department of Justice, Drug Enforcement Administration, Synopsis of Meeting with LAPD detectives Greg Kading and Daryn Dupree, December 18, 2008

Sandy Ribera Handwritten Notes of Meeting with Greg Kading and Perry Sanders, Hilton Garden Hotel, Calabasas, 2011

MICHAEL BERKOW

Email from Lieutenant Amy Midgett, U.S. Coast Guard, August 31, 2018

Email from Michael Berkow to Randall Sullivan, September 5, 2018

ACKNOWLEDGMENTS

Dead Wrong was built on the platform of my earlier book *LAbyrinth*. And *LAbyrinth* could never have been written without the unstinting assistance of the book's dogged protagonist, Russell Poole. Russell was dead by the time I began working on *Dead Wrong*, but he and I had spoken on the phone every month or so for more than a decade before his death, always about some development associated with the investigations of the murders of Tupac Shakur and Notorious B.I.G. He was, in his way, *the* background source for this book.

 I won't be acknowledging here the others who helped me in writing *LAbyrinth*, unless they were significant sources for *Dead Wrong*. But again, people like Kendrick Knox (the former LAPD officer whom I interviewed, more briefly than I would have preferred, for *LAbyrinth*) and Don Vincent (the Los Angeles assistant city attorney whom I interviewed for the *Rolling Stone* article "The Unsolved Murder of Notorious B.I.G."), along with numerous others, provided an underlying understanding of the Biggie murder investigation. In writing *Dead Wrong*, I did draw extensively on interviews I conducted for that second of the two *Rolling Stone* articles I wrote about the murder of Notorious B.I.G..

 When I wrote *LAbyrinth*, many of those I interviewed (and most who refused to be interviewed) expressed their fear of Suge Knight and the Bloods gang. Fifteen years later, when I began work on *Dead Wrong*, those who spoke to me about this case were most afraid of the

Los Angeles Police Department and its political allies, in particular the ones who occupied positions in the federal government.

I applaud the courage of those who talked, especially Phil Carson. For me, there was an eerie echo of Russell Poole's wrenching, career-wrecking experience in Carson's story. The two were quite similar in some ways: both earnest Boy Scout types who tried to be above politics and just do their jobs as they understood them. They were a pair of investigators who couldn't conceive that there was any duty greater than the solving of a homicide. The discovery that this attitude made them not only unusual but actually dangerous in the eyes of others working in law enforcement came as a shock to both men. Their idealism was mere naïveté in the eyes of the people they were working for. Of the two men, Poole paid the higher price and it could be argued that this was by his own choice. Carson, though, may not be done paying. I anticipate that there will be powerfully placed people who will attack him after this book is published. What I wonder is whether those whom he worked with, and who know the truth, will speak up in his defense. The ones I interviewed, to a man and a woman, described Carson as utterly honest—"a guy who couldn't tell you a lie even if he wanted to," as one former colleague at the FBI put it. To the extent they had knowledge, they backed what Carson told me, but did not want their names cited in the book. (I interviewed Cathy Viray and Lou Caprino for *Rolling Stone* back in 2005, and the quotes attributed to them by name came from those interviews.) Carson was actually more sympathetic to his former colleagues than I was, explaining how recent events in Washington, D.C., had made the FBI into an even more treacherously political organization than it had been previously, and that everyone was, as he put it, "running scared." For me, given that an underlying theme of this book is the politicization of law enforcement, and that I believe there were dozens of officers, agents, and officers of the court whose failure to do their jobs—for political reasons—resulted in the murder of a young man going unsolved, this isn't a sufficient explanation. Carson seems sure that those he once worked with will step up if called upon. I hope he's right.

Perry Sanders was my most valuable source in writing this book. Along with his partner Rob Frank, Sanders provided me with an almost blow-by-blow account of the *Wallace v. Los Angeles* lawsuit. He also opened a good many doors for me. One example was getting Eugene Deal on a conference call so that I could ask about the recent claims by Greg Kading that Deal had changed his story. The infuriated big man not only denied this in vivid and profane terms; he also described in hugely entertaining detail what he planned to do to that "lyin' motherfucker Kading" if he ever got in a room with him. It was through Sanders and Frank also that I obtained many of the documents that helped me in writing this book, although the person who actually did the work in that regard was paralegal Audrey Matheny, a woman to whom I owe more than I will likely ever have a chance to repay.

Sanders's and Frank's associate counsels Chris Brizzolara and Bradley Gage also gave me invaluable assistance, particularly in understanding the latter stages of the *Wallace v. Los Angeles* suit and its sad, unsatisfying conclusion. Brizzolara is an especially insightful fellow. I very much appreciate the interview that another of Sanders's associates, Sandra Ribera, gave me, and am enormously grateful that she took the time to dig out the handwritten notes she made of the meeting she and Sanders had with Greg Kading back in 2011.

Sergio Robleto was an absolutely indispensable source and a delightful companion. I helped him get the job as an adviser on the film made from *LAbyrinth*, and hanging out on the set with Sergio was both edifying and a whole lot of fun. Though I spoke with him on the phone half a dozen times afterward, I never saw him face-to-face again. His sudden death shook a lot of people, me included. Sergio's operatives, former Los Ageles County sheriff's deputy Richard Valdemar and former LAPD detective Bruce Stoughton, gave me great interviews. The depth of feeling that Valdemar brought to our conversations about Mike Robinson made a huge impression on me.

The contained fury of former LAPD officer Cliff Armas was just as affecting; no one I interviewed gave me greater insight into how the mostly trumped-up Rampart Scandal infected everything it touched inside the LAPD, and for that matter throughout the city of Los Angeles. Attorney Joseph Avrahamy ran him a close second, however. Although in this book I used only an excerpt from the op-ed Avrahamy wrote for the *Daily News*, my conversation with him echoes in every word I wrote about the Rampart Scandal.

Because I don't believe one can be brave unless one is also frightened, I call Shelby Braverman one of the most courageous people I've ever interviewed. The man had been, as he put it, "broken" by what Bernard Parks and the LAPD had done to him, and he was terribly afraid that the police department might find a way to hurt him again if he spoke to me. But speak to me he did, and I'm very appreciative of it. I appreciate also the help that former LAPD detective Jeff Pailet gave me in arranging interviews with Braverman and with former LAPD sergeant John Cook. Cook is a cautious, careful man, taciturn to a fault. But he told me enough.

Xavier Hermosillo, on the other hand, is extraordinarily loquacious and thank God for that. Hermosillo described the Board of Rights hearing at which Kenneth Boagni and Felipe Sanchez first testified about the involvement of Rafael Perez in the Notorious B.I.G. murder in such vivid detail that I could almost hear the breathing of the people who had been in the room with him. Hermosillo was equally evocative in describing his complaints against Bernard Parks and the process by which he initiated the declaration of a mistrial in *Wallace v. Los Angeles*. The man leaves nothing out. Through him, I found Al Rubalcalva, the former LAPD Internal Affairs investigator who provided the police reports Hermosillo used to block Parks's appointment as LAPD chief back in 1992.

I was unable to interview Bernard Parks. We did have a brief phone conversation in which he refused to answer questions about any of the allegations that were made about him by various others among my sources. "My reputation has already been established and I don't need to defend it to you," Parks told me.

I also could not interview Chuck Philips for this book, though I did interview Philips and his *Los Angeles Times* editor Marc Duvoisin for *Rolling Stone* back in 2005, and I've used parts of those interviews in *Dead Wrong*. I reached out to Philips through every means available to me (two email addresses and his website) and he never replied. I also wrote to Marc Duvoisin at the *San Antonio Express-News*, where he was hired as editor in chief last year, asking not only for an interview with him but also for help in making sure his friend Chuck Philips understood the gravity of his actions as reported in this book. We eventually spoke off the record.

Thanks to Steve Strong for describing Greg Kading's bad behavior in the George Torres case in such authoritative terms.

Thanks also to Richard "R.J." Bond and Jesse Surratt for the information they provided about Kading and his absurd claims of having "solved" the Biggie murder. Bond gets a bad rap even from people who aren't named Greg Kading, but not from me. I know it bothered him that I had so little enthusiasm for his theory of the Tupac murder, but I found R.J. to be extraordinarily knowledgeable and diligent, and a real help to me. Along with Michael Carlin, he gave me a deeper understanding of Russell Poole's last years, months, weeks, and days.

Finally, I want to say thanks again to Voletta Wallace. I spoke to her only once while working on this book, but I felt her support throughout. Seeking justice for her son has cost this woman enormously, but she's never backed down. If only there were more people who believe the truth will set them free so sincerely as Voletta does.